Wisdom, Intelligence, and Creativi[

Intelligence, a Harvard psychologist famously remarked, is what intelligence tests measure. The observation may have been made in jest, but its effects have been all too serious. A multibillion dollar "intelligence testing" industry largely determines which children attend the best schools and universities. And local communities, under government pressure to produce results, institute curricula that teach to the test but leave little room for "luxuries" such as music and the arts. But what if the essential nature of intelligence is grossly distorted by the testing industry? For thirty years, Robert J. Sternberg has been among the most vocal critics of narrow conceptions of intelligence. In his most recent book, *Wisdom, Intelligence, and Creativity Synthesized*, Professor Sternberg critically reviews and summarizes the best research available on human intelligence. He argues that any serious understanding of intelligence must go beyond the standard paper-and-pencil tests currently in use. In addition to analytical and quantitative abilities, a theory of intelligence must take into account people's creative abilities – their ability to go beyond given information and imagine new and exciting ways of reformulating old problems. It must also take into account wisdom – people's ability to weigh options carefully and to act prudently. Understanding one's own intellectual shortcomings and learning how to overcome them, Professor Sternberg argues, is just as important as developing one's strengths. As he weaves his way through decades of important research – including recent international studies – on these questions, Professor Sternberg develops a vision of human intelligence that is far more nuanced and accurate than anything offered previously. *Wisdom, Intelligence, and Creativity Synthesized* will be essential reading for psychologists, cognitive scientists, educators, and organizational researchers.

Robert J. Sternberg is Dean of the School of Arts and Sciences and Professor of Psychology at Tufts University. Prior to being at Tufts, he was IBM Professor of Psychology and Education, Professor of Management in the School of Management, and Director of the Center for the Psychology of Abilities, Competencies, and Expertise at Yale University. This center, now relocated to Tufts, is dedicated to the advancement of theory, research, practice, and policy that advances the notion of intelligence as developing expertise and as a construct that is modifiable and capable, to some extent, of development throughout the lifespan. Author of more than 1,100 articles, chapters, and books, Sternberg's research focuses on intelligence, creativity, and wisdom, and he has studied love and close relationships as well as hate.

Wisdom, Intelligence, and Creativity Synthesized

ROBERT J. STERNBERG

Yale University

 **CAMBRIDGE** UNIVERSITY PRESS

CAMBRIDGE UNIVERSITY PRESS
Cambridge, New York, Melbourne, Madrid, Cape Town,
Singapore, São Paulo, Delhi, Tokyo, Mexico City

Cambridge University Press
32 Avenue of the Americas, New York, NY 10013-2473, USA

www.cambridge.org
Information on this title: www.cambridge.org/9780521002714

© Robert J. Sternberg 2003

First published 2003
Reprinted 2006
First paperback edition 2007
Reprinted 2011

A catalog record for this publication is available from the British Library.

Library of Congress Cataloging in Publication Data

Sternberg, Robert J.
Wisdom, intelligence, and creativity synthesized / Robert J. Sternberg.
    p.   cm.
Includes bibliographical references and index.
ISBN 0-521-80238-5
1. Intellect.   2. Creative ability.   3. Creative thinking.   4. Wisdom.   I. Title.
BF431.S7385   2003
153.9–dc21   2003043751

ISBN 978-0-521-80238-3 Hardback
ISBN 978-0-521-00271-4 Paperback

This book is dedicated to Elena L. Grigorenko

Contents

Preface

Professor Wormbog had every beastie in his collection except one (Mayer, 1976). He had everything from A to Y: an askingforit, a blowfat-glowfish, a croonie, a diddly-dee, an errg, a fydolagump, and everything else up to the yalapappus. But he lacked the crucial Z, the zipperump-a-zoo. He therefore set out to find the missing zipperump-a-zoo and looked everywhere, including the most exotic places in the world. But the zipperump-a-zoo eluded him. Finally he gave up, came back home, and went to sleep, exhausted. As soon as he fell asleep, a whole tribe of zipperump-a-zoos emerged to party, right in his house. They had been there all the time, hiding. In asking in what exotic place they might be, he had neglected to ask whether they might be in the most obvious place of all, right in his own home. Because he had asked the wrong question, he emerged with the wrong answer.

This book represents, in a sense, a recounting of the tale of a search for my own zipperump-a-zoo (Sternberg, 2000b), the nature of the mind – of human intelligence, creativity, and wisdom, and how they interrelate. I have learned a crucial lesson from Professor Wormbog: You will never come up with the right answer if you ask the wrong question. I still have not figured out quite the right question, but that's fortunate because there is still hope for what's left of the second half of my career.

Because this book represents the culmination of all the work on the human mind I have done in the roughly thirty years since I started graduate school, I should like to say something about how the book came to be, to indulge myself in recounting the tale. (In the main text, I stick to theories, data, and interpretations.) I tell the tale from my own point of view, but I wish to emphasize that I have done nothing by myself. Without support from my family, my mentors, research advisors, granting agencies, and most important, my research group, now the PACE Center at Yale, there would be no story to tell. The critical lesson of the tale is that what seems to be a complete answer at one stage of a career seems, at a later stage, to be woefully incomplete.

THE PREHISTORY

The prehistory of my search began when I was a primary school student and turned in a dismal performance on the required group IQ tests. I was so test-anxious I could hardly get myself to answer the test questions. When I heard other students turn the test pages, it was all over for me. For three years, my teachers thought me stupid, and I obliged, pleasing them by confirming their self-fulfilling prophecies for me. They were happy, I was happy; everyone was pretty damn happy.

In grade 4, at age nine, I had a teacher who believed in me, and to please her, I became an "A" student. I also learned that, when authority figures set high expectations for a student, it is amazing how quickly that student can defy earlier low expectations.

By age thirteen, I was determined to understand why I was now achieving at high levels despite my low IQ, so I did a science project on mental testing. I found the Stanford-Binet Intelligence test in the adult section of my town library and thought it would be good practice to give it to some classmates. I chose poorly. The first person I selected was a girl in whom I was romantically interested, and I soon discovered that giving a potential girl friend an IQ test is a bad way to break the ice. The second person I chose tattled on me, and I ended up in serious trouble with the school authorities when they learned I was giving IQ tests to my classmates. After they threatened to burn the book if I ever brought it to school again, I went underground, only to re-emerge some years later.

I also thought it would be a good idea to create a group test comprising not just eight or nine subtests, but two dozen. My idea was to improve IQ testing by giving a wider range of subtests. So I created the Sternberg Test of Mental Abilities (STOMA), no copies of which I have been able to locate in my adulthood. I had asked the wrong question – whether adding more of essentially the same kinds of subtests to create a super-duper-extra-long test would substantially improve reliability or validity. The answer was no. I quickly stumbled into the general (g) factor, which represents the individual-differences variation common to virtually all conventional psychometric tests of intellectual abilities. I was a bit too late. Charles Spearman (1904) had already speculated on the g factor at the turn of the twentieth century, as have many others since. Spearman believed the g factor represents "mental energy." Other psychologists have had other ideas about it, but the question of what it represents remains unresolved even today.

As a youth, I discovered that mental testing has many peculiarities. Over the summer after grade 10, when I was sixteen, I did a project on the effect of distractions on mental ability test scores. I discovered that of four distractions – a car headlamp shining in the eyes, a slowly ticking metronome, a rapidly ticking metronome, and the Beatles singing "She has the Devil in Her Heart" – only one had an effect relative to a control condition in which there were no distractions. Students performed better on both verbal and math ability tests when listening to the Beatles!

The next year, at seventeen, I created a Physics Aptitude Test as a physics project to save my flagging physics grade, and the test was successful, predicting physics grades with a correlation in the mid .60s. The test actually was used by my high school for several years after I created it to help screen for honors physics.

At age twenty, as a junior in college, I thought I really had the solution: The answer to the problem of understanding intelligence was not more tests, but more refined scoring of the items already in tests. So I devised partial systems of scoring psychometric test items, and discovered, as had many of my colleagues at the Educational Testing Service (where I worked for the summer), that partial scoring adds very little reliable or valid variation in test scores. Wrong question again: The answer was not to be found in cosmetic manipulations such as adding more of essentially the same kinds of items or in seeking to extract partial information from such items. And so ended my largely futile prehistory as an apprentice.

THE HISTORY

Stage 1: Componential Analyses of Analytical Abilities

As a first-year graduate student I despaired of having any good ideas for studying intelligence. One day, I saw Betty, my wife at the time, using People Pieces in her work – a math-manipulative material for young children consisting of small square tiles that vary with respect to four binary features – color, height, weight, and sex. I visualized creating analogies from them, and so began my efforts at what I came to call componential analyses of human abilities.

The basic idea of componential analysis is that underlying intelligence is a series of information-processing components. The questions intelligence researchers should be asking are not merely what psychometric factors underlie these tests, but also (a) what information-processing components underlie the tests, (b) on what forms of mental representation these components act, (c) how the components combine into coherent strategies for solving problems, (d) how long each component consumes in real time, and (e) how liable each component is to errors in implementation. I started by describing componential analysis in detail and showing its implementation with various kinds of analogies (such as People Pieces, verbal, and figural ones – Sternberg, 1977).

Componential analyses served many useful purposes. They told psychologists how people were processing IQ-test-like problems in real time. The models accounted for large proportions of both stimulus and person variation in reaction-time data. Interesting specific findings also emerged. For example, I discovered that early real-time information processing in the solution of a given analogy is exhaustive and then later becomes self-terminating. I also found that being smart is not just a matter of being fast: Better reasoners tend to spend relatively more time encoding the terms of analogy problems but relatively less time operating on those encodings (Sternberg & Rifkin, 1979). They want to make sure they have understood what they are doing before they go ahead and do it.

The methodology also enabled me to discover why people may be doing poorly on a given type of test item. For example, is a low verbal-analogies score due to problems understanding the vocabulary required to solve the analogies or is it due to faulty reasoning operating on known vocabulary (Sternberg, 1977)?

Stage 1 of my research was actually divided into two substages. In Substage 1a, I merely posited the existence of information-processing components (Sternberg, 1977). In Substage 1b, I distinguished metacomponents – higher order executive processes that decide what to do, how to do it, and how well it was done; performance components – lower order processes that execute the instructions of the metacomponents; and knowledge-acquisition components, which figure out how to do things in the first place (Sternberg, 1980b). Using this framework, I was able to discover that better reasoners tend, for example, to spend relatively more time on the metacomponent of global planning, but less time on the metacomponent of local planning, than do poorer reasoners (Sternberg, 1981). In other words, the better reasoners realize that they need to plan in advance to conserve time and effort when they later begin getting into the details of the problem. We were also able to isolate the knowledge-acquisition components used in the acquisition of vocabulary from context (Sternberg & Powell, 1983), such as selective encoding of relevant cues in distinction from irrelevant cues for figuring out a word's meaning.

But the wrong questions had once again led to the wrong answers, or, to be more precise, *incomplete* answers. Puzzles were emerging. Why was the regression constant (i.e., the a in the equation $a + bx$) instead of the regression coefficient (i.e., the b in the equation) for the mathematical models we were constructing the best predictor of scores on psychometric tests? Were we just rediscovering g again, but this time as an information-processing construct? Why, when we assessed people's implicit (folk) theories of intelligence, were analytical abilities only a small aspect of what people broadly consider intelligence to be (Okagaki & Sternberg, 1993; Sternberg, 1985b; Sternberg, Conway, Ketron, & Bernstein, 1981; see also Yang & Sternberg,

1997b)? The main factor leading to my puzzlement, however, was really not a research finding, but an observation.

Stage 2: The Triarchic Theory of Human Intelligence

I have always been one to get most of my ideas not from reading academic materials or listening to academic lectures, but from my daily experience. And my experience was not fitting my theory. I was teaching three graduate students who provided a curious contrast. (The names given below are fictitious, although they represent real people.)

One, who I call Alice, was brilliant academically and at the kinds of memory and analytical skills conventional psychometric tests of intelligence emphasize. She started off our graduate program in psychology as one of the top students in the program but ended up as one of the bottom students. The reason was transparent: Alice was brilliant analytically but showed only the most minimal creative skills. I was not convinced that Alice was born creatively retarded. It seemed more likely that Alice had been so over-reinforced for her school smarts during her life that she had never had any incentive to develop or even to find whatever creative skills may have lain latent within her.

Another student, Barbara, was marvelously creative, if we were to believe her portfolio of research work and the recommendations of her undergraduate professors, but her scores on the largely analytical Graduate Record Examination (GRE) were weak. Other professors were reluctant to admit her because of these GRE scores, and Barbara was rejected from our program, with mine the only vote in her favor. I hired her as a research associate, which gave her a chance to show her creative brilliance. Barbara was admitted as the top pick to our graduate program a couple of years later. Some years later, we did a study on twelve years of graduate students in psychology at Yale. The study showed that, although the GRE was a good predictor of first-year grades, it was a satisfactory predictor of little else, such as students' analytical, creative, practical, research, or teaching abilities, or the quality of their dissertations (Sternberg & Williams, 1997). Concerning these other criteria, for men the analytical section (since discontinued) had some predictive power; for women none of the sections had significant predictive power.

The third student, Celia, was admitted not because she was spectacular but because she appeared to be good (but not great) in both analytical and creative skills, and every program needs students who are good in several things, if not great in any of them. But Celia surprised us when she was besieged with job offers. She was the kind of person who could go into a job interview, figure out what her potential employers wanted to hear, and give it to them. In contrast, Paul, a student who was analytically and creatively brilliant, received many job interviews but only one very weak job offer. In some respects the opposite of Celia, he managed to insult his interviewers at every turn. He was as low as Celia was high in practical intelligence.

I now realize that once again I had been asking the wrong question. By asking what information-processing components underlie performance on conventional mental tests, I had been able to identify how people solve such conventional problems. But I had assumed that these tests measured the universe of skills relevant to intelligence, and my assumption was false. By asking the wrong question, I ended up with an incomplete answer.

These observations led to the development of the triarchic theory of human intelligence (Sternberg, 1984, 1985a, 1988c). This theory has three subtheories. A componential subtheory specifies the information-processing components of human intelligence, such as recognizing, defining, and representing problems. An experiential subtheory specifies the regions of experience at which these components are most relevant to the demonstration and assessment of intelligence. These regions are relative novelty and automatization. The former region refers to the solving of problems that are rather different in kind from what one is used to, but not wholly different. A problem that is too novel (e.g., calculus problems for five-year-olds) does not provide a good measure of intelligence. The second region refers to rendering unconscious and automatic a process that starts off as conscious and controlled, such as reading (see Sternberg, 1985a). A contextual subtheory specifies the real-world contextual functions of intelligence: adaptation to existing environments; shaping of existing environments into new and, it is hoped, better environments; and selection of different environments (usually when adaptation and shaping fail).

Analytical abilities are engaged when information-processing components are applied to relatively familiar problems that are largely academic because they are abstracted from the substance of everyday life. Creative abilities are engaged when the components are applied to relatively novel problems. Finally, practical abilities are engaged when the components are applied to adaptation to, shaping of, and selection of everyday environments.

My group expanded its research into the creative and practical domains, with some interesting results, we thought.

In Stage 2a, we focused on creative abilities, which seemed complementary to analytical ones. Some of this research used convergent measures. For example, we might introduce participants to relatively novel concepts, such as Goodman's (1955) concepts of *grue* – say, of the color green until the year 3000 and blue thereafter – and *bleen* – say, of the color blue until the year 3000 and green thereafter. We pointed out that one could not say whether an emerald was green or grue because one would not know until the year 3000 (actually, 2000 in the research, which was done in the 1980s: Sternberg, 1982; Tetewsky & Sternberg, 1986). Or we might introduce participants to the planet Kyron, where there are four kinds of people – *plins*, who are born young and die young; *kwefs*, who are born old and die old; *balts*, who are born young and die old; and *prosses*, who are born old and die young. Participants had to solve reasoning problems that involved these novel concepts. We found that the information-processing component that distinguished the more from the less creative reasoners was the component that measured the ability to transit back and forth between conventional (*green–blue*) and unconventional (*grue–bleen*) thinking. The more creative individuals found it easier to switch back and forth.

In Stage 2b, which largely overlapped with Stage 2a, we focused on practical abilities. The basic idea motivating this research is that practical intelligence derives largely from the acquisition and utilization of *tacit knowledge* – the procedural knowledge not explicitly taught and often not even verbalized that one needs to know to succeed in an environment. For an academic psychologist, for example, tacit knowledge would include knowing how to win acceptance of articles submitted to journals and knowing how to get resources from the Chair of one's department. We represent this knowledge in the form of production systems, which are ordered series of conditional ("if–then") statements. Thus, one keeps asking which piece of tacit knowledge to apply (the "if" antecedent) and executes the tacit knowledge (the "then" consequent) when the right piece of tacit knowledge is found.

We have developed (Sternberg, Wagner, Williams, & Horvath, 1995; Wagner & Sternberg, 1985) and continue to develop (Sternberg et al., 2000) instruments to assess the acquisition and utilization of tacit knowledge. We have now tested thousands of people in more than two dozen occupations, including that of academic psychologist.

The tests are all based on the same notion. Participants are presented with scenarios from the everyday life of people going about their business (as students, as employees, or whatever). The participants then either state a solution to the problem posed in the scenario (in one format), or evaluate the quality of alternative solutions proposed to them (in another format).

The results have been fairly consistent across studies: Tacit knowledge typically does not correlate with IQ-based measures but predicts school and job performance as well as or better than IQ-based measures. The correlations are not always zero. At the lower (but not higher) ranks of military officers, we obtained weak but significant positive correlations. Among children in rural Kenya, we obtained significant negative correlations: The anthropological members of our team – Wenzel Geissler and Ruth Prince – recognized a fundamental fact about family values. The children saw that their path to success was not through obtaining high grades in formal schooling but rather through acquiring the tacit knowledge that led to adaptation to the demands of village life.

In other words, our measures supplement, although obviously do not replace, the IQ-based measures. They are not replacements because we are focusing here on practical abilities, whereas IQ-based measures focus on analytical abilities.

But I eventually came to the conclusion that I was once again asking the wrong question. I was emphasizing analytical, creative, and practical abilities and thinking loosely in terms of some additive combination rule. Observation of effective people in a variety of occupations convinced me that there was no single combination rule, however. For example, my two mentors and greatest role models – Endel Tulving and Gordon Bower – are both wonderfully successful psychologists, but they have gotten to where they are in very different ways. There seems to be an infinite number of combination rules.

Stage 3: The Theory of Successful Intelligence

The theory of successful intelligence (Sternberg, 1997b, 1999d) is in many respects an expansion of the triarchic theory. It states that people are successfully intelligent to the extent that they have the abilities needed to succeed in life, according to their own definition of success within their sociocultural context. They succeed by adapting to, shaping, and selecting environments, which they do by recognizing and then capitalizing on their strengths, and by recognizing and then compensating for or correcting their weaknesses. Thus, there is no one path to success in life. Each person must chart his or her own way, and the job of the teacher is to help students in this endeavor. Teaching in just one way can never work.

Many societies, especially developed ones, tend to focus a spotlight on just one group of students – those with high levels of memory and analytical abilities. But in doing so, they create self-fulfilling prophecies, developing assessments of ability, instruction, and assessments of achievement that identify as intelligent this one group of students. They can create whatever kinds of self-fulfilling prophecies they wish. If they bestow benefits primarily or exclusively on children of certain religions, castes, skin colors, or accents of speech, they quickly find that only those children succeed. They then convince themselves, as did Herrnstein and Murray (1994), that the success of these individuals represents an "invisible hand of nature" rather than a system created by the society.

Our research has shown that analytical, creative, and practical abilities are largely independent. When students' abilities and achievements are assessed not just for memory and analytical abilities, but also for creative and practical abilities, students formerly considered as not very bright can succeed in school at higher levels (Sternberg, Grigorenko, Ferrari, &

Clinkenbeard, 1999). Moreover, students taught for successful intelligence do better across grade levels and subject matter areas, regardless of how their performance is assessed, and even if it is assessed merely for memory learning (Sternberg, Torff, & Grigorenko, 1998a). The students learn better because they can use their abilities more effectively and because the greater interest of the material better motivates them to learn.

Stage 4: The Investment Theory of Creativity and the Propulsion Theory of Creative Contributions

After studying intelligence for a number of years, it became clear to me that there is more to creativity than creative intelligence. There are people who appear to have creative intelligence but are unable to use it effectively in their lives because they have various kinds of blocks. More and more, I came to believe that creativity is a decision.

Eventually, Todd Lubart and I (Sternberg & Lubart, 1991, 1995) proposed an investment theory of creativity, according to which more creative thinkers are those who buy low and sell high in the world of ideas (Sternberg & Lubart, 1995). In other words, they are people who generate ideas that are relatively unpopular (buy low); convince others of the worth of these ideas (sell high); and then move on to the next unpopular idea. We had people write stories with diverse titles such as *The Octopus's Sneakers*; or do art work for topics such as *Earth from an Insect's Point of View*; or produce advertisements for boring products such as a new brand of bow tie; or solve quasi-scientific problems such as how we could tell whether there are extraterrestrial aliens among us seeking to escape detection. Products were evaluated for their novelty and quality.

Two major findings emerged. First, creativity tends to be fairly but not completely domain-specific. Second, it tends to be rather but not totally distinct from psychometrically measured intelligence.

Today, I believe the investment theory was a bit of an oversimplification. Whereas the investment theory holds that creative ideas tend to be unappreciated and devalued, I now believe, according to a new propulsion theory of creative contributions (Sternberg, 1999c; Sternberg, Kaufman, & Pretz, 2002), that whether creative ideas are valued or not depends on which of seven kinds of creative ideas they are. Ideas that are consistent with ongoing paradigms tend to be welcome. Forward incrementations, for example, which move existing paradigms forward, tend to be valued. Redirections, which move existing paradigms in new directions, or re-initiations, which reject current paradigms and start at a different point of departure, tend not to be recognized as creative because they are often too novel for people to appreciate their value. Of course, novelty is no guarantee of quality.

Stage 5: The Balance Theory of Wisdom

My latest work has taken a somewhat different direction. I have come to realize that some of the world's cruelest despots and greediest business tycoons are successfully intelligent. They have played within the socio-cultural rules, which they have largely set. Thus, they have been enormously successful, often at the expense of countless countrymen who are left to their own devices, and often to death. It is for this reason that I have now turned my attention to wisdom (Sternberg, 1998b, 2001a). In my balance theory, I view wisdom as the value-laden application of tacit knowledge not only for one's own benefit (as can be the case with successful intelligence) but also for the benefit of others, in order to attain a common good. The wise person realizes that what matters is not just knowledge, or the intellectual skills one applies to this knowledge, but how the knowledge is used.

IQs have been rising over the past several generations (Flynn, 1987; Neisser, 1998). The perpetuation of ever worse massacres and genocides suggests that wisdom has not been rising concomitantly. If there is anything the world needs, it is wisdom. Without it, I exaggerate not at all in saying that very soon, there may be no world, or at least none with humans populating it. Perhaps the only ones left will be zipperump-a-zoos.

Preparation of this book was supported by Contract DAS W01-00-K-0014 from the U.S. Army Research Institute; by Grant REC-9979843 from the National Science Foundation; by a government grant under the Javits Act Program (Grant No. R206R000001) as administered by the Institute of Educational Sciences, formerly the Office of Educational Research and Improvement, U.S. Department of Education; by a grant from the W. T. Grant Foundation; and by a grant from the College Board. Grantees undertaking such projects are encouraged to express freely their professional judgment. This work, therefore, does not necessarily represent the positions or the policies of any of the funding agencies.

Robert J. Sternberg
March 2003

PART I

INTELLIGENCE

1

Background Work on Intelligence

In the year 2000, Al Gore ran against George W. Bush for the presidency of the United States. Both candidates had highly successful political careers, Gore as a U.S. senator from the state of Tennessee and as vice-president of the United States, Bush as governor of the state of Texas, certainly one of the most complex states in the United States. Their success in politics was not preceded by success in school (Simon, 2000). Both men were mediocre students in college. In four years at Yale University, Bush never received an A, and Gore's grades at Harvard were even lower than Bush's at Yale. During his sophomore year, Gore received one B, two Cs, and a D (on a scale where A is high and D is the lowest passing grade). Their college admission test scores were also undistinguished. Gore received a 625 on the verbal SAT (on a scale where 200 is low, 500 average, and 800 high, and where the standard deviation is 100 points). Bush received a score of 566. Bill Bradley, a former U.S. senator and a Democratic presidential primary candidate, received an even less impressive score of 485.

Are these famous politicians unintelligent, intelligent in some way not measured by conventional tests, or what? What does it mean to be intelligent, anyway, and how does our understanding of the nature of intelligence help us understand concrete cases such as Bradley, Bush, and Gore?

CONCEPTIONS OF THE NATURE OF INTELLIGENCE

Anyone who has seriously studied the history of the United States or of any other country knows that there is not one history of a country but many histories. The history of the United States as told by some American Indians, for example, would look quite different from the history as told by some of the later settlers, and even within these groups, the stories would differ. Similarly, there is no one history of the field of intelligence, but rather, many histories, depending on who is doing the telling. For example, the largely laudatory histories recounted by Carroll (1982, 1993), Herrnstein and Murray (1994), and Jensen (1998, 2002) read very differently from the largely skeptical histories recounted by Gardner (1983, 1999), Gould (1981) or Sacks (1999). And there are differences within these groups of authors.

These differences need mentioning because, although all fields of psychology are perceived through ideological lenses, few fields seem to have lenses with so many colors and, some might argue, with so many different distorting imperfections as do the lenses through which are seen the field of intelligence. The different views come not only from ideological biases affecting what is said, but also from affecting what is included. For example, there is virtually no overlap in the historical data used by Carroll (1993) and those used by Gardner (1983) to support their respective theories of intelligence.

Although no account can be truly value-free, I try in this chapter to clarify values in three ways. First, I attempt to represent the views of the investigators and their times in presenting the history of the field. Second, I critique this past work, but make my own personal opinions clear by labeling evaluative sections "Evaluation." Third, I try to represent multiple points of view in a dialectical fashion (Hegel, 1807/1931; see Sternberg, 1999a), pointing out both the positive and negative sides of various contributions. This representation recognizes that all points of view taken in the past can be viewed, with "20/20 hindsight," as skewed, in much the same way that present points of view will be viewed as skewed in the future. A dialectical form of examination will serve as the basis for the entire chapter. The basic idea is that important ideas, good or bad, eventually serve as the springboard for other new ideas that grow out of unions of past ideas that may once have seemed incompatible.

The emphasis in this chapter is on the background history of the field of intelligence, particularly with reference to theories of intelligence. Readers interested primarily in measurement issues might consult relevant chapters in Sternberg (1982, 1994b, 2000b).

Perhaps the most fundamental dialectic in the field of intelligence arises from the question of how we should conceive of intelligence. Several different positions have been staked out (Sternberg, 1990a). Many of the differences in ideology that arise in accounts of the history of the field of intelligence arise from differences in the model of intelligence to which an investigator adheres. To understand the history of the field of intelligence, one must understand the alternative epistemological models that can give rise to the concept of intelligence. But before addressing these models, consider simply the question of how psychologists in the field of intelligence have defined the construct on which they base their models.

Expert Opinions on the Nature of Intelligence

Historically, one of the most important approaches to figuring out what intelligence is has relied on the opinions of experts. Such opinions are sometimes referred to as *implicit theories*, to distinguish them from the more formal *explicit theories* that serve as the bases for scientific hypotheses and subsequent data collections.

Implicit theories (which can be those of laypersons as well as experts) are important to the history of a field for at least three reasons (Sternberg, Conway, Ketron, & Bernstein, 1981). First, experts' implicit theories are typically what give rise to their explicit theories. Second, much of the history of intelligence research and practice is much more closely based on implicit theories than it is on formal theories. Most of the intelligence tests that have been used, for example, are based more on the opinions of their creators as to what intelligence is than on formal theories. Third, people's everyday judgments of each other's intelligence always have been and continue to be much more strongly guided by their implicit theories of intelligence than by any explicit theories.

Intelligence Operationally Defined. E. G. Boring (1923), in an article in the *New Republic*, proposed that intelligence is what the tests of intelligence test. Boring did not believe that this operational definition was the end of the line for understanding intelligence. On the contrary, he saw it as a "narrow definition, but a point of departure for a rigorous discussion . . . until further scientific discussion allows us to extend [it]" (p. 35). Nevertheless, many psychologists and especially testers and interpreters of tests of intelligence have adopted this definition or something similar to it.

From a scientific point of view, the definition is problematic. First, the definition is circular: It defines intelligence in terms of what intelligence tests test, but what the tests test can only be determined by one's definition of intelligence. Second, the definition legitimates rather than calling into scientific question whatever operations are in use at a given time to measure intelligence. To the extent that the goal of science is to disconfirm existing scientific views (Popper, 1959), such a definition will not be useful. Third, the definition assumes that what intelligence tests test is uniform. But this is not the case. Although tests of intelligence tend to correlate positively with each other (the so-called *positive manifold* first noted by Spearman, 1904), such correlations are far from perfect, even controlling for unreliability. Thus, what intelligence tests test is not just one uniform thing. Moreover, even the most ardent proponents of a general factor of intelligence (a single element common to all of these tests) acknowledge there is more to intelligence than just the general factor.

The 1921 Symposium. Probably the best-known study of experts' definitions of intelligence was one done by the editors of the *Journal of Educational*

Psychology ("Intelligence and its measurement," 1921). Contributors to the symposium were asked to address two issues: (a) what they conceived intelligence to be and how it best could be measured by group tests, and (b) what the most crucial next steps would be in research. Fourteen experts gave their views on the nature of intelligence, with such definitions as the following:

1. the power of good responses from the point of view of truth or facts (E. L. Thorndike)
2. the ability to carry on abstract thinking (L. M. Terman)
3. sensory capacity, capacity for perceptual recognition, quickness, range or flexibility of association, facility and imagination, span of attention, quickness or alertness in response (F. N. Freeman)
4. having learned or ability to learn to adjust oneself to the environment (S. S. Colvin)
5. ability to adapt oneself adequately to relatively new situations in life (R. Pintner)
6. the capacity for knowledge and knowledge possessed (B. A. C. Henmon)
7. a biological mechanism by which the effects of a complexity of stimuli are brought together and given a somewhat unified effect in behavior (J. Peterson)
8. the capacity to inhibit an instinctive adjustment, the capacity to redefine the inhibited instinctive adjustment in the light of imaginally experienced trial and error, and the capacity to realize the modified instinctive adjustment in overt behavior to the advantage of the individual as a social animal (L. L. Thurstone)
9. the capacity to acquire capacity (H. Woodrow)
10. the capacity to learn or to profit by experience (W. F. Dearborn)
11. sensation, perception, association, memory, imagination, discrimination, judgment, and reasoning (N. E. Haggerty)

Others of the contributors to the symposium did not provide clear definitions of intelligence but rather concentrated on how to test it. B. Ruml refused to present a definition of intelligence, arguing that not enough was known about the concept. S. L. Pressey described himself as uninterested in the question, although he became well known for his tests of intelligence.

There have been many definitions of intelligence since those presented in the *Journal* symposium, and an essay has been written on the nature of definitions of intelligence (Miles, 1957). One well-known set of definitions was published in 1986 as an explicit follow-up to the 1921 symposium (Sternberg & Detterman, 1986).

Sternberg and Berg (1986) attempted a comparison of the views of experts (P. Baltes, J. Baron, J. Berry, A. Brown & J. Campione, E. Butterfield, J. Carroll, J. P. Das, D. Detterman, W. Estes, H. Eysenck, H. Gardner,

R. Glaser, J. Goodnow, J. Horn, L. Humphreys, E. Hunt, A. Jensen, J. Pellegrino, R. Schank, R. Snow, R. Sternberg, E. Zigler) with those of the experts in 1921. They reached three general conclusions.

First, there was at least some general agreement across the two symposia regarding the nature of intelligence. When attributes were listed for frequency of mention in the two symposia, the correlation was .50, indicating moderate overlap. Attributes such as adaptation to the environment, basic mental processes, higher order thinking (e.g., reasoning, problem solving, and decision making) were prominent in both symposia.

Second, central themes occurred in both symposia. One theme was the one versus the many: Is intelligence one thing or is it multiple things? How broadly should intelligence be defined? What should be the respective roles of biological versus behavioral attributes in seeking an understanding of intelligence?

Third, despite the similarities in views over the sixty-five years, some salient differences could also be found. Metacognition – conceived of as both knowledge about and control of cognition – played a prominent role in the 1986 symposium but virtually no role at all in 1921. The later symposium also placed a greater emphasis on the role of knowledge and the interaction of mental processes with this knowledge.

Lay Conceptions of Intelligence

In some cases, Western notions about intelligence are not shared by other cultures. For example, the Western emphasis on speed of mental processing (Sternberg, Conway, Ketron, & Bernstein, 1981) is not shared by many cultures. Other cultures may even be suspicious of the quality of work that is done very quickly. They emphasize depth rather than speed of processing. They are not alone: Some prominent Western theorists have pointed out the importance of depth of processing for full command of material (e.g., Craik & Lockhart, 1972).

Yang and Sternberg (1997a) have reviewed Chinese philosophical conceptions of intelligence. The Confucian perspective emphasizes the characteristic of benevolence and of doing what is right. As in the Western notion, the intelligent person spends a great deal of effort in learning, enjoys learning, and persists in lifelong learning with a great deal of enthusiasm. The Taoist tradition, in contrast, emphasizes the importance of humility, freedom from conventional standards of judgment, and full knowledge of oneself as well as of external conditions.

The differences between Eastern and Western conceptions of intelligence have extended beyond ancient times and persist even in the present day. Yang and Sternberg (1997b) studied contemporary Taiwanese Chinese conceptions of intelligence, and found five factors underlying these conceptions: (a) a general cognitive factor, much like the g factor in conventional

Western tests; (b) interpersonal intelligence; (c) intrapersonal intelligence; (d) intellectual self-assertion; and (d) intellectual self-effacement. In a related study but with different results, Chen (1994) found three factors underlying Chinese conceptualizations of intelligence: nonverbal reasoning ability, verbal reasoning ability, and rote memory. The difference may be due to different subpopulations of Chinese, to differences in methodology, or to differences in when the studies were done.

The factors uncovered in both studies differ substantially from those identified in U.S. people's conceptions of intelligence by Sternberg, Conway, Ketron, and Bernstein (1981) – (a) practical problem solving, (b) verbal ability, and (c) social competence – although in both cases, people's implicit theories of intelligence seem to go quite far beyond what conventional psychometric intelligence tests measure. Comparing the Chen (1994) study to the Sternberg and colleagues (1981) study simultaneously naturally must take into account both language and culture.

Chen and Chen (1988) considered only language. They explicitly compared the concepts of intelligence of Chinese graduates from Chinese-language versus English-language schools in Hong Kong. They found that both groups considered nonverbal reasoning skills as the most relevant skill for measuring intelligence. Verbal reasoning and social skills came next, and then numerical skill. Memory was seen as least important. The Chinese-language-schooled group, however, tended to rate verbal skills as less important than did the English-language-schooled group. Moreover, in an earlier study, Chen, Braithwaite, and Huang (1982) found that Chinese students viewed memory for facts as important for intelligence, whereas Australian students viewed these skills as of only trivial importance.

Das (1994), reviewing Eastern notions of intelligence, has suggested that in Buddhist and Hindu philosophies, intelligence involves waking up, noticing, recognizing, understanding, and comprehending, but also includes such things as determination, mental effort, and even feelings and opinions in addition to more intellectual elements.

Differences between cultures in conceptions of intelligence have been recognized for some time. Gill and Keats (1980) noted that Australian university students value academic skills and the ability to adapt to new events as critical to intelligence, whereas Malay students value practical skills, as well as speed (which is more typical of the West than of the East) and creativity. Dasen (1984) found Malay students to emphasize both social and cognitive attributes in their conceptions of intelligence.

The differences between East and West may be due to differences in the kinds of skills valued by the two kinds of cultures (Srivastava & Misra, 1996). Western cultures and their schools emphasize what might be called "technological intelligence" (Mundy-Castle, 1974), and so things like artificial intelligence and so-called smart bombs are viewed, in some sense, as intelligent.

Western schooling also emphasizes other factors (Srivastava & Misra, 1996), such as generalization, or going beyond the information given (Connolly & Bruner, 1974; Goodnow, 1976), speed (Sternberg, 1985a), minimal moves to a solution (Newell & Simon, 1972), and creative thinking (Goodnow, 1976). Moreover, silence is interpreted as a lack of knowledge (Irvine, 1978). In contrast, the Wolof tribe in Africa views people of higher social class and distinction as speaking less (Irvine, 1978). This difference between the Wolof and Western notions suggests the usefulness of looking at African notions of intelligence as a possible contrast to those of the United States.

Studies in Africa in fact provide yet another window on the substantial differences. Ruzgis and Grigorenko (1994) have argued that, in Africa, conceptions of intelligence revolve largely around skills that help to facilitate and maintain harmonious and stable intergroup relations; intragroup relations are probably equally important and at times more so. For example, Serpell (1974, 1982, 1996) found that Chewa adults in Zambia emphasize social responsibilities, cooperativeness, and obedience as important to intelligence; intelligent children are expected to be respectful of adults. Kenyan parents also emphasize responsible participation in family and social life as important aspects of intelligence (Super & Harkness, 1982, 1986, 1993). In Zimbabwe, the word for intelligence, *ngware*, actually means to be prudent and cautious, particularly in social relationships. Among the Baoule, service to the family and community and politeness toward and respect for elders are seen as key to intelligence (Dasen, 1984).

Similar emphasis on social aspects of intelligence has been found as well among two other African groups – the Songhay of Mali and the Samia of Kenya (Putnam & Kilbride, 1980). The Yoruba, another African tribe, emphasize the importance of depth – of listening rather than just talking – to intelligence, and of being able to see all aspects of an issue and to place the issue in its proper overall context (Durojaiye, 1993).

The emphasis on the social aspects of intelligence is not limited to African cultures. Notions of intelligence in many Asian cultures also emphasize the social aspect more than does the conventional Western or IQ-based view (Azuma & Kashiwagi, 1987; Lutz, 1985; Poole, 1985; White, 1985).

It should be noted that neither Africans nor Asians emphasize exclusively social notions of intelligence. Although their conceptions much more emphasize social skills than do the conventional U.S. ideas, at the same time they recognize the importance of cognitive aspects of intelligence. In a study of Kenyan conceptions of intelligence (Grigorenko et al., 2001), it was found that there are four distinct terms constituting conceptions of intelligence among rural Kenyans, *rieko* (knowledge and skills), *luoro* (respect), *winjo* (comprehension of how to handle real-life problems), and *paro* (initiative), with only the first directly referring to knowledge-based skills (including but not limited to the academic).

It is important to recognize that there is no one overall U.S. conception of intelligence. Indeed, Okagaki and Sternberg (1993) found that different ethnic groups in San Jose, California, had rather different conceptions of what it means to be intelligent. Latino parents of schoolchildren tended to emphasize the importance of social-competence skills in their conceptions, whereas Asian parents tended rather heavily to emphasize the importance of cognitive skills. Anglo parents also emphasized cognitive skills. Teachers, representing the dominant culture, more emphasized cognitive than social-competence skills. The rank order of performance among children of various groups (including subgroups within the Latino and Asian groups) could be perfectly predicted by the extent to which their parents shared the teachers' conceptions of intelligence. Teachers tended to reward those children who were socialized into a view of intelligence that happened to correspond to their own. Yet, as we shall argue later, social aspects of intelligence, broadly defined, may be as important as, or even more important than, cognitive aspects of intelligence in later life. Some, however, prefer to study intelligence not in its social aspect, but in its cognitive one.

Definitions of any kind can provide a basis for explicit scientific theory and research, but they do not provide a substitute for them. Thus it was necessary for researchers to move beyond definitions, which they indeed did. Many of them moved to models based on individual differences.

Intelligence as Arising from Individual Differences: The Differential Model

McNemar (1964) was one of the most explicit in speculating on why we even have a concept of intelligence and in linking the rationale for the concept to individual differences. He queried whether identical twins stranded on a desert island and growing up together would ever generate the notion of intelligence if they never encountered individual differences in their mental abilities.

Perhaps without individual differences, societies would never generate the notion of intelligence and languages would contain no corresponding term. Actually, some languages, such as Mandarin Chinese, have no concept that corresponds precisely to the Western notion of intelligence (Yang & Sternberg, 1997a, 1997b), although they have related concepts that are closer, say, to the Western notion of wisdom or other constructs. Whatever may be the case, much of the history of the field of intelligence is based on an epistemological model deriving from the existence of one or more kinds of individual differences.

THE SEMINAL VIEWS OF GALTON AND BINET

If current thinking about the nature of intelligence owes a debt to any scholars it is to Sir Francis Galton and Alfred Binet. These two investigators – Galton at the end of the nineteenth century and Binet at the beginning of the twentieth century – have had a profound impact on thinking about intelligence, an impact felt to this day. Many present conflicting views regarding the nature of intelligence can be traced to a dialectical conflict between Galton and Binet.

Intelligence is Simple: Galton's Theory of Psychophysical Processes

Intelligence as Energy and Sensitivity. The publication of Darwin's (1859) *Origin of Species* had a profound impact on many lines of scientific endeavor. One of these lines of endeavor was the investigation of human intelligence. The book suggested that the capabilities of humans were in some sense continuous with those of lower animals, and hence could be understood through scientific investigation.

Galton (1883) followed up on these notions to propose a theory of the "human faculty and its development." Because Galton also proposed techniques for measuring the "human faculty," his theory could be applied directly to human behavior.

Galton proposed two general qualities that he believed distinguish the more from the less intellectually able. His epistemological rooting, therefore, was in the individual-differences approach. The first quality was *energy*, or the capacity for labor. Galton believed that intellectually gifted individuals in a variety of fields are characterized by remarkable levels of energy. The second general quality was *sensitivity*. Galton observed that the only information that can reach us concerning external events passes through the senses and that the more perceptive the senses are of differences in luminescence, pitch, odor, or whatever, the larger would be the range of information on which intelligence could act. Galton's manner of expression was direct:

The discriminative facility of idiots is curiously low; they hardly distinguish between heat and cold, and their sense of pain is so obtuse that some of the more idiotic seem hardly to know what it is. In their dull lives, such pain as can be excited in them may literally be accepted with a welcome surprise. (p. 28)

For seven years (1884–1890), Galton maintained an anthropometric laboratory at the South Kensington Museum in London where, for a small fee, visitors could have themselves measured on a variety of psychophysical tests. What, exactly, were these tests?

One was for weight discrimination. The apparatus consisted of cases of shot, wool, and wadding. The cases were identical in appearance and differed only in their weight. Participants were tested by a sequencing task. They were given three cases and, with their eyes closed, had to arrange them in proper order of weight. The weights formed a geometric series of heaviness, and the examiner recorded the finest interval that an examinee could discriminate. Galton suggested that similar geometric sequences could be used for testing other senses, such as touch and taste. With touch, Galton proposed the use of wirework of various degrees of fineness, whereas for taste he proposed the use of stock bottles of solutions of salt of various strengths. For olfaction, he suggested the use of bottles of attar of rose mixed in various degrees of dilution.

Galton also contrived a whistle for ascertaining the highest pitch that different individuals could perceive. Tests with the whistle enabled him to discover that people's ability to hear high notes declines considerably as age advances. He also discovered that people are inferior to cats in their ability to perceive tones of high pitch.

It is ironic, perhaps, that a theory that took off from Darwin's theory of evolution ended up in what some might perceive as a predicament, at least for those who believe that evolutionary advance is, in part, a matter of complexity (Kauffman, 1995). In most respects, humans are evolutionarily more complex than cats. Galton's theory, however, would place cats, who are able to hear notes of higher pitch than humans, at a superior level to humans at least with respect to this particular aspect of what Galton alleged to be intelligence.

Cattell's Operationalization of Galton's Theory.   James McKeen Cattell brought many of Galton's ideas across the ocean to the United States. As head of the psychological laboratory at Columbia University, Cattell was in a good position to publicize the psychophysical approach to the theory and measurement of intelligence. J. M. Cattell (1890) proposed a series of fifty psychophysical tests. Four examples were

1. *Dynamometer pressure.* The dynamometer-pressure test measures the pressure resulting from the greatest possible squeeze of one's hand.
2. *Sensation areas.* This test measures the distance on the skin by which two points must be separated in order for them to be felt as separate points. Cattell suggested that the back of the closed right hand between the first and second fingers be used as the basis for measurement.
3. *Least noticeable difference in weight.* This test measures the least noticeable differences in weights by having participants judge weights of small wooden boxes. Participants were handed two such boxes and asked to indicate which was heavier.
4. *Bisection of a 50-cm line.* In this test, participants were required to divide a strip of wood into two equal parts by means of a movable line.

Wissler Blows the Whistle. A student of Cattell's, Clark Wissler (1901), decided to validate Cattell's tests. Using twenty-one of the tests, he investigated among Columbia University undergraduates the correlations of the tests with each other and with college grades. The results were devastating: Test scores neither intercorrelated much among themselves nor did they correlate significantly with undergraduate grades. The lack of correlation could not have been due entirely to unreliability of the grades or to restriction of range, because the grades did correlate among themselves. A new approach seemed to be needed.

Evaluation. Even those later theorists who were to build on Galton's work (e.g., Hunt, Frost, & Lunneborg, 1973) recognized that Galton was overly simplistic in his conception and measurement of intelligence. Galton was also pejorative toward groups whom he believed to be of inferior intelligence. Yet one could argue that Galton set at least three important precedents.

A first precedent was the desirability of precise quantitative measurement. Much of psychological measurement, particularly in the clinical areas, has been more qualitative, or based on dubious rules about translations of qualitative responses to quantitative measurements. Galton's psychometric precision set a different course for research and practice in the field of intelligence. His combination of theory and measurement techniques set a precedent: Many future investigators would tie their theories, strong or weak, to operations that would enable them to measure the intelligence of a variety of human populations.

A second precedent was the interface between theory and application. Galton's Kensington Museum enterprise set a certain kind of tone for the intelligence measurement of the future. No field of psychology, perhaps, has been more market-oriented than has been the measurement of intelligence. Testing of intelligence has been highly influenced by market demands, more so, say, than testing of memory abilities or social skills. It is difficult to study the history of the field of intelligence without considering both theory and practice.

A third precedent was a tendency to conflate scores on tests of intelligence with some kind of personal value. Galton made no attempt to hide his admiration for hereditary geniuses (Galton, 1869) nor to hide his contempt for those at the lower end of the intelligence scale as he perceived it (Galton, 1883). He believed those at the high end of the scale had much more to contribute than those at the low end. The same kinds of judgments do not pervade the literatures of, say, sensation or memory. This tendency to conflate intelligence with some kind of economic or social value to society and perhaps beyond society has continued to the present day (for example, Herrnstein & Murray, 1994; Schmidt & Hunter, 1998).

Intelligence is Complex: Binet's Theory of Judgment

In 1904, the Minister of Public Instruction in Paris established a commission charged with studying or creating tests that would insure that mentally defective children (as they then were called) would receive an adequate education. The commission decided that no child suspected of retardation should be placed in a special class for children with mental retardation without first being given an examination, "from which it could be certified that because of the state of his intelligence, he was unable to profit, in an average measure, from the instruction given in the ordinary schools" (Binet & Simon, 1916a, p. 9).

Binet and Simon devised a test based on a conception of intelligence very different from Galton's and Cattell's. They viewed judgment as central to intelligence. At the same time, they viewed Galton's tests as ridiculous. They cited Helen Keller as an example of someone who was very intelligent but who would have performed terribly on Galton's tests.

Binet and Simon's (1916b) theory of intelligent thinking in many ways foreshadowed later research on the development of metacognition (for example, Brown & DeLoache, 1978; Flavell & Wellman, 1977; Nelson, 1999). According to Binet and Simon (1916a), intelligent thought comprises three distinct elements: direction, adaptation, and control.

Direction consists in knowing what has to be done and how it is to be accomplished. When we are required to add three numbers, for example, we give ourselves a series of instructions on how to proceed, and these instructions form the direction of thought.

Adaptation refers to one's selection and monitoring of one's strategy during task performance. For example, in adding two numbers, one first needs to decide on a strategy to add the numbers. As we add, we need to check (monitor) that we are not repeating the addition of any of the digits we already have added.

Control is the ability to criticize one's own thoughts and actions. This ability often occurs beneath the conscious level. If one notices that the sum one attains is smaller than either number (if the numbers are positive), one recognizes there is a mistake in one's addition and one must add the numbers again.

Binet and Simon (1916a) distinguished between two types of intelligence, ideational intelligence and instinctive intelligence. *Ideational intelligence* operates by means of words and ideas. It uses logical analysis and verbal reasoning. *Instinctive intelligence* operates by means of feeling. It refers not to the instincts attributed to animals and to simple forms of human behavior, but to lack of logical thinking. This two-process kind of model adumbrates many contemporary models of thinking (for example, Epstein, 1985; Evans, 1989; Sloman, 1996), which make similar distinctions.

What are some examples of the kinds of problems found on a Binet-based test (for example, Terman & Merrill, 1937, 1973; Thorndike, Hagen, & Sattler, 1986)? In one version (Terman & Merrill, 1973), two-year-olds are given a three-hold form board, into which they are required to place in the appropriate indentations circular, square, and triangular pieces. Another test requires children to identify body parts on a paper doll. Six years later, by age eight, the character of the test items changes considerably. By age eight, the tests include vocabulary, which requires children to define words; verbal absurdities, which require recognition of why each of a set of statements is foolish; similarities and differences, which require children to say how each of two objects is the same as and different from each other; and comprehension, which requires children to solve practical problems of the sort encountered in everyday life. At age fourteen, there is some overlap with the age eight tests as well as some different kinds. For example, in induction, the experimenter makes a notch in an edge of some folded paper and asks participants how many holes the paper will have when it is unfolded. On a reasoning test, participants need to solve arithmetic word problems. Ingenuity requires individuals to indicate the series of steps that could be used to pour a given amount of water from one container to another.

The early Binet and Simon tests (preceding the finalized ones), like those of Cattell, were soon put to a test, in this case by Sharp (1899). Although her results were not entirely supportive, she generally accepted the view of judgment, rather than psychophysical processes, as underlying intelligence. Most subsequent researchers have accepted this notion as well.

Evaluation.   Binet's work was to have far more influence than Galton's. First, the kinds of test items used by Binet are, for the most part, similar to those used today. From the standpoint of modern test constructors, Binet "largely got it right." Indeed, a current test, the Stanford-Binet Intelligence Scale (4th ed.) (Thorndike, Hagen, & Sattler, 1986) is a direct descendant of the Binet test. The Wechsler tests (Wechsler, 1991), although somewhat different in their conceptualization, owe a great deal to Binet.

Second, Binet grounded his tests in competencies that are central to schooling and perhaps less central to the world of adult work. Such grounding made sense, given the school-based mission with which Binet was entrusted. Although intelligence test scores correlate both with school grades and with work performance, their correlation with school grades is substantially higher, and they correlate better with job training performance than with work performance (see reviews in Mackintosh, 1998; Wagner, 2000).

Third, intelligence tests continue today, as in Binet's time, to be touted as serving a protective function. The goal of Binet's test was to protect children from being improperly classified in school. Today, test users point out how test scores can give opportunities to children who otherwise would not get them. For example, children from lower-level or even middle-level socioeconomic backgrounds, who would not be able to pay for certain kinds of schooling, may receive admission or scholarships on the basis of test scores. At the same time, there is a dialectic in action here, whereby opponents of testing, or at least of certain kinds of testing, would argue that the conventional tests do more damage than good (Gardner, 1983; Sacks, 1999), taking away opportunities rather than providing them to many children.

An important aspect of Binet's theory has been lost to many. This was Binet's belief that intelligence is malleable and could be improved by "mental orthopedics." To this day, many investigators are interested in raising levels of mental functioning (see review by Grotzer & Perkins, 2000). But many other investigators, even those who use Binet-based tests, question whether intelligence is malleable in any major degree (e.g., Jensen, 1969, 1998).

MODELS OF THE NATURE OF INTELLIGENCE

A number of different types of models have been proposed to characterize intelligence (Sternberg, 1990a). What are the principal models, and how are they similar to and different from one another?

Psychometric Models

The early efforts of intelligence theorists largely built on the Binetian school of thought rather than the Galtonian school of thought. The most influential theorist, historically and perhaps even into the present, was also among the first, a British psychologist named Charles Spearman.

Spearman's Two-Factor Theory.   Spearman (1904, 1927) proposed a two-factor theory of intelligence, a theory still very much alive and well today (for example, Brand, 1996; Jensen, 1998, 2002). The theory posits a general factor (g) common to all tasks requiring intelligence and one specific factor (s) unique to each different type of task. Thus, there are two types of factors, rather than, strictly speaking, two factors.

Spearman (1904) got this idea as a result of looking at data processed by a statistical technique of his own invention, *factor analysis*, which attempts to identify latent sources of individual (or other) differences that underlie observed sources of variation in test performance. Spearman observed that when he analyzed a correlation matrix, the two kinds of factors appeared – the general factor common to all the tests, and the specific factors unique to each particular test.

Spearman (1927) admitted he was not sure of what the psychological basis of g is, but suggested that it might be mental energy (a term he never defined very clearly). Whatever it was, it was a unitary and primary source of individual differences in intelligence test performance.

The Theories of Bonds and of Connections

Theory of Bonds. Spearman's theory was soon challenged, and continues to be challenged today (for example, Gardner, 1983; Sternberg, 1999d). One of Spearman's chief critics was British psychologist Sir Godfrey Thomson, who accepted Spearman's statistics but not his interpretation. Thomson (1939) argued that it is possible to have a general psychometric factor in the absence of any kind of general ability. In particular, he argued that *g* is a statistical reality but a psychological artifact. He suggested that the general factor might result from the working of an extremely large number of what he called *bonds*, all of which are sampled simultaneously in intellectual tasks. Imagine, for example, that each of the intellectual tasks found in the test batteries of Spearman and others requires certain mental skills. If each test samples all these mental skills, then their appearance will be perfectly correlated with each other because they always co-occur. Thus, they will give the appearance of a single general factor, when in fact they are multiple.

Although Thomson did not attempt to specify exactly what the bonds might be, it is not hard to speculate on what some of these common elements are. For example, they might include understanding the problems and responding to them.

Theory of Connections. Thorndike, Bregman, Cobb, and Woodyard (1926) proposed a quite similar theory, based on Thorndike's theory of learning. They suggested that

in their deeper nature the higher forms of intellectual operations are identical with mere association or connection forming, depending on the same sort of physiological connections but requiring *many more of them*. By the same argument the person whose intellect is greater or higher or better than that of another person differs from him in the last analysis in having, not a new sort of physiological process, but simply a larger number of connections of the ordinary sort. (p. 415)

According to this theory, then, learned connections, similar to Thomson's bonds, are what underlie individual differences in intelligence.

Thurstone's Theory of Primary Mental Abilities

Louis L. Thurstone, like Spearman, was an ardent advocate of factor analysis as a method of revealing latent psychological structures underlying observable test performances. Thurstone (1938, 1947) believed, however, that it was a mistake to leave the axes of factorial solutions unrotated. He believed that the solution thus obtained was psychologically arbitrary. Instead, he suggested rotation to what he referred to as *simple structure*, which is designed to clean up the columns of a factor pattern matrix so that the factors display either relatively high or low loadings of tests on given factors, rather than large numbers of moderate ones. Using simple-structure rotation, Thurstone and Thurstone (1941) argued for the existence of seven primary mental abilities.

1. *Verbal comprehension:* the ability to understand verbal material. This ability is measured by tests such as vocabulary and reading comprehension.
2. *Verbal fluency:* the ability involved in rapidly producing words, sentences, and other verbal material. This ability is measured by tests such as one that requires the examinee to produce as many words as possible beginning with a certain letter in a short amount of time.
3. *Number:* the ability to compute rapidly. This ability is measured by tests requiring solution of numerical arithmetic problems and simple arithmetic word problems.
4. *Memory:* the ability to remember strings of words, letters, numbers, or other symbols or items. This ability is measured by serial- or free-recall tests.
5. *Perceptual speed:* the ability to recognize letters, numbers, or other symbols rapidly. This ability is measured by proofreading tests, or by tests that require individuals to cross out a given letter (such as *A*) in a string of letters.
6. *Inductive reasoning:* the ability to reason from the specific to the general. This ability is measured by tests such as letter series ("What letter comes next in the following series? b, d, g, k, ...") and number series ("What number comes next in the following series? 4, 12, 10, 30, 28, 84, . . .").
7. *Spatial visualization:* the ability involved in visualizing shapes, rotations of objects, and how pieces of a puzzle would fit together. This ability is measured by tests that require mental rotations or other manipulations of geometric objects.

The argument between Spearman and Thurstone could not be resolved on mathematical grounds, simply because in exploratory factor analysis, any of an infinite number of rotations of axes is acceptable. As an analogy, consider axes used to understand world geography (Vernon, 1971). One can use lines of longitude and latitude, but really, any axes at all could be used, orthogonal or oblique, or even axes that serve different functions, such as in polar coordinates. The locations of points, and the distances between them, do not change in Euclidean space as a result of how the axes are placed.

Because Thurstone's primary mental abilities are intercorrelated, Spearman and others have argued that they are nothing more than varied manifestations of g: Factor analyze these factors, and a general factor will emerge as a second-order factor. Thurstone argued that the primary mental abilities were more basic. Such arguments became largely polemical because there neither was nor is any way of resolving the debate in the terms in which it was presented. Some synthesis was needed for the opposing thesis of g versus the antithesis of primary mental abilities.

Hierarchical Theories

The main synthesis to be proposed was to be hierarchical theories – theories that assume that abilities can be ordered in terms of levels of generality. Rather than arguing which abilities are more fundamental, hierarchical theorists have argued that all the abilities have a place in a hierarchy of abilities from the general to the specific.

Holzinger's Bifactor Theory. Holzinger (1938) proposed a bifactor theory of intelligence, which retained both the general and specific factors of Spearman, but also permitted group factors such as those found in Thurstone's theory. Such factors are common to more than one test, but not to all tests. This theory helped form the basis for other hierarchical theories that replaced it.

Burt's Theory. Sir Cyril Burt (1949), known primarily for his widely questioned work on the heritability of intelligence, suggested that a five-level hierarchy would capture the nature of intelligence. At the top of Burt's hierarchy was "the human mind." At the second level, the "relations level," are g and a practical factor. At the third level are associations, at the fourth level, perception, and at the fifth level, sensation. This model has proved not to be durable and is relatively infrequently cited today.

Vernon's Theory of Verbal : Educational and Spatial : Mechanical Abilities. A more widely adopted model has been that of Vernon (1971), which proposes the general factor, g, at the top of the hierarchy. Below this factor are two group factors, $v:ed$ and $k:m$. The former refers to verbal-educational abilities of the kinds measured by conventional tests of scholastic abilities. The latter refers to spatial-mechanical abilities (with k perhaps inappropriately referring to the nonequivalent term *kinesthetic*).

Cattell's Theory of Fluid and Crystallized Abilities. More widely accepted than any of the above theories is that of Raymond Cattell (1971), which is somewhat similar to Vernon's theory. Cattell's theory proposes general ability at the top of the hierarchy and two abilities immediately beneath it, fluid ability, or g_f, and crystallized ability, or g_c. Fluid ability is the ability to think flexibly and to reason abstractly. It is measured by tests such as number series and figural analogies. Crystallized ability is the accumulated knowledge base one has developed over the course of one's life as the result of the application of fluid ability. It is measured by tests such as vocabulary and general information.

More recent work has suggested that fluid ability is extremely difficult to distinguish statistically from general ability (Gustafsson, 1984, 1988). The tests used to measure fluid ability are often identical to the tests used to measure what is supposed to be pure g. An example of such a test would be the Raven Progressive Matrices (Raven, 1986), which measures people's ability to fill in a missing part of a matrix comprising abstract figural drawings.

Horn (1994) has greatly expanded on the hierarchical theory as originally proposed by Cattell. Most notably, he has suggested that g can be split into three more factors nested under fluid and crystallized abilities. These three other factors are visual thinking (g_v), auditory thinking (g_a), and speed (g_s). The visual thinking factor is probably closer to Vernon's *k:m* factor than it is to the fluid ability factor.

Carroll's Three-Stratum Theory.   Perhaps the most widely accepted hierarchical model today is that proposed by Carroll (1993), which is based on the reanalysis of (more than 450) data sets from the past. At the top of the hierarchy is general ability; in the middle of the hierarchy are various broad abilities, including fluid and crystallized intelligence, learning and memory processes, visual and auditory perception, facile production, and speed. At the bottom of the hierarchy are fairly specific abilities.

Guilford's Structure-of-Intellect Model.   Although many differential theorists followed the option of proposing a hierarchical model, not all did. J. P. Guilford (1967, 1982; Guilford & Hoepfner, 1971) proposed a model with 120 distinct abilities (increased to 150 in 1982 and to 180 in later manifestations). The basic theory organizes abilities along three dimensions: operations, products, and contents. In the best known version of the model, there are five operations, six products, and four contents. The five operations are cognition, memory, divergent production, convergent production, and evaluation. The six products are units, classes, relations, systems, transformations, and implications. The four contents are figural, symbolic, semantic, and behavioral. Because these dimensions are completely crossed with each other, they yield a total of $5 \times 6 \times 4$ or 120 different abilities. For example, inferring a relation in a verbal analogy (such as the relation between BLACK and WHITE in BLACK : WHITE :: HIGH : LOW) would involve cognition of semantic relations.

Guilford's model has not fared well psychometrically. Horn and Knapp (1973) showed that random theories could generate support equal to that obtained by Guilford's model when the same type of rotation was used that Guilford used – so-called "Procrustean rotation." Horn (1967) showed that equal support could be obtained with Guilford's theory, but with data generated randomly rather than with real data. These demonstrations do not prove the model wrong: They show only that the psychometric support that Guilford claimed for his model was not justified by the methods he used.

Guttman's Radex Model.   The last psychometric model to be mentioned is one proposed by Louis Guttman (1954). The model is what Guttman referred to as a radex, or radial representation of complexity.

The radex consists of two parts. The first part Guttman calls a simplex. If one imagines a circle, then the simplex refers to the distance of a given point (ability) from the center of the circle. The closer a given ability is to the center of the circle, the more central that ability is to human intelligence. Thus, g could be viewed as being at the center of the circle, whereas the more peripheral abilities such as perceptual speed would be nearer to the periphery of the circle. Abilities nearer to the periphery of the circle are viewed as being constituents of abilities nearer the center of the circle, so the theory has a hierarchical element.

The second part of the radex is called the circumplex. It refers to the angular orientation of a given ability with respect to the circle. Thus, abilities are viewed as being arranged around the circle with abilities that are more highly related (correlated) nearer to each other in the circle. Thus, the radex functions through a system of polar coordinates. Snow, Kyllonen, and Marshalek (1984) used nonmetric multidimensional scaling on a Thurstonian type of test to demonstrate that the Thurstonian primary mental abilities actually could be mapped into a radex.

Evaluation

Psychometric theories of intelligence have been enormously influential, particularly in North America and in the United Kingdom. In many respects, they have served the field well. First, they have provided a Zeitgeist for three generations of researchers. Second, they have provided a systematic means for studying individual differences. Arguably, no other paradigm has provided a means nearly as systematic or successful in so many respects. Third, the theories cross well between theory and application. Few theories have proved to have as many and as diverse practical applications. Finally, they have provided a model for how theory and measurement can evolve in synchrony.

At the same time, there have been problems with the differential approach. First, although factor analysis, as a method, is neither good nor bad, it has frequently been subject to misuse (Horn & Knapp, 1974; Humphreys, 1962; McNemar, 1951). Second, factor analyses have sometimes been not so much misinterpreted as overinterpreted. What one gets out of a factor analysis is simply a psychometric transformation of what one puts in. It is possible to support many different theories by choosing one's tests with a certain goal in mind. The resulting factors simply reflect the choice of tests and their interrelationships. Third, in exploratory factor analysis, the rotation issue has proven to be a thorny one. Any rotation is mathematically correct and equivalent in Euclidean space. Arguments over which theory is correct often have boiled down to little more than arguments over which rotation is psychologically more justified. But no adequate basis has been found for supporting one rotation as psychologically preferred over all others. Fifth and finally, the whole issue of deriving a theory of intelligence from patterns of individual differences has never received fully adequate examination by differential psychologists. Evolutionary theorists (e.g., Pinker, 1997; see Sternberg & Kaufman, 2001) would argue that intelligence needs to be understood in terms of commonalities, not differences. Experimental psychologists have made the same claim for many decades, preferring to view individual differences as noise in their data. Perhaps the best solution is some kind of synthesis, as recommended by Cronbach (1957). Jean Piaget, disheartened with his observations from work in Binet's laboratory, provided a synthesis of sorts. He combined measurement with a more cognitive framework for understanding intelligence.

INTELLIGENCE AS ARISING FROM COGNITIVE STRUCTURES AND PROCESSES

Cognitive Structures

Piaget (1952, 1972), among others, has staked out an alternative position to the differential one. Piaget, who was never very interested in individual differences, viewed intelligence as arising from cognitive schemas, or structures that mature as a function of the interaction of the organism with the environment.

Equilibration. Piaget (1926, 1928, 1952, 1972), like many other theorists of intelligence, recognized the importance of adaptation to intelligence. Indeed, he believed adaptation to be its most important principle. In adaptation, individuals learn from the environment and learn to address the changes in the environment. Adjustment consists of two complementary processes: assimilation and accommodation. *Assimilation* is the process of absorbing new information and fitting it into an already existing cognitive structure about what the world is like. The complementary process, *accommodation*, involves forming a new cognitive structure in order to understand information. In other words, if no existing cognitive structure seems adequate to understand new information, a new cognitive structure must be formed through the accommodation process.

The complementary processes of assimilation and accommodation, taken together in an interaction, constitute what Piaget referred to as equilibration. *Equilibration* is the balancing of the two and it is through this balance that people either add to old schemas or form new ones. A *schema*, for Piaget, is a mental image or action pattern. It is essentially a way of organizing sensory information. For example, we have schemas for going to the bank, riding a bicycle, eating a meal, visiting a doctor's office, and the like.

Stages of Intellectual Development. Piaget (1972) suggested that the intelligence of children matures through four discrete stages, or periods of development. Each of these periods builds on the preceding one, so that development is essentially cumulative.

The first period is the *sensorimotor period*, which occupies birth through roughly two years of age. By the end of the sensorimotor period, the infant has started to acquire object permanence, or the realization that objects can exist apart from him or herself. In early infancy, the infant does not ascribe a separate reality to objects. Thus, if a toy is hidden under a pillow or behind a barrier, the infant will not search for the toy because as far as he or she is concerned, it no longer exists when it goes out of sight. By the end of the period, the infant knows that a search will lead to finding the object.

The second period is the *preoperational period*, which emerges roughly between ages two and seven. The child is now beginning to represent the world through symbols and images, but the symbols and images are directly dependent on the immediate perception of the child. The child is still essentially egocentric: He or she sees objects and people only from his or her own point of view. Thus, to the extent that thinking takes place, it is egocentric thinking.

The third period is the *concrete-operational period*, which occupies roughly ages seven through eleven. In this period, the child is able to perform concrete mental operations. Thus, the child now can think through sequences of actions or events that previously had to be enacted physically. The hallmark of concrete-operational thought is reversibility. It is now possible for the child to reverse the direction of thought. He or she comes to understand, for example, that subtraction is the reverse of addition and division is the reverse of multiplication. The child can go to the store and back home again or trace out a route on a map and see the way back.

The period is labeled as one of "concrete" operations because operations are performed for objects that are physically present. A major acquisition of the period is conservation, which involves a child's recognition that objects or quantities can remain the same, despite changes in their physical appearance. Suppose, for example, a child is shown two glasses, one short and fat and the other tall and thin. If a preoperational child watches water poured from the short, fat glass to the tall, thin one, he or she will say that the tall, thin glass has more water than the short, fat one had. But the concrete–operational child will recognize that the quantity of water is the same in the new glass as in the old glass, despite the change in physical appearance.

The period of *formal operations* begins to evolve at around eleven years of age and usually will be fairly fully developed by sixteen years of age, although some adults never completely develop formal operations. In the period of formal operations, the child acquires the ability to think abstractly and hypothetically, not just concretely. The individual can view a problem from multiple points of view and think much more systematically than in the past. For example, if asked to provide all possible permutations of the numbers 1, 2, 3, and 4, the child can now implement a systematic strategy for listing all these permutations. In contrast, the concrete–operational child will have essentially listed permutations at random, without a systematic strategy. The child can now think scientifically and use the hypotheticodeductive method to generate and test hypotheses.

Vygotsky and Feuerstein's Theories.   Whereas Piaget has emphasized primarily biological maturation in the development of intelligence, other theorists interested in structures, such as Vygotsky (1978) and Feuerstein (1979), have more emphasized the role of interactions of individuals with the environment. Vygotsky suggested that basic to intelligence is *internalization*, which is the internal reconstruction of an external operation. The basic notion is that we observe those in the social environment around us acting in certain ways and we internalize their actions so that they become a part of us.

Vygotsky (1978) gave an example of internalization in the development of pointing. He suggested that, initially, pointing is nothing more than an unsuccessful attempt to grasp something. The child attempts to grasp an object beyond his reach and fails. When the mother sees the child attempting to grasp the object, she comes to his aid and is likely to point to it. He thereby learns to do the same. Thus, the child's unsuccessful attempt engenders a reaction from the mother or some other individual, which leads to his being able to perform that action. Note that it is the social mediation, rather than the object itself, which provides the basis for the child's learning to point.

Vygotsky also proposed the important notion of a *zone of proximal development*, which refers to functions that have not yet matured but are in the process of maturation. The basic idea is to look not only at developed abilities, but also at abilities that are developing. This zone is often measured as the difference between performance before and after instruction. Thus, instruction is given at the time of testing to measure the individual's ability to learn in the testing environment (Brown & French, 1979; Feuerstein, 1980; Grigorenko & Sternberg, 1998). The research suggests that tests of the zone of proximal development tap abilities not measured by conventional tests.

Related ideas have been proposed by Feuerstein (1979, 1980). Feuerstein has suggested that much of intellectual development derives from the mediation of the environment by the mother or other adults. From Feuerstein's point of view, parents serve an important role in development not only for the experiences with which they provide children, but also for the way they help children understand these experiences. For example, what would be important would be not so much encouraging children to watch educational television or taking children to museums, but rather, helping them interpret what they see on television or in museums.

Evaluation

By any standard, Piaget's contribution to the study of intelligence was profound. First, his theory stands alone in terms of its comprehensiveness in accounting for intellectual development. There is no competition in this respect. Second, even the many individuals who have critiqued Piaget's work have honored it by deeming it worthy of criticism. To the extent that a theory's value is heuristic, in its giving way to subsequent theories, Piaget's work is almost without par. Much research today, especially in Europe, continues in the tradition of Piaget. Neo-Piagetians, although they have changed many of the details, still build on many Piagetian theoretical ideas and tasks for studying development. Third, even the most ardent critics of Piaget would concede that many of his ideas, such as of centration, conservation, and equilibration, were correct and remain alive today in a wide variety of forms. Fourth, Piaget provided an enormous database for developmental psychologists to deal with today. Replications generally have proven to be successful (Siegler, 1998).

Yet the theory of Piaget has not stood the test of time without many scars. Consider some of the main ones.

First, Piaget's interpretations of data have proven to be problematical in many different respects. The list of such critiques is very long. For example, there is evidence that infants achieve object permanence much earlier than Piaget had thought (for example, Baillargeon, 1987; Cornell, 1978). There is also evidence that conservation begins earlier than Piaget suspected (Au, Sidle, & Rollins, 1993). As another example, difficulties that Piaget attributed to reasoning appear in some instances actually to have been due to memory (e.g., Bryant & Trabasso, 1971).

Second, it now appears that children often failed Piagetian tasks not because they were unable to do them, but because they did not understand the task in the way the experimenter intended. Piaget's research points out how important it is to make sure one understands a problem not only from one's own point of view as experimenter, but also from the child's point of view as participant. For example, being asked whether a collection of marbles contains more blue marbles or more marbles can be confusing, even to an adult.

Third, many investigators today question the whole notion of stages of development (for example, Brainerd, 1978; Flavell, 1971). Piaget fudged a bit with the concept of *horizontal décalage*, or nonsimultaneous development of skills within a given stage across domains; many investigators believe that development is simply much more domain-specific than Piaget was willing to admit (e.g., Carey, 1985; Keil, 1989). As another example, children master different kinds of conservation problems at different ages, with the differences appearing in a systematic fashion (Elkind, 1961; Katz & Beilin, 1976; Miller, 1976), with conservation of number appearing before conservation of solid quantity, and conservation of solid quantity before weight.

Fourth, many investigators have found Piaget's theory to better characterize children's competencies than their performance (for example, Green, Ford, & Flamer, 1971). Indeed, Piaget (1972) characterized his model as a competency model. For this reason, it may not be optimally useful in characterizing what children are able to do on a day-to-day basis.

Fifth, although Piaget believed that cognitive development could not be meaningfully accelerated, the evidence suggests the contrary (Beilin, 1980; Field, 1987). Piaget probably took too strong a position in this regard.

Finally, some have questioned the emphasis Piaget placed on logical and scientific thinking (for example, Sternberg, 1990c). People often seem less rational and more oriented toward heuristics than Piaget believed (Gigerenzer, Todd, & the ABC Research Group, 1999).

Vygotsky's theory is, at the turn of the century, more in vogue than Piaget's. It better recognizes the important role of the social-cultural environment in intellectual development. And it also suggests how conventional tests may fail to unearth developing intellectual functions that give children added potential to succeed intellectually. Vygotsky's theory is rather vague, however, and much of the recent development has gone considerably beyond anything Vygotsky proposed. Perhaps if he had not died tragically at an early age (thirty-eight years), he would have extensively amplified on his theory.

Cognitive Processes

A related position is that of cognitive theorists (e.g., Anderson, 1983; Miller, Galanter, & Pribram, 1960; Newell & Simon, 1972), who seek to understand intelligence in terms of the processes of human thought and the architecture that holds these processes together. These theorists may use the software of a computer as a model of the human mind, or in more recent theorizing, the massively parallel operating systems of neural circuitry (for example, Rumelhart, McClelland, & the PDP Research Group, 1986). Much of the history of this field is relatively recent, simply because much of the "early" development of the field has occurred in recent times. The field today, for example, has advanced quite far beyond where it was thirty years ago. At the same time, the origins of the field go back to early in the twentieth century and even beyond, depending on how broad one is in labeling work as related to this approach.

The Origins of the Process-Based Approach in Spearman's Principles of Cognition

Although some psychologists in the nineteenth century were interested in information processing (e.g., Donders, 1868/1969), the connection between information processing and intelligence seems to have been explicitly drawn first by Charles Spearman (1923), also known for initiating serious psychometric theorizing about intelligence.

Spearman (1923) proposed what he believed to be three fundamental qualitative principles of cognition. The first, *apprehension of experience*, is what today might be called the encoding of stimuli (see Sternberg, 1977). It involves perceiving the stimuli and their properties. The second principle, *eduction of relations*, is what today might be labeled inference. It is the inferring of a relation between two or more concepts. The third principle, *eduction of correlates*, is what today might be called application. It is the application of an inferred rule to a new situation. For example, in the analogy, WHITE : BLACK :: GOOD : ?, apprehension of experience would involve reading each of the terms. Eduction of relations would involve inferring the relation between WHITE and BLACK. And eduction of correlates would involve applying the inferred relation to complete the analogy with BAD. Tests that measure these attributes without contamination from many other sources, such as the Raven Progressive Matrices tests, generally provide very good measures of psychometric *g*.

The Cognitive-Correlates Approach

Lee Cronbach (1957) tried to revive interest in the cognitive approach with an article on "the two disciplines of scientific psychology," and there were some fits and starts during the 1960s in an effort to revive this approach. But serious revival can probably be credited in large part to the work of Earl Hunt. Hunt (1980; Hunt, Frost, & Lunneborg, 1973; Hunt, Lunneborg, & Lewis, 1975) was the originator of what has come to be called the *cognitive-correlates approach* to integrating the study of cognitive processing with the study of intelligence (Pellegrino & Glaser, 1979).

The proximal goal of this research is to estimate parameters representing the durations of performance for information-processing components constituting experimental tasks commonly used in the laboratories of cognitive psychologists. These parameters are then used to investigate the extent to which cognitive components correlate with each other across participants and with scores on psychometric measures commonly believed to measure intelligence, such as the Raven Progressive Matrices tests. Consider an example.

In one task – the Posner and Mitchell (1967) letter-matching task – participants are shown pairs of letters such as "A A" or "A a." After each pair, they are asked to respond as rapidly as possible to one of two questions: "Are the letters a physical match?" or "Are the letters a name match?" Note that the first pair of letters provides an affirmative answer to both questions, whereas the second pair of letters provides an affirmative answer only to the second of the two questions. That is, the first pair provides both a physical and a name match, whereas the second pair provides a name match only.

The goal of such a task is to estimate the amount of time a given participant takes to access lexical information – letter names – in memory. The physical-match condition is included to subtract out (control for) sheer time to perceive the letters and respond to questions. The difference between name and physical match time thus provides the parameter estimate of interest for the task. Hunt and his colleagues found that this parameter and similar parameters in other experimental tasks typically correlate about −.3 with scores on psychometric tests of verbal ability.

The precise tasks used in such research have varied. The letter-matching task has been a particularly popular one, as has been the short-term memory scanning task originally proposed by S. Sternberg (1969). Other researchers have preferred simple and choice reaction time tasks (for example, Jensen, 1979, 1982). Most such studies have been conducted with adults, but some have been conducted developmentally with children of various ages (e.g., Keating & Bobbitt, 1978).

The Cognitive-Components Approach

An alternative approach has come to be called the *cognitive-components approach* (Pellegrino & Glaser, 1979). In this approach, participants are tested in their ability to perform tasks of the kinds actually found on standard psychometric tests of mental abilities – for example, analogies, series completions, mental rotations, and syllogisms. Participants typically are timed and response time is the principal dependent variable, with error rate and pattern-of-response choices serving as further dependent variables. This approach was suggested by Sternberg (1977; see also Royer, 1971).

The proximal goal in this research is, first, to formulate a model of information processing in performance on the types of tasks found in conventional psychometric tests of intelligence. Second, it is to test the model at the same time as parameters for the model are estimated. Finally, it is to investigate the extent to which these components correlate across participants with each other and with scores on standard psychometric tests. Because the tasks that are analyzed are usually taken directly from psychometric tests of intelligence or are very similar to such tasks, the major issue in this kind of research is not whether there is any correlation at all between cognitive tasks and psychometric test scores. Rather, the issue is one of isolating the locus or loci of the correlations that are obtained. One seeks to discover what components of information processing are the critical ones from the standpoint of the theory of intelligence (Carroll, 1981; Pellegrino & Glaser, 1979, 1980, 1982; Royer, 1971; Sternberg, 1977, 1980b, 1983; Sternberg & Gardner, 1983).

Consider the analogies task mentioned above. The participant might be presented with an analogy such as WHITE : BLACK :: GOOD : (A) BAD, (B) BETTER. The task is to choose the better of the two response options as quickly as possible. Cognitive-components analysis might extract a number of components from the task, using an expanded version of Spearman's theory (Sternberg, 1977). These components might include (a) the time to *encode* the stimulus terms, (b) the time to *infer* the relation between WHITE and BLACK, (c) the time to *map* the relation from the first half of the analogy to the second, (d) the time to *apply* the inferred relation from GOOD to each of the answer options, (e) the time to *compare* the two response options, (f) the time to *justify* BAD as the preferable option, and (g) the time to *respond* with (A).

The Cognitive-Training Approach

The goal of the *cognitive-training approach* is to infer the components of information processing from how individuals perform when they are trained. According to Campione, Brown, and Ferrara (1982), one starts with a theoretical analysis of a task and a hypothesis about a source of individual differences within that task. It might be assumed, for example, that components A, B, and C are required to carry out Task X and that less able children do poorly because of a weakness in component A. To test this assertion, one might train less able participants in the use of A and then retest them on X. If performance improves, the task analysis is supported. If performance does not improve, then either A was not an important component of the task or participants were originally efficient with regard to A and did not need training, or the training was ineffective (see also Belmont &

Butterfield, 1971; Belmont, Butterfield, & Ferretti, 1982; Borkowski & Wanschura, 1974).

The Cognitive-Contents Approach

In the *cognitive-contents approach*, one seeks to compare the performances of experts and novices in complex tasks such as physics problems (for example, Chi, Feltovich, & Glaser, 1981; Chi, Glaser, & Rees, 1982; Larkin, McDermott, Simon, & Simon, 1980), the selection of moves and strategies in chess and other games (Chase & Simon, 1973; DeGroot, 1965; Reitman, 1976), and the acquisition of domain-related information by groups of people at different levels of expertise (Chiesi, Spilich, & Voss, 1979). The notion underlying such research can be seen as abilities being forms of developing expertise (Sternberg, 1998a). In other words, the experts have developed high levels of intellectual ability in particular domains as results of the development of their expertise. Research on expert–novice differences in a variety of task domains suggests the importance of the amount and form of information storage in long-term memory as key to expert–novice differences.

Evaluation

The information-processing approach to understanding intelligence has been very productive in helping to elucidate the nature of the construct. First, it has been uniquely successful in identifying processes of intelligent thinking. Second, it has not been bound to individual differences as a source of determining the bases of human intelligence. It can detect processes, whether they are shared across individuals or not. Third, it is the approach that seems most conducive to the use of conventional experimental methods of analysis, so it is possible to gain more control in experimentation by the use of these methods than by the use of alternative methods.

The approach also has its weaknesses, though. First, in many cases, information-processing psychologists have not been terribly sensitive to individual differences. Second, information-processing psychologists have often been even less sensitive to contextual variables (see Neisser, 1976; Sternberg, 1997b). Third, although information-processing analyses are not subject to the rotation dilemma, it is possible to have two quite different models that nevertheless account for comparable proportions of variation in the response-time or error-rate data, thereby making the models indistinguishable. In other words, difficulties in distinguishing among models can plague this approach every bit as much as they can plague psychometric models (Anderson, 1983). Finally, the approach simply never produced much in the way of useful tests. More than a quarter of a century after its initiation, the approach has little to show for itself by way of useful or at least marketable products. Perhaps this is because it never worked quite the way it was supposed to. For example, Sternberg (1977) and Sternberg and Gardner (1983) found the individual parameter representing a regression constant showed higher correlations with psychometric tests of abilities than did parameters representing well-defined information-processing components.

BIOLOGICAL BASES OF INTELLIGENCE

Some theorists have argued that notions of intelligence should be based on biological notions, and usually, on scientific knowledge about the brain. The idea here is that the base of intelligence is in the brain and that behavior is interesting in large part as it elucidates the functioning of the brain.

Classical Approaches

One of the earlier theories of brain function was proposed by Halstead (1951). Halstead suggested four biologically based abilities: (a) the integrative field factor (C), (b) the abstraction factor (A), (c) the power factor (P), and (d) the directional factor (D). Halstead attributed all four of these abilities primarily to the cortex of the frontal lobes. Halstead's theory became the basis for a test of cognitive functioning, including intellectual aspects (the Halstead-Reitan Neuropsychological Test Battery).

A more influential theory, perhaps, has been that of Donald Hebb (1949). Hebb suggested the necessity of distinguishing among different intelligences. *Intelligence A* is innate potential. It is biologically determined and represents the capacity for development. Hebb described it as "the possession of a good brain and a good neural metabolism" (p. 294). *Intelligence B* is the functioning of the brain in which development has occurred. It represents an average level of performance by a person who is partially grown. Although some inference is necessary in determining either intelligence, Hebb suggested that inferences about intelligence A are far less direct than inferences about intelligence B. A further distinction could be made with regard to *Intelligence C*, which is the score one obtains on an intelligence test. This intelligence is Boring's intelligence as the tests test it.

A theory with an even greater impact on the field of intelligence research is that of the Russian psychologist, Alexander Luria (1973, 1980). Luria believed that the brain is a highly differentiated system whose parts are responsible for different aspects of a unified whole. In other words, separate cortical regions act together to produce thoughts and actions of various kinds. Luria (1980) suggested that the brain comprises three main units. The first, a unit of arousal, includes the brain stem and midbrain structures. Included within this first unit are the medulla, reticular activating system, pons, thalamus, and hypothalamus. The second unit of the brain is a sensory-input unit, which includes the temporal, parietal, and occipital lobes. The third unit includes the frontal cortex, which is involved in organization and planning. It comprises cortical structures anterior to the central sulcus.

The most active research program based on Luria's theory has been that of J. P. Das and his colleagues (for example, Das, Kirby, & Jarman, 1979; Das, Naglieri, & Kirby, 1994; Naglieri & Das, 1990, 1997). The theory as they conceive it is the PASS theory, referring to *planning, attention, simultaneous processing*, and *successive processing*. The idea is that intelligence requires the ability to plan and to pay attention. It also requires the ability to attend to many aspects of a stimulus, such as a picture, simultaneously, or, in some cases, to process stimuli sequentially, as when one memorizes a string of digits to remember a telephone number. Other research and tests also have been based on Luria's theory (e.g., Kaufman & Kaufman, 1983).

An entirely different approach to understanding intellectual abilities has emphasized the analysis of hemispheric specialization in the brain. This work goes back to a finding of an obscure country doctor in France, Marc Dax, who in 1836 presented a little-noticed paper to a medical society meeting in Montpelier. Dax had treated a number of patients suffering from loss of speech as a result of brain damage. The condition, known today as aphasia, had been reported even in ancient Greece. Dax noticed that in all of more than forty patients with aphasia, there had been damage to the left hemisphere of the brain but not to the right. His results suggested that speech and perhaps verbal intellectual functioning originated in the left hemisphere of the brain.

Perhaps the best known figure in the study of hemispheric specialization is Paul Broca. At a meeting of the French Society of Anthropology, Broca claimed that a patient of his who was suffering a loss of speech was shown post mortem to have a lesion in the left frontal lobe of the brain. At the time no one paid much attention. But Broca soon became involved in a hot controversy over whether functions, in particular speech, are indeed localized in the brain. The area that Broca identified as involved in speech is today referred to as Broca's area. By 1864, Broca was convinced that the left hemisphere is critical for speech. Carl Wernike, a German neurologist of the late nineteenth century, identified language-deficient patients who could speak, but whose speech made no sense. He also traced language ability to the left hemisphere, though to a different precise location, which is now known as Wernicke's area.

Nobel-Prize-winning physiologist and psychologist Roger Sperry (1961) later suggested that the two hemispheres behave in many respects like separate brains, with the left hemisphere more localized for analytical and verbal processing and the right hemisphere more localized for holistic and imaginal processing. Today it is known that this view was an oversimplification, and that the two hemispheres of the brain largely work together (Gazzaniga, Ivry, & Mangun, 1998).

Contemporary Approaches. More recent theories have dealt with more specific aspects of brain or neural functioning. One contemporary biological theory is based on speed of neuronal conduction. For example, one theory has suggested that individual differences in nerve-conduction velocity are basis for individual differences in intelligence (for example, Reed & Jensen, 1992; Vernon & Mori, 1992). Two procedures have been used to measure conduction velocity, either centrally (in the brain) or peripherally (e.g., in the arm).

Reed and Jensen (1992) tested brain nerve conduction velocities via two medium-latency potentials, N70 and P100, which were evoked by pattern-reversal stimulation. Subjects saw a black and white checkerboard pattern in which the black squares would change to white and the white squares to black. Over many trials, responses to these changes were analyzed via electrodes attached to the scalp in four places. Correlations of derived latency measures with IQ were small (generally in the .1 to .2 range of absolute value), but were significant in some cases, suggesting at least a modest relation between the two kinds of measures.

Vernon and Mori (1992) reported on two studies investigating the relation between nerve-conduction velocity in the arm and IQ. In both studies, nerve-conduction velocity was measured in the median nerve of the arm by attaching electrodes to the arm. In the second study, conduction velocity from the wrist to the tip of the finger was also measured. Vernon and Mori found significant correlations with IQ in the .4 range, as well as somewhat smaller correlations (around −.2) with response-time measures. They interpreted their results as supporting the hypothesis of a relation between speed of information transmission in the peripheral nerves and intelligence. These results must be interpreted cautiously, however, as Wickett and Vernon (1994) later tried unsuccessfully to replicate these earlier results.

Other work has emphasized P300 as a measure of intelligence. Higher amplitudes of P300 are suggestive of higher levels of extraction of information from stimuli (Johnson, 1986, 1988) and also more rapid adjustment to novelty in stimuli (Donchin, Ritter, & McCallum, 1978). However, attempts to relate P300 and other measures of amplitudes of evoked potentials to scores on tests of intelligence have led to inconclusive results (Vernon, Wickett, Bazana, & Stelmack, 2000). The field has gotten a mixed reputation because so many successful attempts have later been met with failure to replicate.

There could be a number of reasons for these failures. One is almost certainly that there are just so many possible sites, potentials to measure, and ways of quantifying the data that the huge number of possible correlations creates a greater likelihood of Type 1 errors than would be the case for more typical cases of test-related measurements. Investigators using such methods therefore must take special care to guard against Type 1 errors.

Another approach has been to study *glucose metabolism*. The underlying theory is that when a person processes information, there is more activity in a certain part of the brain. The better the person is at the behavioral activity, the less is the effort required by the brain. Some of the most interesting recent studies of glucose metabolism have been done by Richard Haier and his colleagues. For example, Haier and colleagues (1988) showed that cortical glucose metabolic rates as revealed by positron emission tomography (PET) scan analysis of subjects solving Raven Matrix problems were lower for more intelligent than for less intelligent subjects. These results suggest that the more intelligent participants needed to expend less effort than the less intelligent ones in order to solve the reasoning problems. A later study (Haier, Siegel, Tang, Abel, & Buschsbaum, 1992) showed a similar result for more versus less practiced performers playing the computer game of Tetris. In other words, smart people or intellectually expert people do not have to work so hard as less smart or intellectually expert people at a given problem.

What remains to be shown, however, is the causal direction of this finding. One could sensibly argue that the smart people expend less glucose (as a proxy for effort) because they are smart, rather than that people are smart because they expend less glucose. Or both high IQ and low glucose metabolism may be related to a third causal variable. In other words, we cannot always assume that the biological event is a cause (in the reductionistic sense). It may be, instead, an effect.

Another approach considers *brain size*. The theory is simply that larger brains are able to hold more neurons and, more important, more and more complex intersynaptic connections between neurons. Willerman, Schultz, Rutledge, and Bigler (1991) correlated brain size with Wechsler Adult Intelligence Scale (WAIS-R) IQs, controlling for body size. They found that IQ correlated .65 in men and .35 in women, with a correlation of .51 for both sexes combined. A follow-up analysis of the same forty subjects suggested that, in men, a relatively larger left hemisphere better predicted WAIS-R verbal than it predicted nonverbal ability, whereas in women a larger left hemisphere predicted nonverbal ability better than it predicted verbal ability (Willerman, Schultz, Rutledge, & Bigler, 1992). These brain-size correlations are suggestive, but it is difficult to say what they mean at this point.

Yet another approach that is at least partially biologically based is that of behavior genetics. A fairly complete review of this extensive literature is found in Sternberg and Grigorenko (1997). The basic idea is that it should be possible to disentangle genetic from environmental sources of variation in intelligence. Ultimately, one would hope to locate the genes responsible for intelligence (Plomin, McClearn, & Smith, 1994, 1995; Plomin & Neiderhiser, 1992; Plomin & Petrill, 1997). The literature is complex, but it appears that about half the total variance in IQ scores is accounted for by genetic factors (Loehlin, 1989; Plomin, 1997). This figure may be an underestimate, because the variance includes error variance and because most studies of heritability have been with children, but we know that heritability of IQ is higher for adults than for children (Plomin, 1997). Also, some studies, such as the Texas Adoption Project (Loehlin, Horn, & Willerman, 1997), suggest higher estimates: .78 in the Texas Adoption Project, .75 in the Minnesota Study of Twins Reared Apart (Bouchard, 1997; Bouchard, Lykken, McGue, Segal, & Tellegen, 1990), and .78 in the Swedish Adoption Study of Aging (Pedersen, Plomin, Nesselroade, & McClearn, 1992).

At the same time, some researchers argue that effects of heredity and environment cannot be clearly and validly separated (Bronfenbrenner & Ceci, 1994; Wahlsten & Gottlieb, 1997). Perhaps the direction for future research should be to figure out how heredity and environment work together to produce phenotypic intelligence (Scarr, 1997), concentrating especially on within-family environmental variations, which appear to be more important than between-family variations (Jensen, 1997). Such research requires, at the very least, very carefully prepared tests of intelligence, perhaps some of the newer tests described in the next section.

Evaluation

The biological approach has provided unique insights into the nature of intelligence. Its greatest advantage is its recognition that, at some level, the brain is the seat of intelligence. In modern times, and to a lesser extent in earlier times, it has been possible to pinpoint areas of the brain responsible for various functions. The approach is now probably among the most productive in terms of the sheer amount of research being generated.

The greatest weakness of the approach is not so much a problem of the approach as in its interpretation. Reductionists would like to reduce all understanding of intelligence to understanding of brain function, but it just will not work. If we want to understand how to improve the school learning of a normal child through better teaching, we are not going to find an answer, in the foreseeable future, through the study of the brain. Culture certainly affects what kinds of behavior are viewed as more or less intelligent within a given setting, and again, the biology of the brain will not settle the question of what behavior is considered intelligent within a given culture, or why it is considered to be so.

Another weakness of the approach, or at least of its use, has been invalid inferences. Suppose one finds that a certain evoked potential is correlated with a certain cognitive response. All one knows is that there is a correlation. The potential could cause the response, the response could cause the potential, or both could be based on some higher order factor. Yet, reports based on the biological approach often seem to suggest that the biological response is somehow causal (e.g., Hendrickson & Hendrickson, 1980). Useful though the biological approach may be, it will always need to be supplemented by other approaches.

CULTURE AND SOCIETY

A rather different position has been taken by more anthropologically oriented investigators. Modern investigators trace their work back at the very least to Kroeber and Kluckhohn (1952), who studied culture as patterns of behavior acquired and transmitted by symbols. Much of the work in this approach, like that in the cognitive approach, is relatively recent.

The most extreme position is one of radical cultural relativism, proposed by Berry (1974), which rejects assumed psychological universals across cultural systems and requires the generation from within each cultural system of any behavioral concepts to be applied to it (the so-called emic approach). According to this viewpoint, therefore, intelligence can be understood only from within a culture, not in terms of views imposed from outside that culture (the so-called etic approach). Even in present times, psychologists have argued that the imposition of Western theories or tests on non-Western cultures can result in seriously erroneous conclusions about the capabilities of individuals within those cultures (Greenfield, 1997; Sternberg et al., 2000).

Other theorists have taken a less extreme view. For example, Michael Cole and his colleagues in the Laboratory of Comparative Human Cognition (1982) argued that the radical position does not take into account the fact that cultures interact. Cole and his colleagues believe that a kind of conditional comparativism is important, so long as one is careful in setting the conditions of the comparison.

Cole and his colleagues gave as an example a study done by Super (1976). Super found evidence that African infants sit and walk earlier than do their counterparts in the United States and Europe. But does such a finding mean that African infants are better walkers, in much the same way that North American psychologists have concluded that American children are better thinkers than African children (for example, Herrnstein & Murray, 1994)? On the contrary, Super found that mothers in the culture he studied made a self-conscious effort to teach babies to sit and walk as early as possible. He concluded that the African infants are more advanced because they are specifically taught to sit and walk earlier and are encouraged through the provision of opportunities to practice these behaviors. Other motor behaviors were not more advanced. For example, infants who sat and walked early were actually found to crawl later than did infants in the United States.

Evaluation

The greatest strength of cultural approaches is their recognition that intelligence cannot be understood fully outside its cultural context. However common may be the thought processes that underlie intelligent thinking, the behaviors that are labeled as intelligent by a given culture certainly vary from one place to another, as well as from one epoch to another.

The greatest weakness of cultural approaches is their vagueness. They tend to say more about the context of intelligent behavior than they do about the causes of such behavior. Intelligence probably always will have to be understood at many different levels, and any one level in itself will be inadequate. It is for this reason, presumably, that systems models have become particularly popular in recent years. These models attempt to provide an understanding of intelligence at multiple levels.

SYSTEMS MODELS

The Nature of Systems Models

In recent times, systems models have been proposed as useful bases for understanding intelligence. These models seek to understand the complexity of intelligence from multiple points of view, and generally combine at least two and often more of the models described above.

The Theory of Multiple Intelligences. Gardner (1983, 1993, 1999) has proposed a theory of multiple intelligences, according to which intelligence is not just one thing, but multiple things. According to this theory, there are eight or possibly even ten intelligences – linguistic, logical–mathematical, spatial, musical, bodily–kinesthetic, interpersonal, intrapersonal, naturalist, and possibly existential and spiritual.

True Intelligence. Perkins (1995) has proposed a theory of what he refers to as *true intelligence*, which he believes synthesizes classic views as well as new ones. According to Perkins, there are three basic aspects to intelligence: neural, experiential, and reflective.

Neural intelligence concerns what Perkins believes to be the fact that some people's neurological systems function better than those of others, running faster and with more precision. He mentions "more finely tuned voltages" and "more exquisitely adapted chemical catalysts" as well as a "better pattern of connecticity in the labyrinth of neurons" (Perkins, 1995, p. 97), although it is not entirely clear what any of these terms means. Perkins believes this aspect of intelligence to be largely genetically determined and unlearnable. It seems to be somewhat similar to Cattell's (1971) idea of fluid intelligence.

The experiential aspect of intelligence is what has been learned from experience. It is the extent and organization of the knowledge base, and thus is similar to Cattell's (1971) notion of crystallized intelligence.

The reflective aspect of intelligence refers to the role of strategies in memory and problem solving, and appears to be similar to the construct of metacognition or cognitive monitoring (Brown & DeLoache, 1978; Flavell, 1981).

There have been no published empirical tests of the theory of true intelligence, so it is difficult to evaluate the theory at this time. Like Gardner's (1983) theory, Perkins's theory is based on literature review, and as noted above, such literature reviews often tend to be selective and interpreted so as to maximize the fit of the theory to the available data.

The Bioecological Model of Intelligence.   Ceci (1996) has proposed a bioecological model of intelligence, according to which multiple cognitive potentials, context, and knowledge are all essential bases of individual differences in performance. Each of the multiple cognitive potentials enables relationships to be discovered, thoughts to be monitored, and knowledge to be acquired within a given domain. Although these potentials are biologically based, their development is closely linked to environmental context, and hence it is difficult if not impossible cleanly to separate biological from environmental contributions to intelligence. Moreover, abilities may express themselves very differently in different contexts. For example, children given essentially the same task in the context of a video game and in the context of a laboratory cognitive task performed much better when the task was presented in the video game.

The bioecological model appears in many ways to be more a framework than a theory. At some level, the theory must be right. Certainly, both biological and ecological factors contribute to the development and manifestation of intelligence. Perhaps what the theory needs most at this time are specific and clearly falsifiable predictions that would set it apart from other theories.

Emotional Intelligence.   Emotional intelligence is the ability to perceive accurately, appraise, and express emotion; the ability to access and/or generate feelings when they facilitate thought; the ability to understand emotion and emotional knowledge; and the ability to regulate emotions to promote emotional and intellectual growth (Mayer, Salovey, & Caruso 2000a, 2000b). The concept was introduced by Salovey and Mayer (Mayer & Salovey, 1993; Salovey & Mayer, 1990), and popularized and expanded upon by Goleman (1995).

There is some, although still tentative, evidence for the existence of emotional intelligence. For example, Mayer and Gehr (1996) found that emotional perception of characters in a variety of situations correlates with

SAT scores, with empathy, and with emotional openness. Full convergent-discriminant validation of the construct, however, appears to be needed. The results to date are mixed, with some studies supportive (Mayer, Salovey, & Caruso, 2000a; 2000b) and others not (Davies, Stankov, & Roberts, 1998).

The Theory of Successful Intelligence. Sternberg (1985a, 1988c, 1997b, 1999d) has proposed a theory of successful intelligence, according to which intelligence can be seen in terms of various kinds of information-processing components combining in different ways to generate analytical, creative, and practical abilities. This theory is the subject of the next chapter.

Evaluation

The complexity of systems models is both a blessing and a curse. It is a blessing because it enables such models to recognize the multiple complex levels of intelligence. It is a curse because the models become more difficult to test. One of the most popular models, that of Gardner (1983), was proposed some time ago, but as of this writing, there has not been even one empirical test of the model as a whole, scarcely a commendable record for a scientific theory. This record compares with thousands of predictive empirical tests of psychometric or Piagetian models, and probably hundreds of tests of information-processing models. Sternberg's (1997b) triarchic theory of successful intelligence has been predictively empirically tested numerous times (see, e.g., Sternberg et al., 2000), but because most of these tests have been by members of Sternberg's research group, the results cannot be considered definitive at this time.

CONCLUSION: RELATIONS AMONG THE VARIOUS MODELS OF THE NATURE OF INTELLIGENCE

There are different ways of resolving the conflicts among alternative models of the nature of intelligence.

Different Names

One way of resolving the conflicts is to use different names for different constructs. For example, some researchers stake their claim on a certain number of intelligences or intellectual abilities. Is intelligence, fundamentally, one important thing (Spearman, 1904), or seven things (Gardner, 1983), or maybe ten things (Gardner, 1999), or perhaps 120 things (Guilford, 1967) or even 150 or more things (Guilford, 1982)? Some might say that those who are splitters are actually talking of "talents" rather than intelligence, or that they are merely slicing the same "pie" everyone else is eating, but very thinly.

Sometimes different names are used to reflect the same construct. For example, what was once the Scholastic Aptitude Test became the Scholastic Assessment Test and still later became simply the SAT, an acronym perhaps belatedly asserted to stand for nothing in particular. This illustrates how, over time and place, similar or even identical constructs can be given names in order to reflect temporally or spatially local sensibilities in what constitutes desirable or even acceptable terminology. Many similar efforts, such as referring to what usually is called *intelligence* as *cognitive development* (Thorndike, Hagen, & Sattler, 1986), point out the extent to which the history of intelligence is in part a battle over names.

In a sense, the history of the field of intelligence bifurcates. Some investigators, perhaps starting with Boring (1923), have suggested we define intelligence as what intelligence tests measure and get on with testing it, and other investigators, such as Spearman (1904, 1927) and Thurstone (1938) have viewed the battle over what intelligence is as determining what should be tested.

Fighting for "Truth"

A second response to the differences among theories has been for researchers to stake their ground and then "slug it out" in a perceived fight for the truth. Some of these battles, to be described later, became rather bitter. Underlying them is the notion that only one model or theory embedded under a model could be correct, and the goal of research should be to figure out which one that is.

Dialectical Synthesis

A third response has been to seek some kind of dialectical synthesis among alternative models or theories embedded under these models. There have been different kinds of syntheses.

Approach or Methodology Subject to Improvement. Some investigators have argued that their approach is the best the field can do at the time, but eventually should be replaced. For example, Louis L. Thurstone suggested that factor analysis is useful in the early stages of investigation followed by laboratory research. In other words, the differential approach could be replaced by a more cognitively based one. Thurstone (1947), who was largely a psychometric theorist, argued that

The exploratory nature of factor analysis is often not understood. Factor analysis has its principal usefulness at the borderline of intelligence. It is naturally superseded by rational formulations in terms of the science involved. Factor analysis is useful, especially in those domains where basic and fruitful concepts are essentially lacking and where crucial experiments have been difficult to conceive. . . . But if we have scientific intuition and sufficient ingenuity, the rough factorial map of a new domain will enable us to proceed beyond the exploratory factorial stage to the more direct forms of psychological experimentation in the laboratory. (p. 56)

Coexistence. Other investigators have argued for coexistence. Charles Spearman, for example, had both a differential theory of intelligence (Spearman, 1927) and a cognitively based one (Spearman, 1923) (both of which will be described later). Cronbach (1957) argued for the merger of the fields of differential and experimental psychology.

Synthetic Integration. Perhaps the best way to achieve a certain coherence in the field is to recognize that there is no one right "model" or "approach" and that different ones elucidate different aspects of a very complex phenomenon. Models such as the systems models are useful in attempting integrations, but they fall short in integrating all that we know about intelligence. The time may come when such large-scale integrations can be achieved in ways that are theoretically meritorious and empirically sound. In the meantime, it is likely that many different conceptions of intelligence will compete for the attention of the scientific world as well as of the lay public.

2

The Theory of Successful Intelligence

The theory of successful intelligence views intelligence as broader than do most theories. In general, the conception fits best with the systems theories discussed in Chapter 1.

The Definition of Successful Intelligence

1. *Intelligence is defined in terms of the ability to achieve success in life in terms of one's personal standards, within one's sociocultural context.* The field of intelligence has at times tended to put "the cart before the horse," defining the construct conceptually on the basis of how it is operationalized rather than vice versa. This practice has resulted in tests that stress the academic aspect of intelligence, as one might expect, given the origins of modern intelligence testing in the work of Binet and Simon (1916b) in designing an instrument to distinguish children who would succeed from those who would fail in school. But the construct of intelligence needs to serve a broader purpose, accounting for the bases of success in all one's life.

The use of societal criteria of success (e.g., school grades, personal income) can obscure the fact that these operationalizations often do not capture people's personal notions of success. Some people choose to concentrate on extracurricular activities such as athletics or music and pay less attention to grades in school; others may choose occupations that are personally meaningful to them but that will never yield the income they might gain doing other work. Although scientific analysis of some kinds requires nomothetic operationalizations, the definition of success for an individual is idiographic. In the theory of successful intelligence, however, the conceptualization of intelligence is always within a sociocultural context. Although the processes of intelligence may be common across such contexts, what constitutes success is not. Being a successful member of the clergy of a particular religion may be highly rewarded in one society and viewed as a worthless pursuit in another.

2. *One's ability to achieve success depends on capitalizing on one's strengths and correcting or compensating for one's weaknesses.* Theories of intelligence typically specify some relatively fixed set of abilities, whether one general factor and a number of specific factors (Spearman, 1904), seven multiple factors (Thurstone, 1938), eight multiple intelligences (Gardner, 1983, 1999), or 150 separate intellectual abilities (Guilford, 1982). Such a nomothetic specification is useful in establishing a common set of skills to be tested. But people achieve success, even within a given occupation, in many different ways. For example, successful teachers and researchers achieve success through many different blendings of skills rather than through any single formula that works for all of them.

3. *Balancing abilities is achieved in order to adapt to, shape, and select environments.* Definitions of intelligence traditionally have emphasized the role of adaptation to the environment (Intelligence and its measurement, 1921; Sternberg & Detterman, 1986). But intelligence involves not only modifying oneself to suit the environment (adaptation), but also modifying the environment to suit oneself (shaping), and sometimes, finding a new environment that is a better match to one's skills, values, or desires (selection).

Not all people have equal opportunities to adapt to, shape, and select environments. In general, people of higher socioeconomic standing tend to have more opportunities and people of lower socioeconomic standing have fewer. The economy or political situation of the society can also be factors. Other variables that may affect such opportunities are education and especially literacy, political party, race, religion, and so forth. For example, someone with a college education typically has many more possible career options than does someone who has dropped out of high school. Thus, how and how well an individual adapts to, shapes, and selects environments must always be viewed in terms of the opportunities the individual has.

4. *Success is attained through a balance of analytical, creative, and practical abilities.* Analytical abilities are the abilities primarily measured by traditional tests of abilities. But success in life requires one not only to analyze one's own ideas as well as the ideas of others, but also to generate ideas and to persuade other people of their value. This necessity occurs in the world of work, as when a subordinate tries to convince a superior of the value of his or her plan; in the world of personal relationships, as when a child attempts to convince a parent to do what he or she wants or when a spouse tries to convince the other spouse to do things his or her preferred way; and in the world of school, as when a student writes an essay arguing for a point of view.

Information-Processing Components Underlying
Successful Intelligence

According to the proposed theory of human intelligence and its development (Sternberg, 1980b, 1984, 1985a, 1990a, 1997b, 1999d), a common set of processes underlies all aspects of intelligence. These processes are hypothesized to be universal. For example, although the solutions to problems that are considered intelligent in one culture may be different from the solutions considered to be intelligent in another culture, the need to define problems and translate strategies to solve these problems exists in any culture.

Metacomponents, or executive processes, plan what to do, monitor the plans as they are being carried out, and evaluate them after they are done. Examples of metacomponents are recognizing the existence of a problem, defining the nature of the problem, deciding on a strategy for solving the problem, monitoring the solution of the problem, and evaluating the solution after the problem is solved.

Performance components execute the instructions of the metacomponents. For example, inference is used to decide how two stimuli are related and application is used to apply what one has inferred (Sternberg, 1977). Other examples of performance components are comparison of stimuli, justification of a given response as adequate although not ideal, and actually making the response.

Knowledge-acquisition components are used to learn how to solve problems or simply to acquire declarative knowledge in the first place (Sternberg, 1985a). Selective encoding is used to decide what information is relevant in the context of one's learning. Selective comparison is used to bring old information to bear on new problems. And selective combination is used to put together the selectively encoded and compared information into a single and sometimes insightful solution to a problem.

Although the same processes are used for all three aspects of intelligence universally, these processes are applied to different kinds of tasks and situations depending on whether a given problem requires analytical thinking, creative thinking, practical thinking, or a combination of these kinds of thinking. In particular, analytical thinking is invoked when components are applied to fairly familiar kinds of problems abstracted from everyday life. Creative thinking is invoked when the components are applied to relatively novel kinds of tasks or situations. Practical thinking is invoked when the components are applied to experience to adapt to, shape, and select environments.

Figure 2.1 shows the interrelationships among the elements of the theory: metacomponents and active performance and knowledge-acquisition components, which in turn provide feedback to the metacomponents. When these components are applied to relatively abstract but familiar

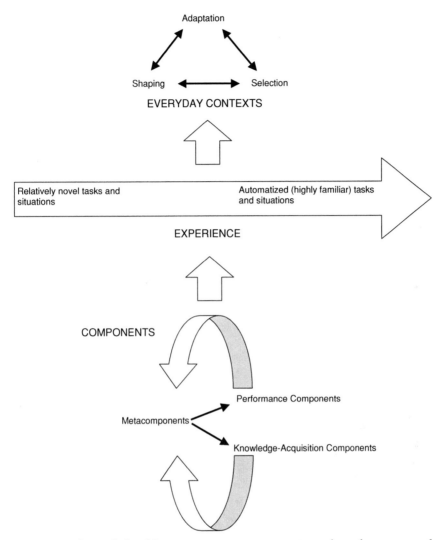

FIGURE 2.1. Interrelationships among metacomponents and performance and knowledge-acquisition components of theory of human intelligence.

problems, the problems call upon analytical abilities. When the components are applied to novel tasks or situations, they call upon creative abilities. And when they are applied to adapt to, shape, or select environments, they call upon practical abilities.

More details regarding the theory can be found in Sternberg (1985a, 1997b). Because the theory of successful intelligence comprises three subtheories – a componential subtheory dealing with the components of intelligence, an experiential subtheory dealing with the importance of coping with relative novelty and of automatization of information processing, and a contextual subtheory dealing with processes of adaptation, shaping, and selection, the theory has been referred to from time to time as *triarchic*.

People who are high in conventional intelligence but low in successful intelligence are susceptible to committing four fallacies in their thinking.

The first, which I call the *stable-trait fallacy*, is the belief that once smart, always smart. They think that because of their high test scores or grades in school, they can pretty much count on being smart forever. As a result, some of them do not actively engage in life-long learning, with unfortunate results. They lose their edge.

The second fallacy is the *general-ability fallacy*, or the belief that if you are smart in one thing, you are smart in everything. People who do well on tests and in school often think that their high levels of performance in these domains mean they will be expert in any domain. Typically, they are wrong.

The third fallacy, the *life-success fallacy*, is based on the belief that if they succeed on tests, the rest is guaranteed. Some of them never learn that conventional intelligence at some level may be necessary for success in life, but is far from sufficient. People cannot succeed in their lives on the basis of IQ alone.

The fourth fallacy is the *moral-equivalence fallacy*, the belief that to be smart is to be good. Herrnstein and Murray (1994) seem to come quite close in their book to committing this fallacy, at times equating the smart with the good. There are many people who are smart, but not good, and vice versa.

INTERNAL VALIDATION OF THE THEORY OF
SUCCESSFUL INTELLIGENCE

Componential Analyses

Componential analyses involve studying the information-processing components underlying performance on cognitive tasks. These kinds of analyses have been used to study both analytical and creative thinking abilities.

Analytical Intelligence. Analytical intelligence is involved when the components of intelligence (which are specified by the componential subtheory of the triarchic theory) are applied to analyze, evaluate, judge, or compare and contrast. It typically is involved when components are applied to relatively familiar kinds of problems where the judgments to be made are of a fairly abstract nature.

In some early work, it was shown how analytical kinds of problems, such as analogies or syllogisms, can be analyzed componentially

(Guyote & Sternberg, 1981; Sternberg, 1977, 1980b, 1983; Sternberg & Gardner, 1983; Sternberg & Turner, 1981), with response times or error rates decomposed to yield their underlying information-processing components. The goal of this research was to understand the information-processing origins of individual differences in (the analytical aspect of) human intelligence. With componential analysis, one could specify sources of individual differences underlying a factor score such as that for "inductive reasoning." For example, response times on analogies (Sternberg, 1977) and linear syllogisms (Sternberg, 1980a) were decomposed into their elementary performance components. The general strategy of such research is to (a) specify an information-processing model of task performance; (b) propose a parameterization of this model, so that each information-processing component is assigned a mathematical parameter corresponding to its latency (and another corresponding to its error rate); and (c) construct cognitive tasks administered in such a way that it is possible through mathematical modeling to isolate the parameters of the mathematical model. It is thus possible to specify, in the solving of various kinds of problems, several sources of important individual or developmental differences (Sternberg, 1977, 1983):

1. What performance components are used?
2. How long does it takes to execute each component?
3. How susceptible is each component to error?
4. How are the components combined into strategies?
5. What are the mental representations on which the components act?

For example, using componential analysis, it was possible to decompose inductive-reasoning performance into a set of underlying information-processing components. The analogy $A : B : C : D_1, D_2, D_3, D_4$ will be used as an example to illustrate the components. These components are (a) *encoding*, the amount of time needed to register each stimulus ($A, B, C, D_1, D_2, D_3, D_4$); (b) *inference*, the amount of time needed to discern the basic relation between given stimuli (A to B); (c) *mapping*, the amount of time needed to transfer the relation from one set of stimuli to another (needed in analogical reasoning) (A to C); (d) *application*, the amount of time needed to apply the relation as inferred (and sometimes as mapped) to a new set of stimuli (A to B to C to ?); (e) *comparison*, the amount of time needed to compare the validity of the response options (D_1, D_2, D_3, D_4); (f) *justification*, the amount of time needed to justify one answer as the best of the bunch (e.g., D_1); and (g) *preparation response*, the amount of time needed to prepare for problem solution and to respond.

Studies of reasoning need not use artificial formats. In a more recent study, Sternberg and a colleague looked at predictions for everyday kinds of situations, such as when milk will spoil (Sternberg & Kalmar, 1997). In this study, the investigators looked at both predictions and postdictions (hypotheses about the past where information about the past is unknown) and found that postdictions took longer to make than did predictions.

Research on the components of human intelligence yielded some interesting results. Consider some examples. First, execution of early components (e.g., inference and mapping) tends exhaustively to consider the attributes of the stimuli, whereas execution of later components (e.g., application) tends to consider the attributes of the stimuli in self-terminating fashion, with only those attributes processed that are essential for reaching a solution (Sternberg, 1977). Second, in a study of the development of figural analogical reasoning, it was found that although children generally became quicker in information processing with age, not all components were executed more rapidly with age (Sternberg & Rifkin, 1979). The encoding component first showed a decrease in component time with age and then an increase. Apparently, older children realized that their best strategy was to spend more time in encoding the terms of a problem so that later they would be able to spend less time in operating on these encodings. A related, third finding was that better reasoners tend to spend relatively more time than do poorer reasoners in global, up-front metacomponential planning, when they solve difficult reasoning problems. Poorer reasoners, on the other hand, tend to spend relatively more time in local planning (Sternberg, 1981). Presumably, the better reasoners recognize that it is better to invest more time up front so as to be able to process a problem more efficiently later on. Fourth, it was also found in a study of the development of verbal analogical reasoning that, as children grew older, their strategies shifted. They relied on word association less and abstract relations more (Sternberg & Nigro, 1980).

Some of the componential studies concentrated on knowledge-acquisition components rather than performance components or meta-components. For example, in one set of studies, the investigators were interested in sources of individual differences in vocabulary (Sternberg & Powell, 1983; Sternberg, Powell, & Kaye, 1983; see also Sternberg, 1987b). The researchers were not content just to view these as individual differences in declarative knowledge. They wanted to understand why it was that some people acquired this declarative knowledge and others did not. What they found is that there are multiple sources of individual and developmental differences. The three main sources are in knowledge-acquisition components, use of context clues, and use of mediating variables. For example, in the sentence, "The blen rises in the east and sets in the west," the knowledge-acquisition component of selective comparison is used to relate prior knowledge about a known concept, the sun, to the unknown word (neologism) in the sentence, "blen." Several context cues appear in the sentence, such as the fact that a blen rises, the fact that it sets, and the information about where it rises and sets. A mediating variable is that the information can occur after the presentation of the unknown word.

Sternberg and his colleagues did research such as that described above because they believed that conventional psychometric research sometimes incorrectly attributed individual and developmental differences. For example, a verbal analogies test that might appear on its surface to measure verbal reasoning might in fact measure primarily vocabulary and general information (Sternberg, 1977). In some populations, reasoning might hardly be a source of individual or developmental differences at all. And if researchers then look at the sources of the individual differences in vocabulary, they would need to understand that the differences in knowledge do not come from nowhere: Some children have much more frequent and better opportunities to learn word meanings than others.

Creative Intelligence. Intelligence tests contain a range of problems, some of them more novel than others. In some of the componential work Sternberg and his colleagues have shown that when one goes beyond the range of unconventionality in the kinds of items that appear on tests of intelligence, one starts to tap sources of individual differences measured little or not at all by the tests. According to the theory of successful intelligence, (creative) intelligence is particularly well measured by problems assessing how well an individual can cope with relative novelty. Thus it is important to include in a battery of tests problems that are relatively novel in nature. These problems can be either convergent or divergent in nature.

In work with convergent problems, Sternberg and his colleagues presented eighty individuals with novel reasoning problems that had a single best answer. For example, they might be told that some objects are green and others blue; but still other objects might be grue, meaning green until the year 2000 and blue thereafter, or bleen, meaning blue until the year 2000 and green thereafter. Or they might be told of four kinds of people on the planet—Kyron, blens, who are born young and die young; kwefs, who are born old and die old; balts, who are born young and die old; and prosses, who are born old and die young (Sternberg, 1982; Tetewsky & Sternberg, 1986). Their task was to predict future states from past states, given incomplete information. In another set of studies, sixty people were given more conventional kinds of inductive reasoning problems, such as analogies, series completions, and classifications and were told to solve them. But the problems had premises preceding them that were either conventional (dancers wear shoes) or novel (dancers eat shoes). The participants had to solve the problems as though the counterfactuals were true (Sternberg & Gastel, 1989a, 1989b).

In these studies, Sternberg and his colleagues found that correlations with conventional kinds of tests depended on how novel or nonentrenched the conventional tests were. The more novel the items, the higher the correlations of the tests with scores on successively more novel conventional tests. Thus, the components isolated for relatively novel items would tend to correlate more highly with more unusual tests of fluid abilities (for example, that of Cattell & Cattell, 1973) than with tests of crystallized abilities. Sternberg and his colleagues also found that when response times on the relatively novel problems were componentially analyzed, some components better measured the creative aspect of intelligence than did others. For example, in the "grue–bleen" task mentioned above, the information-processing component requiring people to switch from conventional green–blue thinking to grue–bleen thinking and then back to green–blue thinking again was a particularly good measure of the ability to cope with novelty.

Componential analyses provide one means of internal validation of the triarchic theory. But their emphasis is on testing specific models of task performance for particular components of information processing. Is it possible internally to validate the triarchic theory as a whole?

Factor Analyses

Internal Validity. Four separate factor-analytic studies support the internal validity of the theory of successful intelligence.

In one study (Sternberg, Grigorenko, Ferrari, & Clinkenbeard, 1999), Sternberg and his colleagues used the so-called Sternberg Triarchic Abilities Test (STAT – Sternberg, 1993) to investigate the internal validity of the theory. Three hundred twenty-six high school students from diverse parts of the United States took the test, which comprised twelve subtests in all. There were four subtests measuring analytical, creative, and practical abilities. For each type of ability, there were three multiple-choice tests and one essay test. The multiple-choice tests, in turn, involved, verbal, quantitative, and figural content. Consider the content of each test:

1. Analytical–Verbal: Figuring out meanings of neologisms (artificial words) from natural contexts. Students see a novel word embedded in a paragraph, and have to infer its meaning from the context.

2. Analytical–Quantitative: Number series. Students have to say what number should come next in a series of numbers.

3. Analytical–Figural: Matrices. Students see a figural matrix with the lower right entry missing. They have to say which of the options fits into the missing space.

4. Practical–Verbal: Everyday reasoning. Students are presented with a set of everyday problems in the life of an adolescent and have to select the option that best solves each problem.

5. Practical–Quantitative: Everyday math. Students are presented with scenarios requiring the use of math in everyday life (e.g., buying tickets for a ball game), and have to solve math problems based on the scenarios.

6. Practical–Figural: Route planning. Students are presented with a map of an area (e.g., an entertainment park) and have to answer questions about navigating effectively through the area depicted by the map.

7. Creative–Verbal: Novel analogies. Students are presented with verbal analogies preceded by counterfactual premises (e.g., money falls off trees). They have to solve the analogies as though the counterfactual premises were true.

8. Creative–Quantitative: Novel number operations. Students are presented with rules for novel number operations, for example, "flix," which involves numerical manipulations that differ as a function of whether the first of two operands is greater than, equal to, or less than the second. Participants have to use the novel number operations to solve presented math problems.

9. Creative–Figural: In each item, participants are first presented with a figural series that involves one or more transformations; they then have to apply the rule of the series to a new figure with a different appearance, and complete the new series.

10. Analytical Essay: This essay requires students to analyze the use of security guards in high schools: What are the advantages and disadvantages and how can these be weighed to make a recommendation?

11. Practical Essay: Give three practical solutions to a problem you are currently having in your life.

12. Creative Essay: Describe the ideal school.

Confirmatory factor analysis on the data was supportive of the triarchic theory of human intelligence, yielding separate and uncorrelated analytical, creative, and practical factors. The lack of correlation was due to the inclusion of essay as well as multiple-choice subtests. Although multiple-choice tests tended to correlate substantially with other multiple-choice tests, their correlations with essay tests were much weaker. The multiple-choice analytical subtest loaded most highly on the analytical factor, but the creative and practical essay subtests loaded most highly on their respective factors. Thus, measurement of creative and practical abilities probably ideally should be accomplished with other kinds of testing instruments that complement multiple-choice instruments.

In a second study, the investigators developed a revised version of the STAT, which, in a preliminary study of fifty-three college students, showed outstanding internal and external validation properties (Grigorenko, Gil, Jarvin, & Sternberg, 2000). This test supplements the creative and practical measures described above with performance-based measures. For example, creative abilities are additionally measured by having people write and tell short stories, by having them do captions for cartoons, and by having them use computer software to design a variety of products, such as greeting cards and a company logo. Practical skills are measured additionally by solving everyday problems presented by means of films, and by an office-based situational-judgment inventory and a college-student situational-judgment inventory. These tests require individuals to make decisions about everyday problems faced in office situations and in school.

Grigorenko and her colleagues found that the creativity tests are moderately correlated with each other and the practical tests are highly correlated with each other. The two kinds of tests are distinct from one another, however. It is interesting that exploratory factor analysis reveals the performance-based assessments tend to cluster separately from multiple-choice assessments measuring the same skills (similar to our earlier findings of essay measures tending to be distinctive from multiple-choice measures). These results further suggest the need for measuring not only a variety of abilities, but also for measuring these abilities through various modalities of testing.

In a third study, conducted with 3,252 students in the United States, Finland, and Spain, Sternberg and his colleagues used the multiple-choice section of the STAT to compare five alternative models of intelligence, again via confirmatory factor analysis. A model featuring a general factor of intelligence fit the data relatively poorly. The triarchic model, allowing for intercorrelation among the analytic, creative, and practical factors, provided the best fit to the data (Sternberg, Castejón, Prieto, Hautamäki, & Grigorenko, 2001).

In a fourth study, Grigorenko and Sternberg (2001) tested 511 Russian school children (ranging in age from eight to seventeen years) as well as 490 mothers and 328 fathers of these children. They used entirely distinct measures of analytical, creative, and practical intelligence. Consider, for example, the tests used for adults. (Similar tests were used for children.)

In these tests, fluid analytical intelligence was measured by two subtests of a test of nonverbal intelligence. The *Test of g: Culture Fair, Level II* (Cattell & Cattell, 1973) is a test of fluid intelligence designed to reduce, as much as possible, the influence of verbal comprehension, culture, and educational level, although no test eliminates such influences. In the first subtest, *Series*, individuals were presented with an incomplete, progressive series of figures. The participants' task was to select, from among the choices provided, the answer that best continued the series. In the *Matrices* subtest, the task was to complete the matrix presented at the left of each row.

The test of crystallized intelligence was adapted from existing traditional tests of analogies and synonyms/antonyms used in Russia. Grigorenko and Sternberg used adaptations of Russian rather than American tests because the vocabulary used in Russia differs from that used in the United States. The first part of the test included twenty verbal analogies (KR20 = 0.83). An example is *circle – ball = square – ? (a) quadrangular, (b) figure, (c) rectangular, (d) solid, (e) cube.* The second part included thirty pairs of words. The participants' task was to specify whether the words in the pair were synonyms or antonyms (KR20 = 0.74). Examples are *latent – hidden*, and *systematic – chaotic*.

The measure of creative intelligence also comprised two parts. The first part asked the participants to describe the world through the eyes of insects. The second part asked participants to describe who might live and what might happen on a planet called "Priumliava." No additional information on the nature of the planet was specified. Each part of the test was scored in three different ways to yield three different scores. The first score was for originality (novelty); the second was for the amount of development in the plot (quality); and the third was for creative use of prior knowledge in these relatively novel kinds of tasks (sophistication). The mean inter-story reliabilities were .69, .75, and .75 for the three respective scores, all of which were statistically significant at the $p < .001$ level.

The measure of practical intelligence was self-report and also comprised two parts. The first part was designed as a twenty-item, self-report instrument, assessing practical skills in the social domain (e.g., effective and successful communication with other people), in the family domain (e.g., how to fix household items, how to run the family budget), and in the domain of effective resolution of sudden problems (e.g., organizing something that has become chaotic). For the subscales, internal-consistency estimates varied from 0.50 to 0.77. In this study, only the total practical intelligence self-report scale was used (Cronbach's alpha = .71). The second part had four vignettes, based on themes that appeared in popular Russian magazines in the context of discussion of adaptive skills in the current society. The four themes were how to maintain the value of one's savings, what to do when one purchases an item and discovers that it is broken, how to locate medical assistance in a time of need, and how to manage a salary bonus one has received for outstanding work. Each vignette was accompanied by five choices and participants had to select the best one. Obviously, there is no one "right" answer in this type of situation. Hence Grigorenko and Sternberg used the most frequently chosen response as the keyed answer. To the extent that this response was suboptimal, this suboptimality would work against the researchers in subsequent analyses relating scores on this test to other predictor and criterion measures.

In this study, exploratory principal-component analysis for both children and adults yielded very similar factor structures. Both varimax and oblimin rotations yielded clear-cut analytical, creative, and practical factors for the tests. Thus, a sample of a different nationality (Russian), a different set of tests, and a different method of analysis (exploratory rather than confirmatory analysis) again supported the theory of successful intelligence.

In a recent collaborative study involving fifteen different high schools, colleges, and universities, we investigated the construct validity of the theory of successful intelligence in the context of predicting college success

(Sternberg & The Rainbow Project Collaborators, in press). The study, involving just over a thousand students, utilized an expanded battery of analytical, creative, and practical assessments to predict first-year college GPA. Our goals in the study were threefold: (a) to construct validate the theory of successful intelligence, (b) to improve prediction of first-year college GPA over and above the prediction obtained through high school grade-point average and SAT, and (c) to increase potential diversity by showing reduced ethnic-group differences on our test.

The test incorporated the Sternberg Triarchic Abilities Test, as described earlier, plus some new tests. The new tests were of creative and practical skills.

For creativity, there were three additional measures. One provided students with unusual titles for short stories. The students were asked to use two of the titles as a basis for writing two very short stories. A second provided pictorial collages. Students were asked to pick two of them, and orally tell a short story based on these collages. A third measure required students to caption cartoons.

There were also three additional practical tests. One required students to indicate how they would solve everyday problems encountered in school. The second required students to indicate how they would solve typical problems encountered in the workplace. The third presented problems students encounter in movies. The movies would stop, and then students would have to indicate how they would solve the problems.

The results were very promising. The Rainbow measures clustered into three factors. One was a strong practical factor. The second was a weaker creative factor. And the third – the analytical factor – was represented by the paper-and-pencil tests. The Rainbow measures significantly and substantially increased prediction of first-year college GPA. The creative measures provided more incremental validity than the practical ones. Oral stories was especially effective as an incremental predictor. And the Rainbow measures showed much less effect of ethnic group than did the SAT. The measures thus appear to provide further construct validation of the theory of successful intelligence.

EXTERNAL VALIDATION OF THE THEORY OF SUCCESSFUL INTELLIGENCE

The external validity of the triarchic theory of successful intelligence has been tested via two methods: correlational studies and instructional studies.

Correlational Studies

Analytical Intelligence. In the componential-analysis work described above, correlations were computed between component scores of individuals and scores on tests of different kinds of psychometric abilities. First, in the studies of inductive reasoning (Sternberg, 1977; Sternberg & Gardner, 1982, 1983), it was found that although inference, mapping, application, comparison, and justification tended to correlate with such tests, the highest correlation typically was with the preparation-response component. This result was puzzling at first, because this component was estimated as the regression constant in the predictive regression equation. This result ended up giving birth to the concept of the metacomponents: higher order processes used to plan, monitor, and evaluate task performance. It was also found, second, that the correlations obtained for all the components showed convergent-discriminant validation: They tended to be significant with psychometric tests of reasoning but not with psychometric tests of perceptual speed (Sternberg, 1977; Sternberg & Gardner, 1983). Moreover, third, significant correlations with vocabulary tended to be obtained only for encoding of verbal stimuli (Sternberg, 1977, Sternberg & Gardner, 1983). Fourth, it was found in studies of linear-syllogistic reasoning (e.g., *John is taller than Mary; Mary is taller than Susan; who is tallest?*) that components of the proposed (mixed linguistic-spatial) model that were supposed to correlate with verbal ability did so and did not correlate with spatial ability; components that were supposed to correlate with spatial ability did so and did not correlate with verbal ability. In other words, it was possible successfully to validate the proposed model of linear-syllogistic reasoning not only in terms of the fit of response time or error data to the predictions of the alternative models, but also in terms of the correlations of component scores with psychometric tests of verbal and spatial abilities (Sternberg, 1980a). Fifth and finally, it was found that there were individual differences in strategies in solving linear syllogisms, whereby some people used a largely linguistic model, others a largely spatial model, and most the proposed linguistic-spatial mixed model. Thus, sometimes, a less than perfect fit of a proposed model to group data may reflect individual differences in strategies among participants.

Creative Intelligence. In our work on external correlates, we found that the best predictor of creative aspects of thinking seemed to be the efficiency with which an individual is able to transition between conventional and unconventional ways of thinking. In particular, in the grue–bleen conceptual-projection task described above, we found that those individuals who were able to transition effectively from "green–blue" to "grue–bleen" thinking and back again tended to be best able to think in creative ways (Sternberg, 1982).

Practical Intelligence. Practical intelligence involves individuals applying their abilities to the kinds of problems that confront them in daily life, on the job or in the home. Practical intelligence involves applying the components of intelligence to experience to (a) adapt to, (b) shape, and (c) select environments. Adaptation is involved when one changes oneself to suit the environment. Shaping is involved when one changes the environment to suit oneself. And selection is involved when one decides to seek out another environment that is a better match to one's needs, abilities, and desires. People differ in their balance of adaptation, shaping, and selection, and in the competence with which they balance among the three possible courses of action.

Much of the work of Sternberg and his colleagues on practical intelligence has centered on the concept of tacit knowledge. They have defined this construct as what one needs to know in order to work effectively in an environment that one is not explicitly taught and that often is not even verbalized (Sternberg et al., 2000; Sternberg & Wagner, 1993; Sternberg, Wagner, & Okagaki, 1993; Sternberg, Wagner, Williams, & Horvath, 1995; Wagner, 1987; Wagner & Sternberg, 1986). Sternberg and his colleagues represent tacit knowledge in the form of production systems, or sequences of "if–then" statements that describe procedures one follows in various kinds of everyday situations.

Sternberg and colleagues typically have measured tacit knowledge using work-related problems that one might encounter on the job. They have measured tacit knowledge for both children and adults, and among adults, for people in over two dozen occupations, such as management, sales, academia, teaching, school administration, secretarial work, and the military. In a typical tacit-knowledge problem, people are asked to read a story about a problem someone faces and to rate, for each statement in a set of statements, how adequate a solution the statement represents. For example, in a paper-and-pencil measure of tacit knowledge for sales, one of the problems deals with sales of photocopy machines. A relatively inexpensive machine is not moving out of the showroom and has become overstocked. The examinee is asked to rate the quality of various solutions for moving the particular model out of the showroom. In a performance-based measure for salespeople, the test taker makes a phone call to a supposed customer, who is actually the examiner. The test taker tries to sell advertising space over the phone. The examiner raises various objections to buying the advertising space. The test taker is evaluated for the quality, rapidity, and fluency of his or her responses.

In the tacit-knowledge studies, Sternberg and his colleagues have found, first, that practical intelligence as embodied in tacit knowledge increases with experience, but it is profiting from experience, rather than experience per se, that results in increases in scores. Some people can be in a job for years and still acquire relatively little tacit knowledge. Second, they also have found that subscores on tests of tacit knowledge – such as for managing oneself, managing others, and managing tasks – correlate significantly with each other. Third, scores on various tests of tacit knowledge, such as for academics and managers, are also correlated fairly substantially (at about the .5 level) with each other. Thus, fourth, tests of tacit knowledge may yield a general factor across these tests. However, fifth, scores on tacit-knowledge tests do not correlate with scores on conventional tests of intelligence, whether the measures used are single-score measures of multiple-ability batteries. Thus, any general factor from the tacit-knowledge tests is not the same as any general factor from tests of academic abilities (suggesting that neither kind of g factor is truly general, but rather, general only across a limited range of measuring instruments). Sixth, despite the lack of correlation of practical-intellectual with conventional measures, the scores on tacit-knowledge tests predict performance on the job as well as or better than do conventional psychometric intelligence tests. In one study done at the Center for Creative Leadership, they further found, seventh, that scores on our tests of tacit knowledge for management were the best single predictor of performance on a managerial simulation. In a hierarchical regression, scores on conventional tests of intelligence, personality, styles, and interpersonal orientation were entered first and scores on the test of tacit knowledge were entered last. Scores on the test of tacit knowledge were the single best predictor of managerial simulation scores. Moreover, these scores also contributed significantly to the prediction even after everything else was entered first into the equation. In recent work on military leadership (Hedlund et al., 1998; Sternberg et al., 2000), it was found, eighth, that scores of 562 participants on tests of tacit knowledge for military leadership predicted ratings of leadership effectiveness, whereas scores on a conventional test of intelligence and on a tacit-knowledge test for managers did not significantly predict the ratings of effectiveness.

One might expect performance on such tests to be hopelessly culture-specific. In other words, it might be expected that what is adaptive in the workplace of one culture may have little to do with what is adaptive in the workplace of another culture. This appears not to be the case, however. In one study, Grigorenko and her colleagues gave a tacit-knowledge test for entry-level employees to workers in a wide variety of jobs in the United States and in Spain. They then correlated preferred responses in the two countries. The correlation was .91, comparable to the reliability of the test (Grigorenko, Gil, Jarvin, & Sternberg, 2000)!

Sternberg and his colleagues have also done studies of social intelligence, which is viewed in the theory of successful intelligence as a part of practical intelligence. In these studies, forty individuals were presented with photos and asked to make judgments about them. In one kind of photo, they were asked to evaluate whether a male–female couple was a genuine couple (i.e., really involved in a romantic relationship) or a phony couple posed by the experimenters. In another kind of photo, they were asked to indicate which of two individuals was the other's supervisor (Barnes & Sternberg, 1989; Sternberg & Smith, 1985). Sternberg and his colleagues found females to be superior to males on these tasks. Scores on the two tasks did not correlate with scores on conventional ability tests, nor did they correlate with each other, suggesting a substantial degree of domain-specificity in the task.

In a study in Usenge, Kenya, near the town of Kisumu, Sternberg and his colleagues were interested in school-age children's ability to adapt to their indigenous environment. They devised a test of practical intelligence for adaptation to the environment (see Sternberg & Grigorenko, 1997; Sternberg, Nokes, et al., 2001). The test of practical intelligence measured children's informal tacit knowledge of natural herbal medicines that the villagers believe can be used to fight various types of infections. At least some of these medicines appear to be effective (Dr. Frederick Okatcha, personal communication) and most villagers certainly believe in their efficacy, as shown by the fact that children in the villages use their knowledge of these medicines an average of once a week in medicating themselves and others. Thus, tests of how to use these medicines constitute effective measures of one aspect of practical intelligence as defined by the villagers as well as their life circumstances in their environmental contexts. Middle-class Westerners might find it quite a challenge to thrive or even survive in these contexts, or, for that matter, in the contexts of urban ghettos often not distant from their comfortable homes.

The researchers measured the Kenyan children's ability to identify the medicines, where they come from, what they are used for, and how they are dosed. Based on work the researchers had done elsewhere, they expected that scores on this test would not correlate with scores on conventional tests of intelligence. In order to test this hypothesis, they also administered to the eighty-five children the Raven Coloured Progressive Matrices Test, which is a measure of fluid or abstract-reasoning-based abilities, as well as the Mill Hill Vocabulary Scale, which is a measure of crystallized or formal-knowledge-based abilities. In addition, they gave the children a comparable test of vocabulary in their own Dholuo language. The Dholuo language is spoken in the home, English in the schools.

The researchers did indeed find no correlation between the test of indigenous tacit knowledge and scores on the fluid-ability tests. But to their surprise, they found statistically significant correlations of the tacit-knowledge tests with the tests of crystallized abilities. The correlations, however, were *negative*. In other words, the higher the children scored on the test of tacit knowledge, the lower they scored, on average, on the tests of crystallized abilities. This surprising result can be interpreted in various ways, but based on the ethnographic observations of the anthropologists on the team, Geissler and Prince, the researchers concluded that a plausible scenario takes into account the expectations of families for their children.

Many children drop out of school before graduation, for financial or other reasons, and many families in the village do not particularly value formal Western schooling. There is no reason they should, as the children of many families will for the most part spend their lives farming or engaged in other occupations that make little or no use of Western schooling. These families emphasize teaching their children the indigenous informal knowledge that will lead to successful adaptation in the environments in which they will really live. Children who spend their time learning the indigenous practical knowledge of the community generally do not invest themselves heavily in doing well in school, whereas children who do well in school generally do not invest themselves so heavily in learning the indigenous knowledge – hence the negative correlations.

The Kenya study suggests that the identification of a general factor of human intelligence may tell us more about how abilities interact with patterns of schooling and especially Western patterns of schooling than it does about the structure of human abilities. In Western schooling, children typically study a variety of subject matters from an early age and thus develop skills in a variety of skill areas. This kind of schooling prepares the children to take a test of intelligence, which typically measures skills in a variety of areas. Often intelligence tests measure skills that children were expected to acquire a few years before taking the intelligence test. But as Rogoff (1990) and others have noted, this pattern of schooling is not universal and has not even been common for much of the history of humankind. Throughout history and in many places still, schooling, especially for boys, takes the form of apprenticeships in which children learn a craft from an early age. They learn what they will need to know to succeed in a trade, but not a lot more. They are not simultaneously engaged in tasks that require the development of the particular blend of skills measured by conventional intelligence tests. Hence it is less likely that one would observe a general factor in their scores, much as the investigators discovered in Kenya. Some years back, Vernon (1971) pointed out that the axes of a factor analysis do not necessarily reveal a latent structure of the mind but rather represent a convenient way of characterizing the organization of mental abilities. Vernon believed that there was no one "right" orientation of axes, and indeed, mathematically, an infinite number of orientations of axes can be fit to any solution in an exploratory factor analysis. Vernon's point seems perhaps to have been forgotten or at least ignored by later theorists.

The test of practical intelligence developed for use in Kenya, as well as some of the other practicality-based tests described in this book, may seem more like tests of achievement or of developing expertise (see Ericsson, 1996; Howe, Davidson, & Sloboda, 1998) than of intelligence. But it can be argued that intelligence is itself a form of developing expertise – that there is no clearcut distinction between the two constructs (Sternberg, 1998b, 1999d). Indeed, one might argue that all measures of intelligence measure a form of developing expertise.

An example of how tests of intelligence measure developing expertise emanates from work Sternberg, Grigorenko, and their colleagues have done in Tanzania. A study done in Tanzania (see Sternberg & Grigorenko,

1997; Sternberg, Grigorenko, et al., 2002) points out the risks of giving tests, scoring them, and interpreting the results as measures of some latent intellectual ability or abilities. The investigators administered to 358 schoolchildren between the ages of eleven and thirteen years near Bagamoyo, Tanzania, tests including a form-board classification test, a linear syllogisms test, and a Twenty Questions Test, which measure the kinds of skills required on conventional tests of intelligence. The investigators obtained scores that they could analyze and evaluate, ranking the children in terms of their supposed general or other abilities. However, they administered the tests dynamically rather than statically (Brown & Ferrara, 1985; Budoff, 1968; Day, Engelhardt, Maxwell, & Bolig, 1997; Feuerstein, 1979; Grigorenko & Sternberg, 1998; Guthke, 1993; Haywood & Tzuriel, 1992; Lidz, 1987, 1991; Tzuriel, 1995; Vygotsky, 1978). Dynamic testing is like conventional static testing in that individuals are tested and inferences about their abilities made. But dynamic tests differ in that children are given some kind of feedback to help them improve their scores. Vygotsky (1978) suggested that the children's ability to profit from the guided instruction they received during the testing session could serve as a measure of their zone of proximal development (ZPD), or the difference between their developed abilities and their latent capacities. In other words, testing and instruction are treated as being of one piece rather than as being distinct processes. This integration makes sense in terms of traditional definitions of intelligence as the ability to learn ("Intelligence and its measurement," 1921; Sternberg & Detterman, 1986). What a dynamic test does is directly measure processes of learning in the context of testing rather than measuring these processes indirectly as the product of past learning. Such measurement is especially important when not all children have had equal opportunities to learn in the past.

In our assessments, children were first given the ability tests. Then they were given a brief period of instruction in which they were able to learn skills that would potentially enable them to improve their scores. Then they were tested again. Because the instruction for each test lasted only about five or ten minutes, one would not expect dramatic gains. Yet, on average, the gains were statistically significant. More important, scores on the pretest showed only weak although significant correlations with scores on the post-test. These correlations, at about the .3 level, suggested that when tests are administered statically to children in developing countries, they may be rather unstable and easily subject to influences of training. The reason could be that the children are not accustomed to taking Western-style tests, and so profit quickly from even small amounts of instruction as to what is expected from them. Of course, the more important question is not whether the scores changed or even correlated with each other, but rather how they correlated with other cognitive measures. In other words, which test was a better predictor of transfer to other cognitive performances, the pretest score or the post-test score? The investigators found the post-test score to be the better predictor.

In interpreting results, whether from developed or developing cultures, it is always important to take into account the physical health of the participants one is testing. In a study we did in Jamaica (Sternberg, Powell, McGrane, & McGregor, 1997), we found that Jamaican schoolchildren who suffered from parasitic illnesses (for the most part, whipworm or Ascaris) did more poorly on higher-level cognitive tests (such as of working memory and reasoning) than did children who did not suffer from these illnesses, even after controlling for socioeconomic status. Why might such a physical illness cause a deficit in higher-level cognitive skills?

Ceci (1996) has shown that increased levels of schooling are associated with higher IQ. Why would there be such a relation? Presumably, in part, because schooling helps children develop the kinds of skills measured by IQ tests, and that are important for survival in school. Children with whipworm-induced and related illnesses are less able to profit from school than are other children. Every day they go to school, they are likely to experience symptoms such as listlessness, stomachache, and difficulties in concentrating, which reduce the extent to which they are able to profit from instruction and thus their ultimate performance on higher-level cognitive tests.

Crystallized-ability tests, such as tests of vocabulary and general information, certainly measure the developing and developed knowledge base. Available data suggest that fluid-ability tests, such as tests of abstract reasoning, measure developing and developed expertise even more strongly than do crystallized-ability tests. Probably the best evidence for this claim is that fluid-ability tests have shown much greater increases in scores over the last several generations than have crystallized-ability tests (Flynn, 1984, 1987, 1998; Neisser, 1998). The relatively brief period of time during which these increases have occurred (about nine points of IQ per generation) suggests an environmental rather than a genetic cause of the increases. And the substantially greater increase for fluid than for crystallized tests suggests that fluid tests, like all other tests, actually measure an expertise acquired through interaction with the environment. This is not to say that genes do not influence intelligence: Almost certainly they do (Bouchard, 1997; Plomin, 1997; Scarr, 1997). The point is that the environment always mediates their influence and tests of intelligence measure gene–environment interaction effects. The measurement of intelligence is by assessment of various forms of developing expertise.

The forms of developing expertise that are viewed as practically or otherwise intelligent may differ from one society to another or from one sector of a given society to another. For example, procedural knowledge about natural herbal medicines, on the one hand, or Western medicines, on the other, may be critical to survival in one society, and irrelevant to survival in another (where one or the other type of medicine is not available). Whereas what constitutes components of intelligence is universal, the content that constitutes the application of these components to adaptation to, shaping, and selection of environments is culturally and even subculturally variable.

In another study – the Grigorenko–Sternberg (2001) study in Russia described above – the analytical, creative, and practical tests the investigators employed were used to predict mental and physical health among the Russian adults. Mental health was measured by widely used paper-and-pencil tests of depression and anxiety and physical health was measured by self-report. The best predictor of mental and physical health was the practical-intelligence measure. Analytical intelligence came second and creative intelligence came third. All three contributed to prediction, however. Thus, the researchers again concluded that a theory of intelligence encompassing all three elements provides a better prediction of success in life than does a theory comprising just the analytical element.

Instructional Studies

Improving School Achievement.   In a first set of studies, researchers explored the question of whether conventional education in school systematically discriminates against children with creative and practical strengths (Sternberg & Clinkenbeard, 1995; Sternberg, Ferrari, Clinkenbeard, & Grigorenko, 1996; Sternberg, Grigorenko, Ferrari, & Clinkenbeard, 1999). Motivating this work was the belief that the systems in most schools strongly tend to favor children with strengths in memory and analytical abilities. However, schools can be unbalanced in other directions as well. One school Sternberg and Grigorenko visited in Russia in 2000 placed a heavy emphasis on the development of creative abilities – much more so than on the development of analytical and practical abilities. While on this trip, they were told of yet another school – catering to the children of Russian businessmen – that strongly emphasized practical abilities, and in which children who were not practically oriented were told that, eventually, they would be working for their classmates who were practically oriented.

In the United States and some other countries, the Sternberg Triarchic Abilities Test, as described earlier in the chapter, was administered to 326 children who were identified by their schools as gifted by any standard whatsoever. Children were selected for a summer program at Yale University in (college-level) psychology if they fell into one of five ability groupings: high analytical, high creative, high practical, high balanced (high in all three abilities), or low balanced (low in all three abilities). The students were divided into four instructional groups. Students in all four groups used the same introductory psychology textbook (a preliminary version of Sternberg [1995]) and listened to the same psychology lectures. What differed among them was the type of afternoon discussion section to which they were assigned, emphasizing either memory, analytical, creative, or practical instruction. For example, in the memory condition, they might be asked to describe the main tenets of a major theory of depression. In the analytical condition, they might be asked to compare and contrast two theories of depression. In the creative condition, they might be asked to formulate their own theory of depression. In the practical condition, they might be asked how they could use what they had learned about depression to help a friend who was depressed.

Students in all four instructional conditions were evaluated in terms of their performance on homework, a midterm exam, a final exam, and an independent project. Each type of work was evaluated for memory, analytical, creative, and practical quality. Thus, all students were evaluated in exactly the same way.

Our results suggested the utility of the theory of successful intelligence. This utility showed itself in several ways.

First, the investigators observed when the students arrived at Yale that those in the high creative and high practical groups were much more diverse in terms of racial, ethnic, socioeconomic, and educational backgrounds than were the students in the high analytical group, suggesting that correlations of measured intelligence with status variables such as these may be reduced by using a broader conception of intelligence. Thus, the kinds of students identified as strong differed in terms of populations from which they were drawn in comparison with students identified as strong solely by analytical measures. More important, just by expanding the range of abilities measured, the investigators discovered intellectual strengths that might not have been apparent through a conventional test.

Second, the investigators found that all three ability tests – analytical, creative, and practical – significantly predicted course performance. When multiple-regression analysis was used, at least two of these ability measures contributed significantly to the prediction of each of the measures of achievement. Perhaps as a reflection of the difficulty of deemphasizing the analytical way of teaching, one of the significant predictors was always the analytical score. (However, in a replication of our study with low-income African-American students from New York, Deborah Coates of the City University of New York found a different pattern of results. Her data indicated that the practical tests were better predictors of course performance than were the analytical measures, suggesting that which ability test predicts which criterion depends on population as well as mode of teaching.)

Third and most important, there was an aptitude-treatment interaction whereby students who were placed in instructional conditions that better matched their pattern of abilities outperformed students who were mismatched. In other words, when students are taught in a way that fits how they think, they do better in school. Children with creative and practical abilities, who are almost never taught or assessed in a way that matches their pattern of abilities, may be at a disadvantage in course after course, year after year.

A follow-up study (Sternberg, Torff, & Grigorenko, 1998a, 1998b) examined learning of social studies and science by third graders and eighth graders. The 225 third graders were students in a very low-income neighborhood in Raleigh, North Carolina. The 142 eighth graders were students who were largely middle- to upper-middle class studying in Baltimore, Maryland, and Fresno, California. In this study, students were assigned to one of three instructional conditions. In the first condition, they were taught the course that basically they would have learned had there been no intervention. The emphasis in the course was on memory. In a second condition, students were taught in a way that emphasized critical (analytical) thinking. In the third condition, they were taught in a way that emphasized analytical, creative, and practical thinking. All students' performances were assessed for memory learning (through multiple-choice assessments) as well as for analytical, creative, and practical learning (through performance assessments).

As expected, students in the successful intelligence (analytical, creative, practical) condition outperformed the other students in terms of the performance assessments. One could argue that this result merely reflected the way they were taught. Nevertheless, the result suggested that teaching for these kinds of thinking succeeded. More important, however, was the result that children in the successful intelligence condition outperformed the other children even on the multiple-choice memory tests. In other words, to the extent that one's goal is just to maximize children's memory for information, teaching for successful intelligence is still superior. It enables children to capitalize on their strengths and to correct or compensate for their weaknesses, and it allows children to encode material in a variety of interesting ways.

Grigorenko and her colleagues have now extended these results to reading curricula at the middle school and the high school level. In a study of 871 middle school students and 432 high school students, researchers taught reading either triarchically or through the regular curriculum. At the middle school level, reading was taught explicitly. At the high school level, reading was infused into instruction in mathematics, physical sciences, social sciences, English, history, foreign languages, and the arts. In all settings, students who were taught triarchially substantially outperformed students who were taught in standard ways (Grigorenko, Sternberg, & Jarvin, 2002).

Thus the results of three sets of studies suggest that the theory of successful intelligence is valid as a whole. Moreover, the results suggest that the theory can make a difference not only in laboratory tests, but in school classrooms and in the everyday life of adults as well.

Improving Abilities.   The kinds of analytical, creative, and practical abilities discussed in this book are not fixed, but rather, modifiable.

Analytical skills can be taught. For example, in one study, Sternberg (1987a) tested whether it is possible to teach people better to decontextualize meanings of unknown words presented in context. In one study, Sternberg gave eighty-one participants in five conditions a pretest on their ability to decontextualize word meanings. Then the participants were divided into five conditions, two of which were control conditions that lacked formal instruction. In one condition, participants were not given any instructional treatment. They were merely asked later to take a post-test. In a second condition, they were given practice as an instructional condition, but there was no formal instruction, per se. In a third condition, they were taught knowledge-acquisition component processes that could be used to decontextualize word meanings. In a fourth condition, they were taught to use context cues. In a fifth condition, they were taught to use mediating variables. Participants in all three of the theory-based formal-instructional conditions outperformed participants in the two control conditions, whose performance did not differ. In other words, theory-based instruction was better than no instruction at all or just practice without formal instruction.

Creative-thinking skills can also be taught and a program has been devised for teaching them (Sternberg & Williams, 1996; see also Sternberg & Grigorenko, 2000). In some relevant work, the investigators divided eighty-six gifted and nongifted fourth grade children into experimental and control groups. All children took pretests on insightful thinking. Then some of the children received their regular school instruction whereas others received instruction on insight skills. After the instruction of whichever kind, all children took a post-test on insight skills. The investigators found that children taught how to solve the insight problems using knowledge-acquisition components gained more from pretest to post-test than did students who were not so taught (Davidson & Sternberg, 1984).

Practical-intelligence skills can also be taught. Williams and her colleagues have developed a program for teaching practical–intellectual skills, aimed at middle school students, that explicitly teaches students "practical intelligence for school" in the contexts of doing homework, taking tests, reading, and writing (Williams et al., 1996). Sternberg and his colleagues have evaluated the program in a variety of settings (Gardner, Krechevsky, Sternberg, & Okagaki, 1994; Sternberg, Okagaki, & Jackson, 1990) and found that students taught via the program outperform students in control groups that did not receive the instruction.

Individuals' use of practical intelligence can be to their own gain in addition to or instead of the gain of others. People can be practically intelligent for themselves at the expense of others. It is for this reason that wisdom needs to be studied in its own right in addition to practical or even successful intelligence (Baltes & Staudinger, 2000; Sternberg, 1998b).

In sum, practical intelligence, like analytical intelligence, is an important antecedent of life success. Because measures of practical intelligence predict everyday behavior at about the same level as do measures of analytical intelligence (and sometimes even better), the sophisticated use of such tests could roughly double the explained variance in various kinds of criteria of success. Using measures of creative intelligence as well might improve prediction still more. Thus, tests based on the construct of successful intelligence might take us to new and higher levels of prediction. At the same time, expansion of conventional tests that stay within the conventional framework of analytical tests based on standard psychometric models do not seem likely to expand greatly our predictive capabilities (Schmidt & Hunter, 1998). But how did psychologists get to where they are, with respect to both levels of prediction and the kinds of standard psychometric tests used to attain these levels of prediction?

THE SOCIETAL DILEMMA OF INTELLIGENCE

The Societal System Created by Tests

Tests of intelligence-related skills predict success in many cultures. People with higher test scores seem to be more successful in a variety of ways and those with lower test scores seem to be less successful (Herrnstein & Murray, 1994; Hunt, 1995). Why are scores on intelligence-related tests closely related to societal success? Consider two points of view.

According to Herrnstein and Murray (1994), Wigdor and Garner (1982), and others, conventional tests of intelligence account for about 10 to 15 percent of the variation, on average, in various kinds of real-world outcomes. This figure increases if one makes various corrections to it (for example, for attenuation in measures or for restriction of range in particular samples). Although this percentage is not particularly large, it is not trivial either. It is difficult to find any other kind of predictor that fares as well. Clearly, the tests have some value (Hunt, 1995; Schmidt & Hunter, 1981, 1998). They predict success in many jobs, and predict success even better in schooling for jobs. Rankings of jobs by prestige usually show higher prestige jobs associated with higher levels of intelligence-related skills. Theorists of intelligence differ as to why the tests have some success in prediction of job level and competency.

The Discovery of an "Invisible Hand of Nature"? Some theorists believe that the role of intelligence in society is along the lines of some kind of natural law. In their book, Herrnstein and Murray (1994) refer to an "invisible hand of nature" guiding events such that people with high IQs tend to rise toward the top socioeconomic strata of a society and people with low IQs tend to fall toward the bottom strata. Jensen (1969, 1998) has made related arguments, as have many others (see, for example, [largely unfavorable] reviews by Gould, 1981; Lemann, 1999; Sacks, 1999; Zenderland, 1998). Herrnstein and Murray present data to support their argument, although many aspects of their data and their interpretations of these data are arguable (Fraser, 1995; Gould, 1995; Jacoby & Glauberman, 1995; Sternberg, 1995).

This point of view has a certain level of plausibility to it. First, more complex jobs almost certainly do require higher levels of intelligence-related skills. Presumably, lawyers need to do more complex mental tasks than do street cleaners. Second, reaching the complex jobs via the educational system almost certainly requires a higher level of mental performance than does reaching less complex jobs. Finally, there is at least some heritable component of intelligence (Plomin, DeFries, McClearn, & Rutter, 1997), so that nature must play some role in who gets what mental skills. Despite this plausibility, there is an alternative point of view.

A Societal Invention?   An alternative point of view is that the sorting influence of intelligence in society is more a societal invention than a discovery of an invisible hand of nature (Sternberg, 1997b). The United States and some other countries have created societies in which test scores matter profoundly. High test scores may be needed for placement in higher tracks in elementary and secondary school. They may be needed for admission to selective undergraduate programs. They may be needed again for admission to selective graduate and professional programs. Highest scores help individuals gain the access routes to many of the highest paying and most prestigious jobs. Low GRE scores, in contrast, may exclude one not only from one selective graduate program, but from many others as well. To the extent that there is error of measurement, it will have comparable effects in many schools.

According to this point of view, there are many able people who may be disenfranchised because the kinds of abilities they have, although important for job performance, are not important for test performance. For example, the kinds of creative and practical skills that matter to success on the job typically are not measured on the tests used for admission to educational programs. At the same time, society may be overvaluing those who have a fairly narrow range of skills, and a range of skills that may not serve them particularly well on the job, even if they do lead to success in school and on the tests.

On this view, it is scarcely surprising that ability tests predict school grades, because the tests originally were explicitly designed for this purpose (Binet & Simon, 1916b). In effect, the United States and other societies have created closed systems: Certain abilities are valued in instruction, for example, memory and analytical abilities. Ability tests are then created that measure these abilities and thus predict school performance. Then assessments of achievement are designed that also assess for these abilities. Little wonder that ability tests are more predictive in school than in the workplace: Within the closed system of the school, a narrow range of abilities leads to success on ability tests, in instruction, and on achievement tests. But these same abilities are less important later on in life.

According to the societal-invention view, closed systems can be and have been constructed to value almost any set of attributes. In some societies, caste is used. Members of certain castes are allowed to rise to the top; members of other castes have no chance. The members of the successful castes believe they are getting their due, much as did the nobility in the Middle Ages who were born at the top and, without thought, subjugated their serfs. Even in the United States, if one were born a slave before 1863, one's IQ would make little difference: One would die a slave. Slave owners and others rationalized the system, as social Darwinists always have, by believing that the fittest were in the roles they rightfully belonged in.

The general conclusion is that societies can and do choose a variety of criteria to sort people. Some societies have used or continue to use caste systems. Others use or have used race, religion, or wealth of parents as bases for sorting people. Many societies use a combination of criteria. Once a system is in place, those who gain access to the power structure, whether through elite education or otherwise, are likely to look for others like themselves to enter into positions of power. The reason, quite simply, is that there probably is no more powerful basis of interpersonal attraction than similarity, so that people in a power structure look for others similar to themselves. The result is a potentially endlessly looping closed system that keeps replicating itself.

INTERIM SUMMARY

The time has come to move beyond conventional theories of intelligence. In this discussion we have provided data suggesting that conventional theories and tests of intelligence are incomplete. The general factor is an artifact of limitations in populations of individuals tested, types of materials with which they are tested, and types of methods used in testing. Our studies show that even when one wants to predict school performance, the conventional tests are somewhat limited in their predictive validity (Sternberg & Williams, 1997). Sternberg has proposed a theory of successful intelligence and its development that fares well in construct validations, whether one tests in the laboratory, in schools, or in the workplace. The greatest obstacle to moving on is in vested interests, both in academia and in the world of tests. Psychologists now have ways to move beyond conventional notions of intelligence; they need only the will.

The time perhaps has come to expand our notion and everyone's notion of what it means to be intelligent. Exactly what kind of expansion should take place? An expansion of the conventional conception of intelligence to include not just memory and analytical abilities, but creative and practical abilities as well has been suggested here. Other expansions are also possible. For example, research is ongoing with regard to emotional intelligence (Mayer, Salovey, & Caruso, 2000a; 2000b; Davies, Stankov, & Roberts, 1998), with promising although as yet mixed results. It is hoped that predictive empirical research will also be forthcoming regarding the theory of multiple intelligences (Gardner, 1983, 1999). Ultimately, the answer to the question of how to expand psychological conceptions of intelligence will depend in part on the imagination of theorists, but more important, on the data showing construct validity, and in particular, incremental internal and external validity over the conventional notions that have dominated theory and research on intelligence to date. The memory and analytical abilities measured by these tests have been and likely will continue to matter for many forms of success in life. They never have been, and are unlikely ever to be, the only intellectual abilities that matter for success. It is for this reason that psychologists have needed and will continue to need theories such as the theory of successful intelligence.

INTELLIGENCE AS DEVELOPING EXPERTISE

The conventional view of intelligence is that it is some relatively stable attribute of individuals that develops as an interaction between heredity and environment. Factor analysis and related techniques can be used on tests of intelligence to determine the structure of intellectual abilities, as illustrated by the massive analysis of Carroll (1993).

The argument of this chapter, following on the theory of successful intelligence and advancing that of Sternberg (1997b), is that this view of what intelligence is and of what intelligence tests measure may be incorrect. An alternative view is that of intelligence as developing expertise and intelligence tests as measuring an aspect – typically a limited aspect – of developing expertise. Developing expertise is defined here as the ongoing process of the acquisition and consolidation of a set of skills needed for a high level of mastery in one or more domains of life performance. Good performance on intelligence tests requires a certain kind of expertise, and to the extent that this expertise overlaps with the expertise required by schooling or by the workplace, there will be a correlation between the tests and performance in school or in the workplace. But such correlations represent no intrinsic relation between intelligence and other kinds of performances, but rather overlaps in the kinds of expertise needed to perform well under different kinds of circumstances. The goal here is to carry the argument made by Sternberg (1998a) a step further by showing that a conjunction of research results that would seem puzzling and contradictory when taken together make sense as a whole when considered from the standpoint of ability tests as measuring developing expertise (Sternberg, 2001b).

There is nothing privileged about intelligence tests. One could as easily use, say, academic achievement to predict intelligence-related scores. For example, it is as simple to use the SAT-II (a measure of achievement) to predict the SAT-I (a measure formerly called the Scholastic Assessment Test and before that the Scholastic Aptitude Test) as vice versa, and the levels of prediction will be the same. Both tests measure achievement, although the kinds of achievements they measure are different.

According to this view, although ability tests may have temporal priority relative to various criteria in their administration (that is, ability tests are administered first, and later, criterion indices of performance, such as grades or achievement test scores, are collected), they have no psychological priority. All the various kinds of assessments are of the same kind psychologically. What distinguishes ability tests from other kinds of assessments is how the ability tests are used (usually predictively) rather than what they measure. There is no qualitative distinction among the various kinds of assessments. All tests measure various kinds of developing expertise.

Conventional tests of intelligence and related abilities measure achievement that individuals should have accomplished several years back (see also Anastasi & Urbina, 1997). Tests such as vocabulary, reading comprehension, verbal analogies, arithmetic problem solving, and the like are all, in part, tests of achievement. Even abstract-reasoning tests measure achievement in dealing with geometric symbols, skills taught in Western schools (Laboratory of Comparative Human Cognition, 1982). One might as well use academic performance to predict ability test scores. The problem regarding the traditional model is not in its statement of a correlation between ability tests and other forms of achievement but in its proposal of a causal relation whereby the tests reflect a construct that is somehow causal of, rather than merely temporally antecedent to, later success. The developing-expertise view in no way rules out the contribution of genetic factors as a source of individual differences in who will be able to develop a given amount of expertise. Many human attributes, including intelligence, reflect the covariation and interaction of genetic and environmental factors. But the contribution of genes to an individual's intelligence cannot be directly measured or even directly estimated. Rather, what is measured is a portion of what is expressed, namely, manifestations of developing expertise, the kind of expertise that potentially leads to reflective practitioners in a variety of fields (Schon, 1983). This approach to measurement is used explicitly by Royer, Carlo, Durfresne, and Mestre (1996), who have shown that it is possible to develop measurements of reading skill reflecting varying levels of developing expertise. In such assessments, outcome measures reflect not simply quantitative assessments of skill, but qualitative differences in the types of developing expertise that have emerged (for example, ability to understand technical text material, ability to draw inferences from this material, or ability to conceive "big ideas" from technical text).

According to this view, measures of intelligence *should* be correlated with later success, because both measures of intelligence and various measures of success require developing expertise of related types. For example, both typically require what I have referred to as *metacomponents* of thinking: recognition of problems, definition of problems, formulation of strategies to solve problems, representation of information, allocation of resources, and monitoring and evaluation of problem solutions. These skills develop as results of gene–environment covariation and interaction. If we wish to call them *intelligence*, that is certainly fine, so long as we recognize that what we are calling intelligence is a form of developing expertise.

A major goal of work under the point of view presented here is to integrate the study of intelligence and related abilities (see reviews in Sternberg, 1990c, 1994a, 2000b) with the study of expertise (Chi, Glaser, & Farr, 1988; Ericsson, 1996; Ericsson & Smith, 1991; Hoffman, 1992). These literatures, typically viewed as distinct, are here viewed as ultimately involved with the same psychological mechanisms.

The Specifics of the Developing-Expertise Model

The specifics of the developing-expertise model are shown in Figure 2.2. The model shows the relation of intelligence to other relevant constructs. At the heart of the model is the notion of *developing expertise* – that individuals are constantly in a process of developing expertise when they work within a given domain. They may and do, differ in rate and asymptote of development. The main constraint in achieving expertise is not some fixed prior level of capacity, but purposeful engagement involving direct instruction, active participation, role modeling, and reward.

Elements of the Model

The model of developing expertise has five key elements (although certainly they do not constitute an exhaustive list of elements in the development of expertise): metacognitive skills, learning skills, thinking skills, knowledge, and motivation. Although it is convenient to separate these five elements, they are fully interactive, as shown in the figure. They influence each other, both directly and indirectly. For example, learning leads to knowledge, but knowledge facilitates further learning.

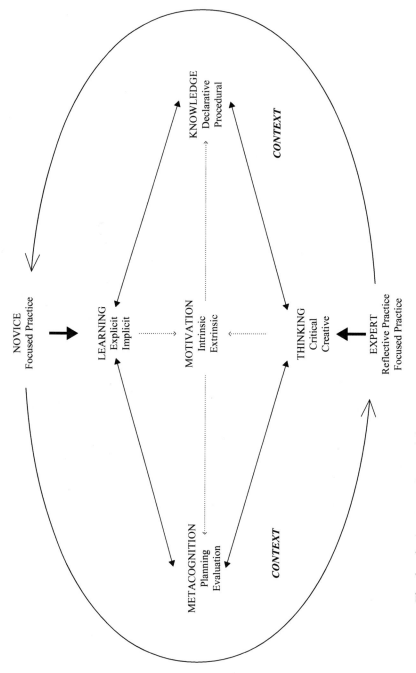

FIGURE 2.2. The developing-expertise model.

These elements are, to a large extent, domain-specific. The development of expertise in one area does not necessarily lead to the development of expertise in another area, although there may be some transfer, depending on the relationship of the areas, a point that has been made with regard to intelligence by others as well (for example, Gardner, 1983).

In the theory of successful intelligence (Sternberg, 1985a, 1997b), intelligence is viewed as having three aspects: analytical, creative, and practical. Our research suggests that the development of expertise in one creative domain (Sternberg & Lubart, 1995) or in one practical domain (Sternberg, Wagner, Williams, & Horvath, 1995) shows modest correlations with the development of expertise in other such domains. Psychometric research suggests more domain-generality for the analytical domain (Jensen, 1998). Moreover, people can show analytical, creative, or practical expertise in one domain without showing all three of these kinds of expertise, or even two of the three.

1. Metacognitive Skills. Metacognitive skills (or metacomponents – Sternberg, 1985a) refer to people's understanding and control of their own cognition. For example, such skills would encompass what an individual knows about writing papers or solving arithmetic word problems, both with regard to the steps that are involved and to how these steps can be executed effectively. Seven metacognitive skills are particularly important, as discussed earlier: problem recognition, problem definition, problem representation, strategy formulation, resource allocation, monitoring of problem solving, and evaluation of problem solving (Sternberg, 1985a, 1986). All these skills are modifiable (Sternberg, 1986, 1988c; Sternberg & Spear-Swerling, 1996).

2. Learning Skills. Learning skills (knowledge-acquisition components) are essential to the model (Sternberg, 1985a, 1986), although they are certainly not the only learning skills that individuals use. Learning skills are sometimes divided into explicit and implicit ones. Explicit learning is what occurs when we make an effort to learn; implicit learning is what occurs when we pick up information incidentally, without any systematic effort. Examples of learning skills are selective encoding, which involves distinguishing relevant from irrelevant information; selective combination, which involves putting together the relevant information; and selective comparison, which involves relating new information to information already stored in memory (Sternberg, 1985a).

3. Thinking Skills. There are three main kinds of thinking skills (or performance components) that individuals need to master (Sternberg, 1985a, 1986, 1994b). It is important to note that these are sets of, rather than individual, thinking skills. Critical (analytical) thinking skills include analyzing, critiquing, judging, evaluating, comparing and contrasting, and assessing. Creative thinking skills include creating, discovering, inventing, imagining, supposing, and hypothesizing. Practical thinking skills include applying, using, utilizing, and practicing (Sternberg, 1997b). They are the first step in the translation of thought into real-world action.

4. Knowledge. There are two main kinds of knowledge that are relevant in academic situations. Declarative knowledge is of facts, concepts, principles, laws, and the like. It is "knowing that." Procedural knowledge is of procedures and strategies. It is "knowing how." Of particular importance is procedural tacit knowledge, which involves knowing how the system in which one is operating functions (Sternberg, Wagner, Williams, & Horvath, 1995).

5. Motivation. One can distinguish among several different kinds of motivation. A first kind of motivation is achievement motivation (McClelland, 1985; McClelland, Atkinson, Clark, & Lowell, 1976). People who are high in achievement motivation seek moderate challenges and risks. They are attracted to tasks that are neither very easy nor very hard. They are strivers – constantly trying to better themselves and their accomplishments. A second kind of motivation is competence (self-efficacy) motivation, which refers to persons' beliefs in their own ability to solve the problem at hand (Bandura, 1977, 1996). Experts need to develop a sense of their own efficacy to solve difficult tasks in their domain of expertise. This kind of self-efficacy can result from both intrinsic and extrinsic rewards (Amabile, 1996; Sternberg & Lubart, 1996). Other kinds of motivation are important, too. Motivation is perhaps the indispensable element needed for school success. Without it, the student never even tries to learn.

6. Context. All the elements discussed above are characteristics of the learner. Returning to the issues raised at the beginning of this chapter, a problem with conventional tests is that they assume that individuals operate in a more or less decontextualized environment. A test score is interpreted largely in terms of the individual's internal attributes. But a test measures much more, and the assumption of a fixed or uniform context across test takers is not realistic. Contextual factors that can affect test performance include native language, emphasis of test on speedy performance, importance to the test taker of success on the test, and familiarity with the kinds of material on the test.

Interactions of Elements

The novice works toward expertise through deliberate practice. But this practice requires an interaction of all five of the key elements. At the center, driving the elements, is motivation. Without it, the elements remain inert. Eventually, one reaches a kind of expertise, at which one becomes a reflective practitioner of a certain set of skills. But expertise occurs at many levels. The expert first-year graduate or law student, for example, is still a far cry from the expert professional. People thus proceed through many cycles on the way to successively higher levels of expertise. They do so through the elements in the figure.

Motivation drives metacognitive skills, which in turn activate learning and thinking skills, which then provide feedback to the metacognitive skills, enabling one's level of expertise to increase (see also Sternberg, 1985a). The declarative and procedural knowledge acquired through the extension of the thinking and learning skills also results in these skills being used more effectively in the future.

All these processes are affected by, and can in turn affect, the context in which they operate. For example, if a learning experience is in English but the learner has only limited English proficiency, his or her learning will be inferior to that of someone with more advanced English-language skills. Or if material is presented orally to someone who is a better visual learner, the quality of that individual's performance will be reduced.

How does this model of developing expertise relate to the construct of intelligence?

The *g* Factor and the Structure of Abilities

Some intelligence theorists point to the stability of the alleged general factor of human intelligence as evidence for the existence of some kind of stable and overriding structure of human intelligence. But the existence of a *g* factor may reflect little more than an interaction between whatever latent (and not directly measurable) abilities individuals have and the kinds of expertise that are developed in school. With different forms of schooling, *g* could be made either stronger or weaker. In effect, Western forms and related forms of schooling may, in part, create the *g* phenomenon by providing a kind of schooling that teaches in conjunction the various kinds of skills measured by tests of intellectual abilities.

Suppose, for example, that children were selected from an early age to be schooled for a certain trade. Throughout most of human history, this is in fact the way most children were schooled. Boys, at least, were apprenticed at an early age to a master who would teach them a trade. There was no point in their learning skills that would be irrelevant to their lives.

To bring the example into the present, imagine that we decided that certain students from an early age would study English (or some other native language) to develop language expertise; other students would study mathematics to develop their mathematical expertise. Still other students might specialize in developing spatial expertise to be used in flying airplanes or doing shop work or whatever. Instead of specialization beginning at the university level, it would begin from the age of first schooling.

This point of view is related to, but different from, that typically associated with the theory of crystallized and fluid intelligence (Cattell, 1971; Horn, 1994). In that theory, fluid ability is viewed as an ability to acquire and reason with information whereas crystallized ability is viewed as the information so acquired. According to this view, schooling primarily develops crystallized ability, based in part on the fluid ability the individual brings to bear on school-like tasks. In the theory proposed here, however, both fluid and crystallized ability are roughly equally susceptible to development through schooling or other means societies create for developing expertise. One could argue that the greater validity of the position presented here is shown by the near-ubiquitous Flynn effect (mentioned earlier – Flynn, 1987; Neisser, 1998), which documents massive gains in IQ around the world throughout most of the twentieth century. The effect must be due to environment, because large genetic changes worldwide in such a short time frame are virtually impossible. It is interesting that the gains are substantially larger in fluid abilities than in crystallized abilities, suggesting that fluid abilities are likely to be as susceptible as or probably more susceptible than crystalloid abilities to environmental influences. Clearly, the notion of fluid abilities as some basic genetic potential one brings into the world, whose development is expressed in crystallized abilities, does not work.

In sum, intelligence in the theory of successful intelligence is viewed not as fixed, but as flexible and modifiable. How can it be modified?

DEVELOPING SUCCESSFUL INTELLIGENCE

Our goal is to raise the achievement of all students by teaching them in a way that matches the way they learn. The question is, how to do it? We think we have a way. Of course, it is not the only way. But so far, it seems to work for a wide variety of students of varied ages and in diverse subject-matter areas.

The Problem: Schools that Work for Some Students but Not for Others

The problem is that some children seem to benefit just fine from the schooling they get, but others do not. Teachers try very hard to reach all students, but rather frequently find that there are some students who just seem hard to reach. There can be many reasons for this – disabilities, disorders, motivational problems, health problems, and so forth. One reason, though, can be the mismatch between a pattern of strengths and weaknesses on the part of the student and the particular range of methods a teacher is using.

"Teaching for successful intelligence" provides a series of techniques for reaching as many students as possible (Sternberg & Grigorenko, 2000; Sternberg & Spear-Swerling, 1996; Sternberg & Williams, 1996).

The theory of successful intelligence holds that some students who do not do well in conventional courses may, in fact, have the ability to succeed if they are taught in a way that better fits their patterns of abilities. For example, when I took my introductory psychology course, I was very motivated to become a psychologist. I received a grade of "C" in the course. The grade was extremely discouraging to me, as was my instructor's comment that "There is a famous Sternberg in psychology, and judging from this grade, there won't be another one." I decided that I did not have the ability to major in psychology, so I switched to mathematics. This was a fortunate decision for me, because on the midterm in advanced mathematics, I got a grade of "F." Now, the "C" was looking pretty good, so I switched back to psychology. I received higher grades in subsequent courses, and today, I am a psychologist and was just recently elected president of the American Psychological Association, a national organization of about 155,000 psychologists. Incidentally, Phil Zimbardo, past president of the Association, also received a grade of "C" in his introductory psychology course.

The problem is that many children who might like to study a given subject area – whether language arts, mathematics, history, science, foreign language, or whatever – may give up because they think they cannot succeed in studying it. They may either stop taking courses in the subject area, or just give up in the courses they are taking. Teaching for successful intelligence can give these students the chance to succeed that they might not otherwise have.

What is Teaching for Successful Intelligence?

Teaching for successful intelligence involves a way of looking at the teaching–learning process that broadens the kinds of activities and assessments teachers traditionally employ. Many good teachers "teach for successful intelligence" spontaneously. But, for one reason or another, most do not. Teaching for successful intelligence involves, at minimum, using a set of prompts that encourages students to engage in memory learning as well as analytical, creative, and practical learning.[1]

The key strategies are these:

Strategy 1: Teaching for Memory Learning
Most conventional teaching is teaching for memory learning. Teaching for successful intelligence does not ask teachers to stop what they are already doing. Rather, it asks them to build on it. Teaching for memory is the

---

[1] Because of space limitations, it is not possible to describe each of the kinds of teaching in detail. More details are contained in Sternberg and Grigorenko (2000).

foundation for all other teaching, because students cannot think critically (or any other way) about what they know if they do not know anything. Teaching for memory basically involves assisting or assessing students' memory of the *who* (for example, "Who did something?"), *what* (for example, "What did they do?"), *where* ("Where did they do it?"), *when* ("When did they do it?"), *why* ("Why did they do it?"), and *how* ("How did they do it?") of learning.

Here are some examples of teaching and assessing for memory learning:

- *Recall* a fact they have learned, such as the name of the king of England during the American Revolution, or the product of 7×8, or the chemical formula for sodium.
- *Recognize* a fact they have learned, such as which of the following countries is in Central America: Bolivia, Ecuador, Guatemala, or Brazil; or whether the product of 7×8 is 54, 56, 48, or 60; or whether the chemical formula for sodium is So, Na, Sd, or Nd.
- *Match* one set of items of one kind with another set of items of another kind, such as the list of the elements hydrogen, sodium, oxygen, and potassium with the list of abbreviations H, K, Na, and O.
- *Verify* statements, such as whether the statement "Vladimir Putin is currently the president of Russia," or "The atomic number for uranium is 100," is true or false.
- *Repeat* what you have learned, such as a poem, an article of the Constitution, a scientific formula, or a mathematical formula.

Research suggests that there are certain things teachers can do to help students maximize their memory-based learning (see Williams & Sternberg, 2002). These things include encouraging students (a) to space their learning over time and study sessions rather than massing it into a small number of study sessions, (b) to avoid studying materials that are similar (for example, French and Spanish) in close temporal proximity, to avoid confusion (or, in technical terms, proactive [forward] and retroactive [backward] interference), and to study the most important information near the beginning and the end of a session (the so-called serial-position effect, which gives a benefit to things studied near the beginning or ending of a session).

Strategy 2: Teaching for Analytical Learning
Teachers who teach for successful intelligence do not teach only for memory, because some students are not particularly adept as memory learners. I, myself, was not, as I mentioned above, and am not to this day. Many students have the ability to learn, but fail miserably when they sit down and try to memorize a set of isolated facts, or even when they are asked merely to recall a set of isolated facts.

Here are examples of teaching and assessing for analytical learning and thinking:

- *Analyze* an issue, such as why genocides continue to occur even today, or why certain elements are radioactive, or why children still find *Tom Sawyer* entertaining, or how to solve a particular algebraic factoring problem.
- *Evaluate* an issue, such as why unlimited political contributions can lead to corruption in a political system, how the Internet is vulnerable to catastrophic sabotage, what part of speech a certain word is, or how best to make a cake.
- *Explain* how the British Parliamentary system works, or why a wool blanket produces static electricity, or how to solve an arithmetic word problem, or why a character in a short story acted the way she did.
- *Compare and contrast* two or more items, such as the systems of government in China and England, or igneous and sedimentary rocks, or two different ways of proving a geometric theorem, or two novels.
- *Judge* the value of the characteristics of something, such as a law, or a scientific experiment, or a poem, or the metric system of measurement.

We have found it useful, in teaching for analytical thinking, to teach students how to use a problem-solving cycle in their thinking. The steps of the problem-solving cycle are what we refer to as metacomponents, or higher-order executive processes that are used to plan, monitor, and evaluate problem solving (Sternberg, 1985a). First, students need to recognize the existence of a problem (for example, the need to write a term paper). Second, they need to define exactly what the problem is (for example, what the topic of the term paper will be). Third, they need to allocate resources for the problem (for example, how much time to spend on the term paper). Fourth, they need to represent information about the problem (for example, using note cards, outlines, etc.). Fifth, they need to formulate a strategy for solving the problem (getting the paper done). Sixth, they need to monitor their progress as they solve the problem (is the paper getting done, or has one gotten stuck on some aspect of it?). Finally, they need to evaluate their work after it is done (proofread the paper and see how it reads).

Strategy 3: Teaching for Creative Learning
Teaching for successful intelligence also involves encouraging students to use and develop their creative-thinking skills. Such skills involve production of ideas that are novel, high in quality, and appropriate to the task at hand (Sternberg & Lubart, 1995). Teachers who teach for successful intelligence recognize that some students learn best when they are allowed to find their own way to learning material, and when they are left free to explore ideas that go beyond those in books or lectures.

Here are some examples of teaching and assessing for creative learning and thinking:

- *Create* a game for learning the names of the states, or a poem, or a haiku or a new numerical operation, or a scientific experiment.
- *Invent* a toy, or a new way of solving a difficult mathematics problem, or a new system of government that builds on old systems.
- *Explore* new ways of solving a mathematics problem beyond those taught by the teacher, or how to achieve a certain chemical reaction, or different ways of reading so as to improve your reading comprehension, or the nature of volcanoes.
- *Imagine* what it would be like to live in another country, or what will happen if temperatures on the Earth keep rising, or what Picasso might have been thinking when he painted *Guernica*, or what might happen if the government of England made it a crime to speak ill of the government.
- *Suppose* that people were paid to inform on their neighbors to the political party in power – what would happen?, or that all lakes instantly dried up – what would happen?, or that schools stopped teaching mathematics – what would happen, or that Germany had won World War II – what would have happened?
- *Synthesize* your knowledge of the Gulf War and the recent war in Afghanistan to propose a set of battle techniques likely to work in many unfamiliar terrains.

I believe that, to a large extent, creative thinking represents a decision to do thinking certain ways and to do certain things. To teach students to think creatively, they need to learn to make these decisions (Sternberg, 2000a). These decisions include, among other things, (a) redefining problems rather than merely accepting the way problems are presented, (b) being willing to take intellectual risks, (c) being willing to surmount obstacles when people criticize one's attempts at being creative, (d) being willing to work to persuade people of the value of one's creative ideas, and (e) believing that one truly has the potential to produce creative ideas in the first place.

Strategy 4: Teaching for Practical Learning
Some students are primarily practical learners. They do not catch on unless they see some kind of practical use for what they are learning. That is, they learn best if the material facilitates their adaptation to, shaping of, and selection of environments (Sternberg et al., 2000).

Here are some examples of teaching and assessing for practical learning and thinking:

- *Put into practice* what you have learned about measurement in baking a cake; your foreign-language instruction in speaking with a foreigner;

your knowledge of soils to determine whether a particular plant can grow adequately in a given soil.

- *Use* your knowledge of percentages or decimals in computing discounts; a lesson learned by a character in a novel in your own life; your knowledge of the effects of particulate matter in the atmosphere on vision to figure out whether a car driving behind you in the fog is substantially closer than it appears to be.
- *Utilize* a physical formula to figure out the speed at which a falling object will actually hit the ground; your understanding of cultural customs to figure out why someone from another culture behaves in a way you consider to be strange; the lesson you learned from a fable or a proverb to change your behavior with other people.
- *Implement* a plan for holding a classroom election; a strategy for conserving energy in your home; what you have learned in a driver education class in your actual driving; a psychological strategy for persuading people to contribute to charity.
- *Apply* your knowledge of political campaigns in history to run for class president; your knowledge of the principles of mixture problems to mixing paints to achieve a certain color; your understanding of the principles of good speaking to give a persuasive talk.

Part of teaching for practical thinking is teaching students to adopt certain attitudes in their intellectual work (Sternberg, 1986). These attitudes include ones such as (a) combating the tendency to procrastinate, (b) organizing oneself to get one's work done, (c) figuring out how one learns best, (d) avoiding the tendency to use self-pity as an excuse for working hard, and (e) avoiding blaming others for one's own failings.

Some General Principles

In teaching for successful intelligence, one is helping all students make the most of their skills by addressing all students at least some of the time. It is important to realize that teaching for successful intelligence does not mean teaching everything three times. Rather, one balances one's teaching strategies, so that one is teaching in each of the ways part of the time. An advantage of this procedure is that one does not have to know each student's exact strengths and weaknesses. By teaching in all of the ways, one is addressing some students' strengths at the same time one is addressing other students' weaknesses. Balancing teaching strategies guarantees that one will be addressing each student's strength at least some of the time. But one does not want to teach only to strengths, as students also need to learn how to compensate for and correct weaknesses.

It is also important to ensure that one's assessment practices match one's teaching practices. Sometimes, teachers teach in one way but assess in another way. For example, they may encourage critical thinking in class, but then give tests that merely measure recall. Students quickly learn that the real game of getting good marks is not the apparent game. The students then respond to the way they are assessed, not to the way they are taught. So it is crucial that the teacher value the same things in his or her assessment as in his or her teaching.

Comparison to Other Pedagogical Theories

No psychological theory or set of teaching techniques is completely new. Rather, theories and the teaching techniques that derive from them build on each other. It is thus useful to point out similarities and differences between teaching for successful intelligence and other ways of teaching, based on different theories.

One well-known theory is that of Bloom (1976; Bloom, Engelhart, Frost, Hill, & Krathwohl, 1956), known as Bloom's taxonomy. Bloom proposes a six-level taxonomy: knowledge, comprehension, application, analysis, synthesis, and evaluation. Teaching for memory is related to teaching for knowledge and comprehension; teaching for analytical thinking, to teaching for analysis and evaluation; teaching for creative thinking, to teaching for synthesis; and teaching for practical thinking, to teaching for application.

There are a few differences between the current theory and Bloom's. Here are four main ones.

First, the theory of successful intelligence does not view the three kinds of abilities as "hierarchically related." For example, one does not need to think for application (practically – lower in Bloom's hierarchy) in order to think for synthesis (creatively – higher in Bloom's hierarchy). On the contrary, much creative thinking is not necessarily practical at all (for example, most academic scholarship), and much practical thinking is not necessarily creative (for example, the thinking involved in filling out bureaucratic forms).

Second, the theory of successful intelligence parses skills differently. Analysis and evaluation are separated by synthesis in Bloom's theory, but in the theory of successful intelligence, they are seen as more related to each other than either is to synthetic thinking.

Third, the concepts of analytical, creative, and practical thinking are each somewhat broader than the terms of Bloom's taxonomy. As shown above, each of the three kinds of teaching includes, but is not limited to, the terms in Bloom's taxonomy. For example, synthesis is part of teaching for creative thinking, but only a small part of it.

Fourth, the techniques involved in teaching for successful intelligence derive from a theory of intelligence that has been tested in many different ways. Bloom's theory is not and was not intended to be a theory of intelligence.

Another related theory is that of Gardner (1983, 1993, 1999). Gardner's theory of multiple intelligences, like the theory of successful intelligence, attempts to extend our thinking about the nature of intelligence. Again, though, there are some key differences.

First, Gardner's theory deals with domains, positing linguistic intelligence, logical/mathematical intelligence, spatial intelligence, musical intelligence, naturalistic intelligence, bodily-kinesthetic intelligence, interpersonal intelligence, intrapersonal intelligence, and possibly existential intelligence. The theory of successful intelligence specifies classes of processes. Thus, at one level, the theories are largely complementary. One can teach analytically, creatively, or practically, for example, in the linguistic domain (analytical – analyze a poem, creative – write a short story, practical – write a persuasive essay), or in any other domain.

Second, Gardner includes as intelligences sets of skills that perhaps would not be viewed as intelligences in the theory of successful intelligence. For example, to survive in the world, everyone has to have at least some ability to think analytically, creatively, and practically. But it is not clear that, to survive in the world, everyone has to think musically.

Third, the theory of successful intelligence has been extensively validated predictively, and these predictions have been largely upheld. For example, in a series of studies, we have shown that the exploratory and confirmatory factor structures of sets of tests designed to measure triarchic abilities do indeed provide distinct factors corresponding to analytical, creative, and practical abilities, and that the model proposing these three separate factors is superior to alternative factorial models (Sternberg, Castejón, Prieto, Hautamäki, & Grigorenko, 2001; Sternberg, Grigorenko, Ferrari, & Clinkenbeard, 1999). In other studies, we have shown that the theory holds up cross culturally, for example, that the analytical and practical aspects of intelligence can be distinguished as well in countries outside the United States as they can in the United States (for example, Grigorenko & Sternberg, 2001; Sternberg et al., 2001). I am unaware of any predictive tests of the theory of multiple intelligences. Although such tests may seem like an abstract detail to many teachers, validation of a theory helps ensure that it does, indeed, characterize how people really think, rather than merely the investigators' or others' opinions of how they really think.

Generally, then, there are similarities and differences between the theory of successful intelligence, on the one hand, and two others theories – those of Bloom and Gardner – on the other. Effective teachers will probably not totally "buy into" any one theory. Rather they will select techniques from each theory that work most effectively for them.

The truth is that most educational programs are based on *no* theory. They are simply programs that their proponents believe to be successful, often without any data to back their efficacy. Why base an educational program on a theory in the first place? There are at least four reasons.

First, a theory potentially suggests what should be taught, how it should be taught, when it should be taught, to whom it should be taught, and why it should be taught. Atheoretical programs do not have this kind of motivation. Second, in a theory-based program, it is possible to state what the essential aspects of the program are (that is, those based on the theory) and what the nonessential aspects are. With an atheoretical program, it is hard to distinguish what is necessary from what is not. Third, a theory-based program suggests what forms assessments should take to match instruction. Atheoretical programs do not suggest assessment options. Finally, use of a theory-based program can advance scientific knowledge by testing the theory. If the theory is good, the program should work. If the program does not work, either the theory is wrong or the operationalization of the theory is inadequate. Atheoretical programs do not advance science in this way.

Why Teaching for Successful Intelligence is Successful

Earlier, we presented data regarding the success of teaching for successful intelligence. Why does teaching for successful intelligence work? There are at least six reasons:

- *Helping students capitalize on strengths.* Teaching for successful intelligence helps students learn in ways that work for them, rather than forcing them to learn in ways that do not work.
- *Helping students correct or compensate for weaknesses.* Teaching for successful intelligence helps students correct deficient skills, or at least to develop methods of compensation for these skills.
- *Multiple encodings.* This form of teaching encourages students to encode material not just in one way, but in three or four different ways (memory, analytical, creative, practical), so the students are more likely to retrieve the material when they need it.
- *Deeper encodings.* Teaching in this way also helps students encode material more deeply because the presentation of the material is more meaningful and more closely related to what they already know.
- *Motivation.* Teaching for successful intelligence is more interesting to most students, and hence motivates them more.
- *Job relevance.* Much of what students learn, and the way they learn it, bears little resemblance to what they will need to succeed on the job. For example, a typical introductory psychology course may require the

memorization of a great amount of material, but psychologists do not spend much of their time memorizing books or retrieving facts from books. Teaching for successful intelligence better helps students prepare for what they later will need to do on the job.

Objections

When any new system for teaching and assessment is introduced, teachers and administrators sometimes have objections. What kinds of objections have we encountered with the system of teaching for successful intelligence, and what are our replies? Here are five typical objections.

- *It is only for gifted students.* Some teachers believe that their students have enough of a problem learning the conventional way. Why introduce other ways that will just confuse them, especially teaching for creative thinking, which these teachers may see as high-falutin'? But these teachers have things backwards. The problem is that many students simply do not learn well in conventional ways. Teaching in other ways, rather than confusing them, enlightens them. Unless they are taught in other ways, they will just not learn much. And teaching for creative thinking is not high-falutin'. In these times of rapid change, all students need to learn to think in a way that maximizes their flexibility.
- *It is only for weak students.* Then there are teachers who say that teaching for successful intelligence is only for weak students. Their regular students learn just fine with the current system. But do they really learn so well? And is it ever the case that their learning cannot be improved? We believe that teaching always can be improved, and that teaching for successful intelligence is one way of doing it. Moreover, many good students are "good" in the sense of having developed adequate memory and analytical skills. But later in life, they will need creative and practical skills too. Schools should help students develop these skills.
- *It takes too much time to teach everything three ways.* This objection is based on a misunderstanding of what teaching for successful intelligence requires. It does not require everything be taught three times in three ways. Rather, the idea is for teachers to alternate, so that some material is being taught one way, other material, another way.
- *It is too hard to do.* Good teachers naturally teach for successful intelligence. They need only the bare minimum of instruction. Other teachers need more time to catch on. But once one catches on – which usually does not take an inordinate amount of time – it becomes like second nature. It is no harder, and perhaps even easier, than teaching in the regular way, because one begins to see alternative natural ways of teaching the same material.

- *My supervisor (principal, director, etc.) will not allow it.* This might be true in some instances. But our experience has been that school administrators are open to almost any form of teaching that is ethical so long as it improves student achievement and motivation.

CONCLUSION

Successful intelligence involves teaching students for memory, as well as analytically, creatively, and practically. It does not mean teaching everything in three ways. Rather, it means alternating teaching strategies so that teaching reaches (almost) every student at least some of the time. Teaching for successful intelligence also means helping students to capitalize on their strengths and to correct or compensate for their weaknesses. We believe we have good evidence to support teaching for successful intelligence. It improves learning outcomes, even if the only outcome measure is straightforward memory learning. We therefore encourage teachers seriously to consider use of this teaching method in their classrooms – at all grade levels and for all subject matter.

At this time, we have active research sites testing the efficacy of innovative aspects of our programs in many parts of the United States and abroad. We also have developed a software system, "CORE," which enables teachers to communicate with us and with each other if they encounter any problems while using our materials. In this way, they can get immediate feedback to help them solve problems, rather than waiting until someone can help them, perhaps much later.

Teaching for successful intelligence potentially provides benefits at multiple levels. It helps students to achieve at a level commensurate with their skills, rather than letting valuable skills, which could be used in facilitating learning, go to waste. It helps schools reach higher levels of achievement as a whole. And in these days of school accountability, reaching higher average scores is a goal virtually every school wants to reach. Finally, it helps society make better use of its human resources. There is no reason for a society to waste its most precious resource – its human talent. Teaching for successful intelligence helps ensure that talent will not go to waste.

PART II

CREATIVITY

3

Background Work on Creativity

Creativity is the ability to produce work that is novel (that is, original, unexpected), high in quality, and appropriate (that is, useful, meets task constraints) (Lubart, 1994; Ochse, 1990; Sternberg, 1988b, 1999b; Sternberg & Lubart, 1995, 1996). Creativity is a topic of wide scope, important at both the individual and societal levels for a wide range of task domains. At an individual level, creativity is relevant, for example, when solving problems on the job and in daily life. At a societal level, creativity can lead to new scientific findings, new movements in art, new inventions, and new social programs. The economic importance of creativity is clear because new products or services create jobs. Furthermore, individuals, organizations, and societies must adapt existing resources to changing task demands to remain competitive.

CREATIVITY AS A NEGLECTED RESEARCH TOPIC

As the first half of the twentieth century gave way to the second half, J. P. Guilford (1950), in his APA presidential address, challenged psychologists to address what he found to be a neglected but extremely important attribute: creativity. Guilford reported that less than two-tenths of one percent of the entries in *Psychological Abstracts* up to 1950 focused on creativity.

Interest in creativity research began to grow somewhat in the 1950s and a few research institutes concerned with creativity were founded. However, several indicators of work on creativity show that it remained a relatively marginal topic in psychology, at least until recently. Robert Sternberg and Todd Lubart (1996) analyzed the number of creativity references in *Psychological Abstracts* from 1975 to 1994. To conduct this analysis, they searched the computerized PsychLit database of journal articles using the database keywords of "creativity," "divergent thinking," and "creativity

This chapter was written in part in collaboration with Todd I. Lubart.

measurement." These terms are assigned by the database to articles whose content concerns primarily the subject of creativity. They also identified additional entries that contained the word stem "creativ-" somewhere in the title or abstract of the article but were not indexed by one of the keywords for creativity. They examined a random subset of these additional entries and found that they did not concern creativity to any notable extent and should be excluded from the set of articles on the subject. This analysis showed that approximately one-half of one percent of the articles indexed in *Psychological Abstracts* from 1975 to 1994 concerned creativity. For comparative purposes, articles on reading accounted for approximately one and one-half percent of the entries in *Psychological Abstracts* during the same twenty-year period, three times greater than for creativity.

If we look at introductory psychology textbooks as another index, we find that creativity is barely covered. Whereas intelligence, for example, gets a chapter or a major part of one, creativity gets a few paragraphs, if that (for example, Gleitman, 1986). Major psychology departments rarely give courses on creativity, although such courses are sometimes offered in educational psychology programs.

If creativity is so important to society, why has it traditionally been one of psychology's orphans? We believe that, historically, the study of creativity has had several strikes against it. We attempt to elicit what these strikes might be by reviewing briefly some of the history of the study of creativity (see Albert & Runco, 1999, for more details). During our analysis, we consider several of the main approaches to studying creativity, including mystical, pragmatic, psychoanalytic, psychometric, cognitive, and social–personality approaches. We then consider what we believe to be the most promising approach for future work on creativity, the confluence approach.

MYSTICAL APPROACHES TO THE STUDY OF CREATIVITY

The study of creativity has always been tinged – some might say tainted – with associations to mystical beliefs. Perhaps the earliest accounts of creativity were based on divine intervention. The creative person was seen as an empty vessel that a divine being filled with inspiration. The individual poured out the inspired ideas, forming an otherworldly product.

In this vein, Plato argued that a poet is able to create only that which the Muse dictates, and even today, people sometimes refer to their own muse as a source of inspiration. In Plato's view, one person might be inspired to create choral songs, another, epic poems (Rothenberg & Hausman, 1976). Mystical sources have often been suggested in creators' introspective reports (Ghiselin, 1985). For example, Rudyard Kipling referred to the "Daemon" that lives in the writer's pen: "My Daemon was with me in the Jungle Books, Kim, and both Puck books, and good care I took to walk delicately, lest he should withdraw.... When your Daemon is in charge, do not think consciously. Drift, wait, and obey" (Kipling, 1937/1985, p. 162).

The mystical approaches to the study of creativity have probably made it harder for scientists to be heard. Many people seem to believe, as they believe for love (see Sternberg, 1988a, 1988b), that creativity is something that just doesn't lend itself to scientific study, because it is a more spiritual process. We believe that it has been hard for scientific work to shake the deep-seated view of some that scientists are treading where they should not.

PRAGMATIC APPROACHES

Equally damaging for the scientific study of creativity, in our view, has been the takeover of the field, in the popular mind, by those who follow what might be referred to as a pragmatic approach. Those taking this approach have been concerned primarily with developing creativity, secondarily with understanding it, but almost not at all with testing the validity of their ideas about it.

Perhaps the foremost proponent of this approach is Edward De Bono, whose work on *lateral thinking* – seeing things broadly and from varied viewpoints – as well as other aspects of creativity has had what appears to be considerable commercial success (De Bono, 1971, 1985, 1992). De Bono's concern is not with theory, but with practice. Thus, for example, he suggests using a tool such as PMI to focus on the aspects of an idea that are pluses, minuses, and interesting. Or he suggests using the word *po*, derived from hypothesis, suppose, possible, and poetry, to provoke rather than judge ideas. Another tool, that of "thinking hats," has individuals metaphorically wear different hats, such as a white hat for data-based thinking, a red hat for intuitive thinking, a black hat for critical thinking, and a green hat for generative thinking, to stimulate seeing things from different points of view.

De Bono is not alone in this enterprise. Osborn (1953), based on his experiences in advertising agencies, developed the technique of brainstorming to encourage people to solve problems creatively by seeking many possible solutions in an atmosphere constructive rather than critical and inhibitory. Gordon (1961) developed a method called synectics, which involves primarily seeing analogies but also stimulating creative thinking.

More recently, authors such as Adams (1974) and von Oech (1983) have suggested that people often construct a series of false beliefs that interfere with creative functioning. For example, some people believe that there is only one "right" answer and that ambiguity must be avoided whenever possible. People can become creative by identifying and removing these mental blocks. Von Oech (1986) has also suggested that we need to adopt the roles of explorer, artist, judge, and warrior in order to foster our creative productivity.

These approaches have had considerable public visibility, in much the way that Leo Buscaglia gave visibility to the study of love. And they may well be useful. From our point of view as psychologists, however, the approaches lack any basis in serious psychological theory nor have there been serious empirical attempts to validate them. Techniques can work in the absence of psychological theory or validation, but the effect of such approaches is often to leave people associating a phenomenon with commercialization, and to see it as less than a serious endeavor for psychological study.

THE PSYCHODYNAMIC APPROACH

The psychodynamic approach can be considered the first of the major twentieth-century theoretical approaches to the study of creativity. Based on the idea that creativity arises from the tension between conscious reality and unconscious drives, Freud (1908/1959) proposed that writers and artists produce creative work as a way to express their unconscious wishes in a publicly acceptable fashion. These unconscious wishes may concern power, riches, fame, honor, or love (Vernon, 1970). Case studies of eminent creators, such as Leonardo da Vinci (Freud, 1910/1964), were used to support these ideas.

Later, the psychoanalytic approach introduced the concepts of adaptive regression and elaboration for creativity (Kris, 1952). *Adaptive regression*, the primary process, refers to the intrusion of unmodulated thoughts in consciousness. Unmodulated thoughts can occur during active problem solving, but often occur during sleep, intoxication from drugs, fantasies or daydreams, or psychoses. *Elaboration*, the secondary process, refers to the reworking and transformation of primary-process material through reality-oriented, ego-controlled thinking. Other theorists (for example, Kubie, 1958) emphasized that the preconscious, which falls between conscious reality and the encrypted unconscious, is the true source of creativity because thoughts are loose and vague but interpretable. In contrast to Freud, Kubie claimed that unconscious conflicts actually have a negative effect on creativity because they lead to fixated, repetitive thoughts. Recent work has recognized the importance of both the primary and secondary processes (Noy, 1969; Rothenberg, 1979; Suler, 1980; Werner & Kaplan, 1963).

Although the psychodynamic approach may offer some insights into creativity, psychodynamic theory was not at the center of the emerging scientific psychology. The early twentieth-century schools of psychology, such as structuralism, functionalism, and behaviorism, devoted practically no resources at all to the study of creativity. The Gestaltists studied a portion of creativity – insight – but their study never went much beyond labeling, as opposed to characterizing the nature of insight.

Further isolating creativity research, the psychodynamic approach and other early work on creativity relied on case studies of eminent creators. This methodology has been criticized historically because of the difficulty of measuring proposed theoretical constructs (such as primary process thought), and the amount of selection and interpretation that can occur in a case study (Weisberg, 1993). Although there is nothing a priori wrong with case study methods, the emerging scientific psychology valued controlled, experimental methods. Thus both theoretical and methodological issues served to isolate the study of creativity from mainstream psychology.

PSYCHOMETRIC APPROACHES

When we think of creativity, eminent artists or scientists such as Michelangelo or Einstein immediately come to mind. These highly creative people are rare, however, and difficult to study in the psychological laboratory. In his APA address, Guilford (1950) noted that the difficulty of studying highly creative people in the laboratory had limited research on creativity. He proposed that creativity could be studied in everyday subjects using paper-and-pencil tasks. One of these was the Unusual Uses Test, in which an examinee thinks of as many uses for a common object (such as a brick) as possible. Many researchers adopted Guilford's suggestion and "divergent thinking" tasks quickly became the main instruments for measuring creative thinking. The tests were a convenient way of comparing people on a standard "creativity" scale.

Building on Guilford's work, Torrance (1974) developed the *Torrance Tests of Creative Thinking*. These tests consist of several relatively simple verbal and figural tasks that involve divergent thinking plus other problem-solving skills. The tests can be scored for fluency (total number of relevant responses), flexibility (number of different categories of relevant responses), originality (the statistical rarity of the responses), and elaboration (amount of detail in the responses). Some of the subtests from the Torrance battery include:

1. Asking questions: The examinee writes out all the questions he or she can think of, based on a drawing of a scene.
2. Product improvement: The examinee lists ways to change a toy monkey so that children will have more fun playing with it.
3. Unusual uses: The examinee lists interesting and unusual uses for a cardboard box.
4. Circles: The examinee expands empty circles into different drawings and titles them.

Catherine Cox (1926), working with Lewis Terman, believed that exceptionally creative people are also exceptionally intelligent. She published

IQ estimates for 301 of the most eminent persons who lived between 1450 and 1850. They selected their names from a list of one thousand prepared by James McKeen Cattell, who determined eminence by the amount of space allotted in biographical dictionaries. From Cattell's list, they deleted hereditary aristocracy and nobility unless those individuals distinguished themselves beyond the status due to their birth, those born before 1450, those with a rank of over No. 510 on the original list, and eleven names for whom no adequate records of creative contributors were available. These deletions left 282 persons whose IQs were summarized as Group A. In addition, they discussed a Group B, which consisted of 19 miscellaneous cases from those over No. 510 on the original list, bringing the grand total to 301.

To estimate IQ, Cox, Terman, and Maud Merrill (Cox, 1926) examined biographies, letters, and other writings and records for evidence of the earliest period of instruction; the nature of the earliest learning; the earliest productions; age of first reading and of first mathematical performance; typical precocious activities; unusually intelligent applications of knowledge; the recognition of similarities or differences; the amount and character of the reading; the range of interests; school standing and progress; early maturity of attitude or judgment; the tendency to discriminate, to generalize, or to theorize; and family standing. Their IQ estimates are necessarily subjective. In a sense, though, the estimates have an ecological validity with regard to real-life intelligence that is not seen in standard IQ tests. The final estimated IQs were averaged from the individual estimates of the three expert raters mentioned above, Cox, Terman, and Merrill. Interrater reliability was .90 for the childhood estimate and .89 for the young adulthood estimate (calculated from intercorrelations in Cox, 1926, pp. 67–68).

An example of some of the factors that contributed to their estimates can be seen in a description of Francis Galton, whose IQ Terman estimated to be 200. "Francis knew his capital letters by twelve months and both his alphabets by eighteen months; . . . he could read a little book, *Cobwebs to Catch Flies*, when $2\frac{1}{2}$ years old, and could sign his name before 3 years" (Cox, 1926, pp. 41–42). By four years of age, he could say all the Latin substantives, adjectives, and active verbs; could add and multiply; read a little French; and knew the clock. At five, he was quoting from Walter Scott. By six, he was familiar with the *Iliad* and the *Odyssey*. At seven, he was reading Shakespeare for fun and could memorize a page by reading it twice. Clearly, Galton's record is one of an exceptional child.

Cox concluded that the average IQ of the group, 135 for childhood and 145 for young adulthood, was probably too low because of instructions to regress toward the mean of 100 for unselected populations (whereas this group's means were 135 and 145) whenever data were unavailable. Also, unreliability of the data may have caused regression to the mean. One of the problems Cox noted in the data was a strong correlation, .77, between IQ and the reliability of the available data: The more reliable the data, the higher the IQ, and the higher the IQ, the more reliable the data on which it was based. She concluded that if more reliable data had been available, all the IQs would have been estimated as higher. She therefore corrected the original estimates, bringing the group average up to 155 for childhood and 165 for young adulthood.

As Cox was careful to point out, the IQs are not estimates of the actual person's IQ, but rather, estimates of the record of that person. "The IQ of Newton or of Lincoln recorded in these pages is the IQ of the Newton or of the Lincoln of whom we have record. But the records are admittedly incomplete" (Cox, 1926, p. 8).

Cox found the correlation between IQ and rank order of eminence to be .16, plus or minus .039 (Cox, 1926, p. 55), after correcting for unreliability of the data. Dean Simonton (1976) reexamined the Cox data using multiple regression techniques. He showed that the correlation between intelligence and ranked eminence that Cox found was an artifact of unreliability of data and, especially, of a time-wise sampling bias – those more recently born had both lower estimated IQs and lower ranks of estimated eminence. In Simonton's analysis, the relationship between intelligence and ranked eminence was zero if birth year was controlled for (Simonton, 1976, pp. 223–224). In any case, Cox recognized the role of factors other than IQ in eminence and concluded that "high but not the highest intelligence, combined with the greatest degree of persistence, will achieve greater eminence than the highest degree of intelligence with somewhat less persistence" (Cox, 1926, p. 187).

Three basic findings concerning conventional conceptions of intelligence as measured by IQ and creativity are generally agreed on (see, for example, Barron & Harrington, 1981; Lubart, 1994). First, creative people tend to show above average IQs, often above 120 (see Renzulli, 1986). This figure is not a cutoff, but rather an expression of the fact that people with low or even average IQs do not seem to be well represented among the ranks of highly creative individuals. Cox's (1926) geniuses had an estimated average IQ of 165. Barron estimated the mean IQ of his creative writers to be 140 or higher, based on their scores on the Terman Concept Mastery Test (Barron, 1963, p. 242). The other groups in the IPAR studies, that is, mathematicians and research scientists, were also above average in intelligence. Anne Roe (1952, 1972), who did similarly thorough assessments of eminent scientists before the IPAR group was set up, estimated IQs for her participants that ranged between 121 and 194, with medians between 137 and 166, depending on whether the IQ test was verbal, spatial, or mathematical.

Second, above an IQ of 120, IQ does not seem to matter as much to creativity as it does below 120. In other words, creativity may be more highly correlated with IQ below an IQ of 120, but only weakly or not at all correlated with it above an IQ of 120. (This relationship is often called the threshold theory. See the contrast with Hayes's [1989] certification theory discussed below). In the architects study, in which the average IQ was 130 (significantly above average), the correlation between intelligence and creativity was −.08, not significantly different from zero (Barron, 1969, p. 42). But in the military officer study, in which participants were of average intelligence, the correlation was .33 (Barron, 1963, p. 219). These results suggest that extremely highly creative people often have high IQs, but not necessarily that people with high IQs tend to be extremely creative.

Some investigators (for example, Simonton, 1994; Sternberg, 1996) have suggested that very high IQ may actually interfere with creativity. Those who have very high IQs may be so highly rewarded for their IQ-like (analytical) skills that they fail to develop their creative potential. In a reexamination of the Cox (1926) data, Simonton (1976) found that the eminent leaders showed a significant negative correlation, −.29, between their IQs and eminence. Simonton explained that

leaders must be understood by a large mass of people before they can achieve eminence, unlike the creators, who need only appeal to an intellectual elite. . . . Scientific, philosophical, literary, artistic, and musical creators do not have to achieve eminence in their own lifetime to earn posterity's recognition, whereas military, political, or religious leaders must have contemporary followers to attain eminence. (Simonton, 1976, pp. 220–222)

Third, the correlation between IQ and creativity is variable, usually ranging from weak to moderate (Flescher, 1963; Getzels & Jackson, 1962; Guilford, 1967; Herr, Moore, & Hasen, 1965; Torrance, 1962; Wallach & Kogan, 1965; Yamamoto, 1964). The correlation depends in part on what aspects of creativity and intelligence are being measured, and how they are being measured as well as in what field the creativity is manifested. The role of intelligence is different in art and music, for instance, than it is in mathematics and science (McNemar, 1964).

An obvious drawback to the tests used and assessments done by Roe and Guilford is the time and expense involved in administering them as well as the subjective scoring. In contrast, Mednick (1962) produced a thirty-item, objectively scored, forty-minute test of creative ability called the Remote Associates Test (RAT). The test is based on his theory that the creative thinking process is the "forming of associative elements into new combinations which either meet specified requirements or are in some way useful. The more mutually remote the elements of the new combination, the more creative the process or solution" (Mednick, 1962). Because the ability to make these combinations and arrive at a creative solution necessarily depends on the existence of the stuff of the combinations, that is, the associative elements, in a person's knowledge base and because the probability and speed of attainment of a creative solution are influenced by the organization of the person's associations, Mednick's theory suggests that creativity and intelligence are very related; they are overlapping sets.

In the RAT the test-taker supplies a fourth word that is remotely associated with three given words. Samples (not actual test items) of given words are:

1) rat   blue   cottage

2) surprise   line   birthday

3) out   dog   cat

(Answers are *1. cheese; 2. party; 3. house.*)

Moderate correlations of .55, .43, and .41 have been shown between the RAT and the WISC (Wechsler Intelligence Scale for Children), the SAT verbal, and the Lorge-Thorndike Verbal intelligence measures, respectively (Mednick & Andrews, 1967). Correlations with quantitative intelligence measures were lower (r = .20–.34). Correlations with other measures of creative performance have been more variable (Andrews, 1975).

This psychometric revolution for measuring creativity had both positive and negative effects on the field. On the positive side, the tests facilitated research by providing a brief, easy to administer, objectively scorable assessment device. Furthermore, research was now possible with "everyday" people (that is, noneminent samples). However, there were some negative effects as well. First, some researchers criticized brief paper-and-pencil tests as trivial, inadequate measures of creativity; larger productions such as actual drawings or writing samples should be used instead. Second, other critics suggested that neither fluency, flexibility, originality, nor elaboration scores captured the concept of creativity. In fact, the definition and criteria for creativity are a matter of ongoing debate and relying on the objectively defined statistical rarity of a response with regard to all the responses of a subject population is only one of many options. Other possibilities include using the social consensus of judges. Third, some researchers rejected the assumption that noneminent samples could shed light on eminent levels of creativity, which was the ultimate goal for many studies of creativity. Thus a certain malaise developed toward, and continues to accompany, the paper-and-pencil assessment of creativity. Some psychologists, at least, avoided this measurement quagmire in favor of less problematic research topics.

COGNITIVE APPROACHES

The cognitive approach to creativity seeks to understand the mental representations and processes underlying creative thought. By studying, say, perception, or memory, one would already be studying the bases of creativity; thus, the study of creativity would merely represent an extension, and perhaps not a very large one, of work already being done under another guise. For example, in the cognitive area, creativity was often subsumed under the study of intelligence. We do not argue with the idea that creativity and intelligence are related to each other. However, the subsumption has often been so powerful that researchers such as Wallach and Kogan (1965), among others, had to write at length on why creativity and intelligence should be viewed as distinct entities. In more recent cognitive work, Weisberg (1986, 1988, 1993, 1999) has proposed that creativity involves essentially ordinary cognitive processes yielding extraordinary products. Weisberg attempted to show that the insights depend on subjects using conventional cognitive processes (such as analogical transfer) applied to knowledge already stored in memory. He did so through the use of case studies of eminent creators and laboratory research, such as studies with Duncker's (1945) candle problem. This problem requires participants to attach a candle to a wall using only objects available in a picture (candle, box of tacks, and book of matches). Langley and colleagues (1987) made a similar claim about the ordinary nature of creative thinking.

As a concrete example of this approach, Weisberg and Alba (1981) had people solve the notorious nine-dot problem. In this problem, people are asked to connect all the dots, which are arranged in the shape of a square with three rows of three dots each, using no more than four straight lines, never arriving at a given dot twice, and never lifting their pencil from the page. The problem can be solved only if people allow their line segments to go outside the periphery of the dots. Typically, the solution of this task had been viewed as hinging on the insight that one had to go "outside the box." Weisberg and Alba showed that even when people were given the insight, they still had difficulty in solving the problem. In other words, whatever is required to solve the nine-dot problem, it is not just some kind of extraordinary insight.

There have been studies with both human subjects and computer simulations of creative thought. Approaches based on the study of human subjects are perhaps prototypically exemplified by the work of Finke, Ward, and Smith (1992) (see also contributions to Smith, Ward, & Finke, 1995; Sternberg & Davidson, 1994; Ward, Smith, & Finke, 1999). Finke and his colleagues have proposed what they call the *Geneplore model*, according to which there are two main processing phases in creative thought: a generative phase and an exploratory phase. In the generative phase, an individual constructs mental representations referred to as preinventive structures, which have properties promoting creative discoveries. In the exploratory phase, these properties are used to come up with creative ideas. A number of mental processes may enter into these phases of creative invention, such as retrieval, association, synthesis, transformation, analogical transfer, and categorical reduction (that is, mentally reducing objects or elements to more primitive categorical descriptions). In a typical experimental test based on the model (see, for example, Finke, 1990), participants will be shown parts of objects, such as a circle, a cube, a parallelogram, and a cylinder. On a given trial, three parts will be named, and participants will be asked to imagine combining the parts to produce a practical object or device. For example, participants might imagine a tool, a weapon, or a piece of furniture. The objects thus produced are then rated by judges for their practicality and originality.

Computer-simulation approaches, reviewed by Boden (1992, 1999), have as their goal the production of creative thought by a computer in a manner that simulates what people do. Langley, Simon, Bradshaw, and Zytgow (1987), for example, developed a set of programs that rediscover basic scientific laws. These computational models rely on heuristics – problem-solving guidelines – for searching a data set or conceptual space and finding hidden relationships between input variables. The initial program, called BACON, uses heuristics such as "if the value of two numerical terms increases together, consider their ratio" to search data for patterns. One of BACON's accomplishments has been to examine observational data on the orbits of planets available to Kepler and to rediscover Kepler's third law of planetary motion. This program is unlike creative functioning, however, in that the problems are given to it in structured form, whereas creative functioning is largely about figuring out what the problems are. Further programs have extended the search heuristics, the ability to transform data sets, and the ability to reason with qualitative data and scientific concepts. There are also models concerning an artistic domain. For example, Johnson-Laird (1988) developed a jazz improvisation program in which novel deviations from the basic jazz chord sequences are guided by harmonic constraints (or tacit principles of jazz) and random choice when several allowable directions for the improvisation exist.

SOCIAL-PERSONALITY APPROACHES

Developing in parallel with the cognitive approach, work in the social–personality approach has focused on personality variables, motivational variables, and the sociocultural environment as sources of creativity. Researchers such as Amabile (1983), Barron (1968, 1969), Eysenck (1993), Gough (1979), MacKinnon (1965) and others have noted that certain personality traits often characterize creative people. Through correlational studies and research contrasting high- and low-creative samples (at both eminent and everyday levels), a large set of potentially relevant traits has been identified (Barron & Harrington, 1981). These traits include independence of judgment, self-confidence, attraction to complexity, aesthetic orientation, and risk taking.

Proposals regarding self-actualization and creativity can also be considered within the personality tradition. According to Maslow (1968), boldness, courage, freedom, spontaneity, self-acceptance, and other traits lead a person to realize his or her full potential. Rogers (1954) described the tendency toward self-actualization as having motivational force and being promoted by a supportive, evaluation-free environment.

Focusing on motivation for creativity, a number of theorists have hypothesized the relevance of intrinsic motivation (Amabile, 1983; Crutchfield, 1962; Golann, 1962), need for order (Barron, 1963), need for achievement (McClelland, Atkinson, Clark, & Lowell, 1953), and other motives. Amabile (1983; Hennessey & Amabile, 1988) and her colleagues have conducted seminal research on intrinsic and extrinsic motivation. Studies using motivational training and other techniques have manipulated these motivations and observed effects on creative performance tasks, such as writing poems and making collages.

Finally, the relevance of the social environment to creativity has also been an active area of research. At the societal level, Simonton (1984, 1988, 1994, 1999) has conducted numerous studies in which eminent levels of creativity over large spans of time in diverse cultures have been statistically linked to environmental variables. These variables include, among others, cultural diversity, war, availability of role models, availability of resources (such as financial support), and number of competitors in a domain. Cross-cultural comparisons (for example, Lubart, 1990) and anthropological case studies (for example, Maduro, 1976; Silver, 1981) have demonstrated cultural variability in the expression of creativity. Moreover, they have shown that cultures differ simply in how much they value the creative enterprise.

The cognitive and social–personality approaches have each provided valuable insights into creativity. If you look for research that investigates both cognitive and social-personality variables at the same time, however, you would find only a handful of studies. The cognitive work on creativity has tended to ignore the personality and social system, and the social–personality approaches have tended to have little or nothing to say about the mental representations and processes underlying creativity.

Looking beyond the field of psychology, Wehner, Csikszentmihalyi, and Magyari-Beck (1991) examined 100 recent doctoral dissertations on creativity. They found a "parochial isolation" of the various studies concerning creativity. There were relevant dissertations from psychology, education, business, history, history of science, and other fields, such as sociology and political science. The different fields tended to use different terms, however, and focus on different aspects of what seemed to be the same basic phenomenon. For example, business dissertations used the term "innovation" and tended to look at the organizational level whereas psychology dissertations used the term "creativity" and looked at the level of the individual. Wehner, Csikszentmihalyi, and Magyari-Beck (1991) describe the situation with creativity research in terms of the fable of the blind men and the elephant. "We touch different parts of the same beast and derive distorted pictures of the whole from what we know: 'The elephant is like a snake,' says the one who only holds its tail; 'The elephant is like a wall,' says the one who touches its flanks" (p. 270).

EVOLUTIONARY APPROACHES TO CREATIVITY

The evolutionary approach to creativity was instigated by Donald Campbell (1960), who suggested that the same mechanisms that have been applied to the study of the evolution of organisms could be applied to the evolution of ideas. This idea has been enthusiastically picked up by a number of investigators (Perkins, 1995; Simonton, 1995, 1998, 1999).

The idea underlying this approach is that there are two basic steps in the generation and propagation of creative ideas. The first is *blind variation*, by which the creator generates an idea without any real idea of whether the idea would be successful (selected for) in the world of ideas. Indeed, Dean Simonton (1996) argues that creators do not have the slightest idea which of their ideas will succeed. As a result, their best bet for producing lasting ideas is to go for a large quantity of ideas. The reason is that their hit rate remains relatively constant through their professional life span. In other words, they have a fixed proportion of ideas that will succeed. The more ideas they have in all, the more ideas they have that will achieve success.

The second step is *selective retention*. In this step, the field in which the creator works either retains the idea for the future or lets it die out. Those ideas that are selectively retained are the ones that are judged to be novel and of value, that is, creative. This process as well as blind generation are described further by Cziko (1998).

Does an evolutionary model really adequately describe creativity? Robert Sternberg (1997b) argues that it does not, and David Perkins (1998) also has doubts. Sternberg argues that it seems utterly implausible that great creators such as Mozart, Einstein, or Picasso were using nothing more than blind variation to come up with their ideas. Good creators, like experts of any kind, may or may not have more ideas than other people have, but they have better ideas, ones that are more likely to be selectively retained. And the reason they are more likely to be selectively retained is that they were not produced in a blind fashion. This debate is by no means resolved, however, and is likely to continue into the future for some time to come.

Were it the case that an understanding of creativity required a multi-disciplinary approach, the result of a unidisciplinary approach might be that we would view a part of the whole as the whole. At the same time, though, we would have an incomplete explanation of the phenomenon we are seeking to explain, leaving dissatisfied those who do not subscribe to the particular discipline doing the explaining. We believe that tradition-ally this has been the case for creativity. Recently, theorists have begun to develop confluence approaches to creativity, which we now discuss.

CONFLUENCE APPROACHES TO THE STUDY OF CREATIVITY

Many recent works on creativity hypothesize that multiple components must converge for creativity to occur (Amabile, 1983; Csikszentmihalyi, 1988; Gardner, 1993; Gruber, 1989; Gruber & Wallace, 1999; Lubart, 1994; Mumford & Gustafson, 1988; Perkins, 1981; Simonton, 1988; Sternberg, 1985a; Sternberg & Lubart, 1991, 1995; Weisberg, 1993; Woodman & Schoenfeldt, 1989). Sternberg (1985b), for example, examined laypersons' and experts' conceptions of the creative person. People's implicit theo-ries contain a combination of cognitive and personality elements, such as "connects ideas," "sees similarities and differences," "has flexibility," "has aesthetic taste," "is unorthodox," "is motivated," "is inquisitive," and "questions societal norms."

At the level of explicit theories, Amabile (1983, 1996; Collins & Amabile, 1999) describes creativity as the confluence of intrinsic moti-vation, domain-relevant knowledge and abilities, and creativity-relevant skills. The creativity-relevant skills include (a) a cognitive style that in-volves coping with complexities and breaking one's mental set during problem solving, (b) knowledge of heuristics for generating novel ideas, such as trying a counterintuitive approach, and (c) a work style charac-terized by concentrated effort, an ability to set aside problems, and high energy.

Gruber and his colleagues (Gruber, 1981, 1989; Gruber & Davis, 1988) have proposed a developmental *evolving-systems model* for understand-ing creativity. A person's knowledge, purpose, and affect grow over time, amplify deviations that an individual encounters, and lead to creative prod-ucts. Developmental changes in the knowledge system have been docu-mented in cases such as Charles Darwin on evolution. Purpose refers to a set of interrelated goals, which also develop and guide an individual's behavior. Finally, the affect or mood system notes the influence of joy or frustration on the projects undertaken.

Csikszentmihalyi (1988, 1996) has taken a different "systems" approach and highlights the interaction of the individual, domain, and field. An in-dividual draws on information in a domain and transforms or extends it via cognitive processes, personality traits, and motivation. The field, consisting of people who control or influence a domain (for example, art critics and gallery owners), evaluates and selects new ideas. The domain, a culturally defined symbol system, preserves and transmits creative prod-ucts to other individuals and future generations. Gardner (1993; see also Policastro & Gardner, 1999) has conducted case studies that suggest that the development of creative projects may stem from an anomaly within a system (for example, tension between competing critics in a field) or moderate asynchronies between the individual, domain, and field (for example, unusual individual talent for a domain). In particular, Gardner (1993) has analyzed the lives of seven individuals who made highly creative contributions in the twentieth century, each specializing in one of the multiple intelligences (Gardner, 1983): Sigmund Freud (intrapersonal), Albert Einstein (logical–mathematical), Pablo Picasso (spatial), Igor Stravinsky (musical), T. S. Eliot (linguistic), Martha Graham (bodily–kinesthetic), and Mohandas Gandhi (interpersonal). Charles Darwin would be an example of someone with extremely high naturalist intelligence. Gardner points out, however, that most of these individuals actually had strengths in more than one intelligence, and that they had notable weaknesses in others (for example, Freud's weaknesses may have been in spatial and musical intelligences).

Although creativity can be understood in terms of uses of the multiple intelligences to generate new and even revolutionary ideas, Gardner's (1993) analysis goes well beyond the intellectual. For example, Gardner pointed out two major themes in the behavior of these creative giants. First, they tended to have a matrix of support at the time of their creative breakthroughs. Second, they tended to drive a "Faustian bargain" whereby they gave up many of the pleasures people typically enjoy in life in order to attain extraordinary success in their careers. It is not clear that these attributes are intrinsic to creativity, per se, however: Rather, they seem to be associated with those who have been driven to exploit their creative gifts in a way that leads them to attain eminence.

Gardner further followed Csikszentmihalyi (1988, 1996) in distinguishing between the importance of the domain (the body of knowledge about a particular subject area) and the field (the context in which this body of knowledge is studied and elaborated on, including the persons working with the domain, such as critics, publishers, and other "gate keepers"). Both are important to the development, and ultimately, the recognition of creativity.

A final confluence theory considered here is Sternberg and Lubart's (1991, 1995) *investment theory of creativity*. This theory is discussed in the next chapter.

In general, confluence theories of creativity offer the possibility of accounting for diverse aspects of creativity (Lubart, 1994). For example, analyses of scientific and artistic achievements suggest that the median creativity of work in a domain tends to fall toward the lower end of the distribution and the upper – high creativity – tail extends quite far. This pattern can be explained through the need for multiple components of creativity to co-occur in order for the highest levels of creativity to be achieved. As another example, the partial domain-specificity of creativity that is often observed can be explained through the mixture of some relatively domain-specific components for creativity such as knowledge and other more domain-general components such as, perhaps, the personality trait of perseverance. Creativity, then, is largely something that people show in a particular domain.

TYPES OF CREATIVE CONTRIBUTIONS

Generally, we think of creative contributions as being of a single kind. A number of researchers on creativity have questioned this assumption, however. There are a number of ways of distinguishing among types of creative contributions. It is important to remember, though, that creative contributions can be viewed in different ways at different times. At a given time, the field can never be sure whose work will withstand the judgments of the field over time (such as that of Mozart) and whose work will not (such as that of Salieri) (Therivel, 1999).

Theorists of creativity and related topics have recognized that there are different types of creative contributions (see reviews in Ochse, 1990; Sternberg, 1988b; Weisberg, 1993). For example, Kuhn (1970) distinguished between normal and revolutionary science. Normal science expands on or otherwise elaborates on an already existing paradigm of scientific research, whereas revolutionary science proposes a new paradigm. The same kind of distinction can be applied to the arts and letters.

Gardner (1993, 1994) has also described different types of creative contributions individuals can make. They include (a) solving a well-defined problem, (b) devising an encompassing theory, (c) creating a "frozen work," (d) performing a ritualized work, and (e) rendering a "high-stakes" performance.

Other bases for distinguishing among types of creative contributions also exist. For example, psychoeconomic models such as those of Rubenson and Runco (1992) and Sternberg and Lubart (1991, 1995, 1996) can distinguish different types of contributions in terms of the parameters of the models. In the Sternberg-Lubart model, contributions might differ in the extent to which they "defy the crowd" or in the extent to which they redefine how a field perceives a set of problems.

Simonton's (1997) model of creativity also proposes parameters of creativity, and that contributions might be seen as differing in terms of the extent to which they vary from other contributions and in the extent to which they are selected for recognition by a field of endeavor (see also Campbell, 1960; Perkins, 1995; Simonton, 1997). But in no case were these models intended explicitly to distinguish among types of creative contributions.

Maslow (1967) distinguished more generally between two types of creativity, which he referred to as primary and secondary. Primary creativity is the kind a person uses to become self-actualized – to find fulfillment in him- or herself and in his or her life. Secondary creativity is the kind with which scholars in the field are more familiar – the kind that leads to creative achievements typically recognized by a field.

Ward, Smith, and Finke (1999) have noted that there is evidence to favor the roles of both focusing (Bowers et al., 1990; Kaplan & Simon, 1990) and exploratory thinking (Bransford & Stein, 1984; Getzels & Csikszentmiyalyi, 1976) in creative thinking. In focusing, one concentrates on pursuing a single problem-solving approach, whereas in exploratory thinking one considers many such approaches. A second distinction made by Ward and his colleagues is between domain-specific (Clement, 1989; Langley, Simon, Bradshaw, & Zytkow, 1987; Perkins, 1981; Weisberg, 1986) and universal (Finke, 1990, 1995; Guilford, 1968; Koestler, 1964) creativity skills. Finally, Ward and his colleagues distinguish between unstructured (Bateson, 1979; Findlay & Lumsden, 1988; Johnson-Laird, 1988) and structured or systematic (Perkins, 1981; Ward, 1994; Weisberg, 1986) creativity.

SUMMARY

Creativity is the ability to produce novel, high-quality, task-appropriate products. Creativity has been a relatively neglected topic in psychology. Among those who have studied creativity, a number of different approaches have been used. Mystical approaches have suggested that creativity has ineffable properties that are impervious to scientific investigation. Pragmatic approaches generally focus on the use of creativity and how to increase creativity. Psychodynamic approaches focus on the unconscious processes underlying creativity. Psychometric approaches concentrate on how creativity can be measured. Cognitive approaches deal with the information processing and mental representations underlying creativity. Social–personality approaches deal with the roles of other people and of personality traits as well as motivation. Evolutionary approaches view creativity as an adaptation that enhances an individual's chances of survival and hence of reproduction. And confluence approaches integrate these various other approaches.

4

The Investment Theory of Creativity as a Decision

What is creativity and how does it develop? Underlying this chapter is a single central notion – that, to a large extent, creativity is a decision. The chapter is divided into three parts: the decision to be creative, the decision of how to be creative, and implementation of these decisions.

Our investment theory (Sternberg & Lubart, 1991, 1995) concerns the *decision to be creative*. Called the investment theory, it is based on the notion that creative people *decide* to buy low and sell high in the world of ideas – that is, they generate ideas that tend to "defy the crowd" (buy low), and then, when they have persuaded many people, they sell high, meaning they move on to the next unpopular idea (see also Rubenson & Runco, 1992). I first describe the proposed theory. Then I describe empirical work supporting at least some aspects of the theory.

I consider creativity in both a minor ("little c") and a major ("big C") sense. The difference between the two often is whether a contribution is creative only with respect to myself or with respect to a field as well. Psychologically, however, the processes may be quite similar or the same. From the point of view of the field the contributions are quite different.

Research within the investment framework has yielded support for this model (Lubart & Sternberg, 1995). This research has used tasks such as (a) writing short stories using unusual titles (for example, "The Octopus' Sneakers"), (b) drawing pictures with unusual themes (for example, the earth from an insect's point of view), (c) devising creative advertisements for boring products (for example, cufflinks), and (d) solving unusual scientific problems (for example, how we could tell if someone had been on the moon within the past month). This research showed creative performance to be moderately domain specific, and to be predicted by a combination of certain resources, as described next.

Work on the nature and testing of the investment theory was done in collaboration with Todd I. Lubart. Work on developing creative thinking has been done in collaboration with Wendy Williams and Elena L. Grigorenko.

According to the investment theory, creativity requires a confluence of six distinct but interrelated resources: intellectual abilities, knowledge, styles of thinking, personality, motivation, and environment. Although levels of these resources are sources of individual differences, often the decision to use a resource is a more important source of individual differences. Below I discuss the resources and the role of decision making in each.

Intellectual skills. Three intellectual skills are particularly important (Sternberg, 1985a): (a) the creative skill to see problems in new ways and to escape the bounds of conventional thinking; (b) the analytic skill to recognize which of one's ideas are worth pursuing and which are not; and (c) the practical–contextual skill to know how to persuade others of the value of one's ideas. The confluence of these three skills is important. Using analytic skills in the absence of the other two results in powerful critical, but not creative, thinking. Using creative skill in the absence of the other two results in new ideas that are not subjected to the scrutiny required to improve them and make them work. And using practical–contextual skill alone may result in societal acceptance of ideas not because the ideas are good, but because they have been well and powerfully presented.

To be creative, one must first *decide* to generate new ideas, analyze these ideas, and sell the ideas to others. In other words, a person may have synthetic, analytical, or practical skills, but not apply them to problems that potentially involve creativity. For example, one may decide to follow other people's ideas rather than synthesize one's own; or not to subject one's ideas to a careful evaluation; or to expect other people to listen to one's ideas and therefore decide not to try to persuade other people of their value. The skill is not enough: One first needs to make the decision to use the skill. Our studies on the role of intelligence in creativity are discussed in Chapter 2. They emphasize the ability to switch between conventional and unconventional modes of thinking.

One aspect of switching between conventional and unconventional thinking is the decision that one is willing and able to think in unconventional ways, that one is willing to accept thinking in terms different from those to which one is accustomed and with which one feels comfortable. People show reliable individual differences in the willingness to do so (Dweck, 1999). Some people (what Dweck calls "entity theorists") prefer to operate primarily or even exclusively in domains relatively familiar to them. Other people (what Dweck calls "incremental theorists") seek out new challenges and new conceptual domains within which to work.

Knowledge. Concerning knowledge, on the one hand, one needs to know enough about a field to move it forward. One cannot move beyond where a field is if one doesn't know where it is. On the other hand, knowledge about a field can result in a closed and entrenched perspective, confining a person to the way in which he or she has seen problems in the past

(Frensch & Sternberg, 1989). Thus, one needs to decide to use one's past knowledge, but also *decide* not to let the knowledge become a hindrance rather than a help. Everyone has a knowledge base. How they choose to use it is a decision they must make.

Thinking styles. Thinking styles are preferred ways of using one's skills. In essence, they are *decisions* about how to deploy the skills available to one. With regard to thinking styles, a legislative style is particularly important for creativity (Sternberg, 1988b, 1997b), that is, a preference for thinking and a decision to think in new ways. This preference needs to be distinguished from the ability to think creatively: Someone may like to think along new lines, but not think well, or vice versa. It also helps to become a major creative thinker if one is able to think globally as well as locally, distinguishing the forest from the trees and thereby recognizing which questions are important and which ones are not.

Personality. Numerous research investigations (summarized in Lubart, 1994, and Sternberg & Lubart, 1991, 1995) have supported the importance of certain personality attributes for creative functioning. These attributes include, but are not limited to, willingness to overcome obstacles, willingness to take sensible risks, willingness to tolerate ambiguity, and self-efficacy. In particular, buying low and selling high typically means defying the crowd, so one has to be willing to stand up to conventions if one wants to think and act in creative ways. Often, creative people seek opposition, in that they decide to think in ways that countervail how others think. Note that none of the attributes of creative thinking is fixed. One can *decide* to overcome obstacles, take sensible risks, and so forth.

Motivation. Intrinsic, task-focused motivation is also essential to creativity. The research of Amabile (1983) and others has shown the importance of such motivation for creative work, and has suggested that people rarely do truly creative work in an area unless they really love what they are doing and focus on the work rather than the potential rewards. Motivation is not something inherent in a person: One *decides* to be motivated by one thing or another. Often, people who need to work in a certain area that does not particularly interest them will decide that, given the need to work in that area, they had better find a way to make it interest them. They will then look for some angle on the work they need to do that makes this work appeal to rather than bore them.

Environment. Finally, one needs an environment that is supportive and rewarding of creative ideas. One could have all of the internal resources needed in order to think creatively, but without some environmental support (such as a forum for proposing those ideas), the creativity that a person has within him or her might never be displayed.

Environments typically are not fully supportive of the use of one's creativity. The obstacles in a given environment may be minor, as when an individual receives negative feedback on his or her creative thinking, or major, as when one's well-being or even life are threatened if one thinks in a manner that defies convention. The individual therefore must *decide* how to respond in the face of the pretty close to omnipresent environmental challenges that exist. Some people let unfavorable forces in the environment block their creative output; others do not.

Confluence. Concerning the confluence of these six components, creativity is hypothesized to involve more than a simple sum of a person's level on each component. First, there may be thresholds for some components (for example, knowledge) below which creativity is not possible regardless of the levels on other components. Second, partial compensation may occur in which a strength on one component (for example, motivation) counteracts a weakness on another component (for example, environment). Third, interactions may also occur between components, such as intelligence and motivation, in which high levels on both components could multiplicatively enhance creativity.

Creative ideas are both novel and valuable. But they are often rejected when the creative innovator stands up to vested interests and defies the crowd (cf. Csikszentmihalyi, 1988). The crowd does not maliciously or willfully reject creative notions. Rather, it does not realize, and often does not want to realize, that the proposed idea represents a valid and advanced way of thinking. Society often perceives opposition to the status quo as annoying, offensive, and reason enough to ignore innovative ideas.

Evidence abounds that creative ideas are often rejected (Sternberg & Lubart, 1995). Initial reviews of major works of literature and art are often negative. Toni Morrison's *Tar Baby* received negative reviews when it was first published, as did Sylvia Plath's *The Bell Jar*. The first exhibition in Munich of the work of Norwegian painter Edvard Munch opened and closed the same day because of the strong negative response from the critics. Some of the greatest scientific papers have been rejected not just by one, but by several journals before being published. For example, John Garcia, a distinguished biopsychologist, was immediately denounced when he first proposed that a form of learning called classical conditioning could be produced in a single trial of learning (Garcia & Koelling, 1966).

From the investment view, then, the creative person buys low by presenting an idea that initially is not valued and then attempting to convince others of its value. After convincing others that the idea is valuable, which increases the perceived value of the investment, the creative person sells high by leaving the idea to others and moving on to another idea. People typically want others to love their ideas, but immediate universal applause for an idea often indicates that it is not particularly creative.

Creativity is as much a decision about and an attitude toward life as it is a matter of ability. Creativity is often obvious in young children, but it may be harder to find in older children and adults because their creative potential has been suppressed by a society that encourages intellectual conformity.

Creativity, according to the investment theory, is in large part a decision. The view of creativity as a decision suggests that creativity can be developed. I have proposed twenty-one ways to develop creativity as a decision (Sternberg, 2001c). Here they are.

The Strategies

Redefine Problems.   Redefining a problem means taking a problem and turning it on its head. Many times in life individuals have a problem and they just don't see how to solve it. They are stuck in a box. Redefining a problem essentially means extricating oneself from the box. It is an aspect of problem finding, as opposed merely to problem solving. This process is the divergent part of creative thinking.

A good example of redefining a problem is summed up in the story of an executive at one of the biggest automobile companies in the Detroit area. The executive held a high-level position, and he loved his job and the money he made on the job. He despised the person he worked for, however, and because of this, he decided to find a new job. He went to a headhunter, who assured him that a new job could be easily arranged. After this meeting the executive went home and talked to his wife, who was teaching a unit on redefining problems as part of a course she was teaching on Intelligence Applied (Sternberg, 1986). The executive realized that he could apply what his wife was teaching to his own problem. He returned to the headhunter and gave the headhunter his boss's name. The headhunter found a new job for the executive's boss, which the boss – having no idea of what was going on – accepted. The executive then got his boss's job. He had decided for creativity by redefining a problem.

There are many ways teachers and parents can encourage children to define and redefine problems for themselves, rather than – as is so often the case – doing it for them. Teachers and parents can promote creative performance by encouraging their children to define and redefine *their own* problems and projects. Adults can encourage creative thinking by having children choose their own topics for papers or presentations, choose their own ways of solving problems, and sometimes by having them choose again if they discover that their selection was a mistake.

Adults cannot always offer children choices, but giving choices is the only way for children to learn how to choose. A real choice is not deciding between drawing a cat or a dog, nor is it picking one state in the United States to present at a project fair. It is deciding what to draw or what topic on which to do a project. Giving children latitude in making choices helps them to develop taste and good judgment, both of which are essential elements of creativity.

At some point everyone makes a mistake in choosing a project or in the method he or she selects to complete it. Teachers and parents should remember that an important part of creativity is the analytic part – learning to recognize a mistake – and give children the chance and the opportunity to redefine their choices.

Question and Analyze Assumptions. Everyone has assumptions. Often one does not know he or she has these assumptions because they are widely shared. Creative people question assumptions and eventually lead others to do the same. Questioning assumptions is part of the analytical thinking involved in creativity. When Copernicus suggested that Earth revolves around the sun, the suggestion was viewed as preposterous because everyone could see that the sun revolves around Earth. Galileo's ideas, including the relative rates of falling objects, caused him to be denounced as a heretic. When an employee questions the way his boss manages the business, the boss does not smile. The employee is questioning assumptions that the boss and others simply accept – assumptions that they do not wish to open up to questions.

Sometimes it is not until many years later that society realizes the limitations or errors of their assumptions and the value of the creative person's thoughts. Those who question assumptions promote cultural, technological, and other forms of advancement.

Teachers and parents can be role models for questioning assumptions by showing children that what they assume they know, they really do not know. Children shouldn't question every assumption. There are times to question and try to reshape the environment, and there are times to adapt to it. Some creative people question so many things so often that others stop taking them seriously. Everyone must learn which assumptions are worth questioning and which battles are worth fighting. Sometimes it's better for individuals to leave the inconsequential assumptions alone so that they have an audience when they find something worth the effort.

Teachers and parents can help children develop this talent by making questioning a part of the daily exchange. It is more important for children to learn what questions to ask – and how to ask them – than to learn the answers. Adults can help children evaluate their questions by discouraging the idea that the adults ask questions and children simply answer them. Adults need to avoid perpetuating the belief that their role is to teach children the facts, and instead help them understand that what matters is the ability to use facts. This can help children learn how to formulate good questions and how to answer questions.

Society tends to make a pedagogical mistake by emphasizing the answering and not the asking of questions. The good student is perceived as the one who rapidly furnishes the right answers. The expert in a field thus becomes the extension of the expert student – the one who knows and can recite a lot of information. As John Dewey (1933) recognized, how one thinks is often more important than what one thinks. Schools need to teach children how to ask the right questions (questions that are good, thought-provoking, and interesting) and lessen the emphasis on rote learning.

Do Not Assume That Creative Ideas Sell Themselves: Sell Them.   As Galileo, Edvard Munch, Toni Morrison, Sylvia Plath, and millions of others have discovered, creative ideas do not sell themselves. On the contrary, creative ideas are usually viewed with suspicion and distrust. Moreover, those who propose such ideas may be viewed with suspicion and distrust as well. Because people are comfortable with the ways they already think, and because they probably have a vested interest in it, it can be extremely difficult to dislodge them from that current way.

Thus, children need to learn how to persuade other people of the value of their ideas as part of the practical aspect of creative thinking. If children do a science project, it is a good idea for them to present it and demonstrate why it makes an important contribution. If they create a piece of artwork, they should be prepared to describe why they think it has value. If they develop a plan for a new form of government, they should explain why it is better than the existing form. At times, teachers may find themselves having to justify their ideas about teaching to their principal. They should prepare their children for the same kind of experience.

Encourage Idea Generation.   As mentioned earlier, creative people demonstrate a "legislative" style of thinking: They like to generate ideas (Sternberg, 1997a). The environment for generating ideas can be constructively critical, but it must not be harshly or destructively critical. Children need to acknowledge that some ideas are better than others. Adults and children should collaborate to identify and encourage any creative aspects of ideas that are presented. When suggested ideas don't seem to have much value, teachers should not just criticize. They should suggest new approaches, preferably ones that incorporate at least some aspects of the previous ideas that seemed in themselves not to have much value. Children should be praised for generating ideas, regardless of whether some are silly or unrelated, while being encouraged to identify and develop their best ideas into high-quality projects.

Recognize That Knowledge Is a Double-Edged Sword and Act Accordingly.   Some years ago, I was visiting a very famous psychologist who lives abroad. As part of the tour he had planned for me, he invited me to visit the local zoo. We went past the cages of the primates, who were at the time engaged in what euphemistically could be called "strange and unnatural sexual behavior." I averted my eyes, but my host did not. After observing the primates for a short amount of time, he astonished me by analyzing their sexual behavior in terms of his theory of intelligence. I realized then, as I have many times since, how knowledge and expertise can be a double-edged sword.

On the one hand, one cannot be creative without knowledge. Quite simply, one cannot go beyond the existing state of knowledge if one does not know what that state is. Many children have ideas that are creative with respect to themselves, but not with respect to the field because others have had the same ideas before. Those with a greater knowledge base can be creative in ways that those who are still learning about the basics of the field cannot be.

At the same time, those who have an expert level of knowledge can experience tunnel vision, narrow thinking, and entrenchment. Experts can become so stuck in a way of thinking that they become unable to extricate themselves from it. In a study of expert and novice bridge players, for example (Frensch & Sternberg, 1989), we found that experts outperformed novices under regular circumstances. When a superficial change was made in the surface structure of the game, the experts and novices were both hurt slightly in their playing, but quickly recovered. When a profound, deep-structural change was made in the game, the experts initially were hurt more than the novices, although they later recovered. The reason, presumably, is that experts make more and deeper use of the existing structure, and hence have to reformulate their thinking more than do novices when there is a deep-structural change in the rules of the game.

Encourage Children to Identify and Surmount Obstacles. Buying low and selling high means defying the crowd. And people who defy the crowd – people who think creatively – almost inevitably encounter resistance. The question is not whether one will encounter obstacles; one will. When one buys low, one defies the crowd, and generally engenders in others a reaction of, at best, puzzlement, and, at worst, hostility. The question is whether the creative thinker has the fortitude to persevere. I have often wondered why so many people start off their careers doing creative work and then vanish from the radar screen. I think I know at least one reason why: Sooner or later, they decide that being creative is not worth the resistance and punishment. The truly creative thinkers pay the short-term price because they recognize that they can make a difference in the long term, although it is often a long while before the value of creative ideas is recognized and appreciated.

Parents and teachers can prepare children for these types of experiences by describing obstacles that they, their friends, and well-known figures in society have faced while trying to be creative; otherwise, children may think they are the only ones confronted by obstacles. Teachers should include stories about people who weren't supportive, about bad grades for unwelcome ideas, and about frosty receptions to what they may have thought were their best ideas. To help children deal with obstacles, parents and teachers can remind them of the many creative people whose ideas were initially shunned and help them to develop an inner sense of awe of the creative act. Suggesting that children reduce their concern over what others think is also valuable. However, it is often difficult for children to lessen their dependence on the opinions of their peers.

When children attempt to surmount an obstacle, they should be praised for the effort, whether or not they were entirely successful. Teachers and parents can point out aspects of the effort that were successful and why, and suggest other ways to confront the obstacles. Having the class brainstorm about ways to confront a given obstacle can get the class thinking about the many strategies people can use to confront problems. Some obstacles are within oneself, such as performance anxiety. Other obstacles are external, such as the bad opinions of others. Whether internal or external, obstacles must be overcome.

Encourage Sensible Risk-Taking.   I took a risk as an assistant professor when I decided to study intelligence. The field of intelligence has low prestige within academic psychology. When I was being considered for tenure, it came to my attention that my university was receiving letters that questioned why it would want to give tenure to someone in such a marginal and unprestigious field. I sought advice from a senior professor, Wendell Garner, telling him that perhaps I had made a mistake in labeling my work as being about intelligence. I could have done essentially the same work but labeled it as "thinking" or "problem solving" – fields with more prestige. He reminded me that I had come to Yale wanting to make a difference in the field of intelligence. I had made a difference, but now I was afraid it might cost me my job. I was right: I had taken a risk. But he maintained that there was only one thing I could do – exactly what I was doing. If this field meant so much to me, then I needed to pursue it, even if it meant losing my job. I am still at the university, but other risks I have taken have not turned out so well. When taking risks, one must realize that some of them just will not work, and that is the cost of doing creative work.

When creative people defy the crowd by buying low and selling high, they take risks in much the same way as do people who invest. Some such investments simply may not pan out. The person may generate an idea that is unpopular and stays unpopular over the long term. Defying the crowd means risking the crowd's disdain for "buying" into the wrong idea, or even its wrath. But there are levels of sensibility to keep in mind when defying the crowd. Creative people may take sensible risks and produce ideas that others ultimately admire and respect as trend-setting. But sometimes they make mistakes, fail, and fall flat on their faces.

I emphasize the importance of sensible risk-taking because I am not talking about risking life and limb for creativity. To help children learn to take sensible risks, adults can encourage them to take some intellectual risks with courses, with activities, and with what they say to adults – to develop a sense of how to assess risks.

Nearly every major discovery or invention entailed some risk. When a movie theater was the only place to see a movie, someone created the idea of the home video machine. Skeptics questioned if anyone would want to see movies on a small screen. Another initially risky idea was the home computer. Many wondered if anyone would have enough use for a home computer to justify the cost. These ideas were once risks but are now ingrained in our society.

Few children are willing to take risks in school, because they learn that taking risks can be costly. Perfect test scores and papers receive praise and open up future possibilities. Failure to attain a certain academic standard is perceived as deriving from a lack of ability and motivation and may lead to scorn and lessened opportunities. Why risk taking hard courses or saying things that teachers may not like when that may lead to low grades or even failure? Teachers may inadvertently advocate that children "play it safe" when they give assignments without choices and allow only particular answers to questions. Thus, teachers need not only encourage sensible risk-taking, but also reward it.

Encourage Tolerance of Ambiguity.   People often like things to be in black and white. They like to think a country is good or bad (ally or enemy) or that a given idea in education works or does not work. The problem is that there are a lot of grays in creative work, just as there are when one invests in a stock whose value may or may not go up. Many stocks are low-valued. The ambiguities arise as to which will go up, when they will go up, and, even, for some individuals, what they can do to make them go up. Artists working on new paintings and writers working on new books often report feeling scattered and unsure in their thoughts. They need to figure out whether they are even on the right track. Scientists often are not sure whether the theory they have developed is exactly correct. These creative thinkers need to tolerate the ambiguity and uncertainty until they get the idea just right.

A creative idea tends to come in bits and pieces and develops over time. The period in which the idea is developing tends to be uncomfortable, however. Without time or the ability to tolerate ambiguity, many may jump to a less than optimal solution. When a student has almost the right topic for a paper or almost the right science project, it's tempting for teachers to accept the near miss. To help children become creative, teachers need to encourage the children to accept and extend the period in which their ideas do not quite converge. Children need to be taught that uncertainty and discomfort are a part of living a creative life. Ultimately, they will benefit from their tolerance of ambiguity by coming up with better ideas.

Help Children Build Self-Efficacy.   Many people eventually reach a point where they feel as if no one believes in them. I reach this point frequently, feeling that no one values what I am doing. Because creative work often doesn't get a warm reception, it is extremely important that creative people believe in the value of what they are doing. This is not to say that individuals should believe that every idea they have is a good idea. Rather, individuals need to believe that, ultimately, they have the ability to make a difference.

The main limitation on what children can do is what they think they can do. All children have the capacity to be creators and to experience the joy associated with making something new, but first they must be given a strong base for creativity. Sometimes teachers and parents unintentionally limit what children can do by sending messages that express or imply limits on children's potential accomplishments. Instead, these adults need to help children believe in their own ability to be creative.

I have found that probably the best predictor of success among my children is not their ability, but their belief in their ability to succeed. If children are encouraged to succeed and to believe in their own ability to succeed, they very likely will find the success that otherwise would elude them.

Help Children Find What They Love to Do.   Teachers must help children find what excites them to unleash their best creative performances. In the investment metaphor, one needs to find an area in which to invest about which one feels some excitement, so that one will do what one can to maximize the value of one's investments. Teachers need to remember that what they happen to teach may not be what really excites the children they are teaching. People who truly excel creatively in a pursuit, whether vocational or avocational, almost always genuinely love what they do. Certainly, the most creative people are intrinsically motivated in their work (Amabile, 1996). Less creative people often pick a career for the money or prestige and are bored with or loathe their careers. Most often, these people do not do work that makes a difference in their field.

I often meet students who are pursuing a certain career interest not because it is what they want to do, but because it is what their parents or other authority figures expect them to do. I always feel sorry for such students, because I know that although they may do good work in that field, they almost certainly will not do great work. It is hard for people to do great work in a field that simply does not interest them.

Encouraging the child's interests rather than one's own is easier said than done. When my son was young, I was heartened that he wanted to play the piano. I play the piano, and was glad that he wanted to play the piano, too. But then he stopped practicing and ultimately quit, and I felt badly. A short time thereafter he informed me that he wanted to play the trumpet. I reacted very negatively, pointing out to him that he had already quit the piano and probably would quit the trumpet, too.

I then found myself wondering why I had been so harsh. How could I have said such a thing? But then I quickly understood it. If someone else's child wanted to play the trumpet, that was fine. But I couldn't imagine any Sternberg child playing the trumpet. It did not fit my ideal image of a Sternberg child. I realized I was being narrow-minded and doing exactly the opposite of what I had told everyone else to do. It's one thing to talk the talk, another to walk the walk. I backpedaled, and Seth started playing the trumpet.

Eventually, he did, in fact, quit the trumpet. Finding the right thing is frustrating work! Seth eventually did find the right thing. Today he is a college student and already has started two businesses. I don't like businesses at all. But businesses and my son are the right thing – absolutely. He is doing what is right for him. Whether it is right for me doesn't matter.

Helping children find what they really love to do is often hard and frustrating work. Yet, sharing the frustration with them now is better than leaving them to face it alone later. To help children uncover their true interests, teachers can ask them to demonstrate a special talent or ability for the class, and explain that it doesn't matter what they do (within reason), only that they love the activity.

Teach Children the Importance of Delaying Gratification. Part of being creative means being able to work on a project or task for a long time without immediate or interim rewards, just as in investing one often must wait quite a while for the value of a stock to rise. Children must learn that rewards are not always immediate and that there are benefits to delaying gratification. In the short term, people are often ignored when they do creative work or even punished for doing it.

Many people believe that they should reward children immediately for a good performance, and that children should expect rewards. This style of teaching and parenting emphasizes the here and now and often comes at the expense of what is best in the long term.

An important lesson in life – and one that is intimately related to developing the discipline to do creative work – is to learn to wait for rewards. The greatest rewards are often those that are delayed. Teachers can give their children examples of delayed gratification in their lives and in the lives of creative individuals and help them apply these examples to their own lives.

Hard work often does not bring immediate rewards. Children do not immediately become expert baseball players, dancers, musicians, or sculptors. And the reward of becoming an expert can seem very far away. Children often succumb to the temptations of the moment, such as watching television or playing video games. The people who make the most of their abilities are those who wait for a reward and recognize that few serious challenges can be met in a moment. Ninth-grade children may not see the benefits of hard work, but the advantages of solid academic performance will be obvious when they apply to college.

The short-term focus of most school assignments does little to teach children the value of delaying gratification. Projects are clearly superior in meeting this goal, but it is difficult for teachers to assign home projects if they are not confident of parental involvement and support. By working on a task for many weeks or months, children learn the value of making incremental efforts for long-term gains.

I can relate to the concept of delayed gratification. Some years ago I contracted with a publisher to develop a test of intelligence based on my theory of intelligence (Sternberg, 1985a). Things were going well until the president of the company left and a new president took over. Shortly after that, my project was canceled. The company's perception was that there was not enough of a potential market for a test of intelligence based on my theory of analytical, creative, and practical abilities. My perception was that the company and some of its market were stuck in the past, endlessly replicating the construction and use of the kinds of tests that have been constructed and used since the turn of the century.

Whoever may have been right, a colleague and I ultimately decided that if we wanted to make this test work, we would have to look elsewhere. Years later, the College Board provided funding for the testing project, and it is now evolving again. But I had to wait many years to see progress resume.

Role-Model Creativity.   There are many ways teachers and parents can provide an environment that fosters creativity (Sternberg & Williams, 1996). The most powerful way for teachers to develop creativity in children is to *role model creativity.* Children develop creativity not when they are told to, but when they are shown how.

The teachers most people probably remember from their school days are not those who crammed the most content into their lectures. The teachers most people remember are those whose thoughts and actions served as a role model. Most likely they balanced teaching content with teaching children how to think with and about that content. The Nobel laureates, before they received their prizes, made excellent role models in large part because they were outstanding examples of creativity in action that students could emulate (Zuckerman, 1977, 1983).

Cross-Fertilize Ideas.   Teachers can also stimulate creativity by helping children *to cross-fertilize in their thinking*, to think across subjects and disciplines. The traditional school environment often has separate classrooms and classmates for different subjects and seems to influence children into thinking that learning occurs in discrete boxes – the math box, the social studies box, and the science box. Creative ideas and insights often result, however, from integrating material across subject areas, not from memorizing and reciting material.

Teaching children to cross-fertilize draws on their skills, interests, and abilities, regardless of the subject. If children are having trouble understanding math, teachers might ask them to draft test questions related to their special interests. For example, they might ask the baseball fan to devise geometry problems based on a game. The context may spur creative ideas because the student finds the topic (baseball) enjoyable and it may counteract some of the anxiety caused by geometry. Cross-fertilization motivates children who aren't interested in subjects taught in the abstract.

One way teachers can promote cross-fertilization in the classroom is to ask children to identify their best and worst academic areas. Children can then be asked to come up with project ideas in their weak area based on ideas borrowed from one of their strongest areas. For example, teachers can explain to children that they can apply their interest in science to social studies by analyzing the scientific aspects of trends in national politics.

Allow Time for Creative Thinking.   Teachers also need *to allow children the time to think creatively*. Often, creativity requires time for incubation (Wallas, 1926). Many societies today are societies in a hurry. People eat fast food, rush from one place to another, and value quickness. One way to say someone is smart is to say that the person is *quick* (Sternberg 1985a), a clear indication of an emphasis on time. This is also indicated by the format of many of the standardized tests used – lots of multiple-choice problems squeezed into a brief time slot.

Most creative insights do not happen in a rush (Gruber & Davis, 1988). People need time to understand a problem and to toss it around. If children are asked to think creatively, they need time to do it well. If teachers stuff questions into their tests or give their children more homework than they can complete, they are not allowing them time to think creatively.

Instruct and Assess for Creativity.   Teachers also should *instruct and assess for creativity*. If teachers give only multiple-choice tests, children quickly learn the type of thinking that teachers value, no matter what they say. If teachers want to encourage creativity, they need to include at least some opportunities for creative thought in assignments and tests. Questions that require factual recall, analytic thinking, *and* creative thinking should be asked. For example, children might be asked to learn about a law, analyze the law, and then think about how the law might be improved.

Reward Creativity. Teachers also need *to reward creativity.* They may choose differentially to reward the different kinds of creative contributions, depending on the circumstances and the students. For example, if teachers ask students to be bold in their thinking, the teachers may choose to reward conceptual replications less than bolder redirections (at levels of innovation characteristic of students, of course). Thus, teachers may choose not to limit their rewards to "crowd-defying creativity," but may choose to allocate rewards, depending on circumstances and expectations for particular students. It is not enough to talk about the value of creativity. Children are used to authority figures who say one thing and do another. They are exquisitely sensitive to what teachers value when it comes to the bottom line – the grade or evaluation.

Creative efforts should be rewarded. For example, teachers can assign a project and remind children that they are looking for them to demonstrate their knowledge, analytical and writing skills, and creativity. They should let children know that creativity does not depend on the teacher's agreement with what children write, but rather with ideas they express that represent a synthesis between existing ideas and their own thoughts. Teachers need to care only that the ideas are creative from the student's perspective, not necessarily creative with regard to the state-of-the-art findings in the field. Children may generate an idea that someone else has already had, but if the idea is an original to the student, the student has been creative.

Some teachers complain that they cannot apply as much objectivity to grading creative responses as they can to multiple-choice or short-answer responses. They are correct in that there is some sacrifice of objectivity. However, research shows that evaluators are remarkably consistent in their assessments of creativity (Amabile, 1996; Sternberg & Lubart, 1995). If the goal of assessment is to instruct children, then it is better to ask for creative work and evaluate it with somewhat less objectivity than to evaluate children exclusively on uncreative work. Teachers should let children know that there is no completely objective way to evaluate creativity.

Allow Mistakes. Teachers also need *to allow mistakes.* Buying low and selling high carries a risk. Many ideas are unpopular simply because they are not good. People often think a certain way because that way works better than other ways. But once in a while, a great thinker comes along – a Freud, a Piaget, a Chomsky, or an Einstein – and shows us a new way to think. These thinkers made contributions because they allowed themselves and their collaborators to take risks and make mistakes.

Many of Freud's and Piaget's ideas turned out to be wrong. Freud confused Victorian issues regarding sexuality with universal conflicts and

Piaget misjudged the ages at which children could perform certain cognitive feats. Their ideas were great not because they lasted forever, but because they became the basis for other ideas. Freud's and Piaget's mistakes allowed others to profit from their ideas.

Although being successful often involves making mistakes along the way, schools are often unforgiving of mistakes. Errors on schoolwork are often marked with a large and pronounced X. When a student responds to a question with an incorrect answer, some teachers pounce on the student for not having read or understood the material, as classmates snicker. In hundreds of ways and in thousands of instances over the course of a school career, children learn that it is not alright to make mistakes. The result is that they become afraid to risk the independent and the sometimes-flawed thinking that leads to creativity.

When children make mistakes, teachers should ask them to analyze and discuss the mistakes. Often, mistakes or weak ideas contain the germ of correct answers or good ideas. In Japan, teachers spend entire class periods asking children to analyze the mistakes in their mathematical thinking. For the teacher who wants to make a difference, exploring mistakes can be an opportunity for learning and growing.

Take Responsibility for Both Successes and Failures.   Another aspect of teaching children to be creative is teaching them *to take responsibility for both successes and failures*. Teaching children how to take responsibility means teaching children to (1) understand their creative process, (2) criticize themselves, and (3) take pride in their best creative work. Unfortunately, many teachers and parents look for – or allow children to look for – an outside enemy responsible for failures.

It sounds trite to say that teachers should teach children to take responsibility for themselves, but sometimes there is a gap between what people know and how they translate thought into action. In practice, people differ widely in the extent to which they take responsibility for the causes and consequences of their actions. Creative people need to take responsibility for themselves and for their ideas.

Encourage Creative Collaboration.   Teachers can also work *to encourage creative collaboration* (Chadwick & Courtivron, 1996; John-Steiner, 2000). Creative performance is often viewed as a solitary occupation. We may picture the writer writing alone in a studio, the artist painting in a solitary loft, or the musician practicing endlessly in a small music room. In reality, people often work in groups. Collaboration can spur creativity. Teachers can encourage children to learn by example by collaborating with creative people.

Imagine Things from Others' Points of View.   Children also need to learn how *to imagine things from other viewpoints.* An essential aspect of working with other people and getting the most out of collaborative creative activity is to imagine oneself in other people's shoes. Individuals can broaden their perspective by learning to see the world from different points of view. Teachers and parents should encourage their children to see the importance of understanding, respecting, and responding to other people's points of view. This is important, as many bright and potentially creative children never achieve success because they do not develop practical intelligence (Sternberg, 1985a, 1997b). They may do well in school and on tests, but they may never learn how to get along with others or to see things and themselves as others see them.

Maximize Person–Environment Fit.   Teachers also need to help children recognize person–environment fit. What is judged as creative is an interaction between a person and the environment (Csikszentmihalyi, 1988, 1996; Gardner, 1993; Sternberg & Lubart, 1995). The very same product that is rewarded as creative in one time or place may be scorned in another.

In the movie *The Dead Poets Society*, a teacher the audience might well judge to be creative is viewed as incompetent by the school's administration. Similar experiences occur many times a day in many settings. There is no absolute standard for what constitutes creative work. The same product or idea may be valued or devalued in different environments. The lesson is that individuals need to find a setting in which their creative talents and unique contributions are rewarded, or they need to modify their environment.

I once had a student to whom I gave consummately bad advice concerning environment. She had two job offers. One was from an institution that was very prestigious, but not a good fit to the kind of work she valued. The other institution was a bit less prestigious, but was a much better fit to her values. I advised her to take the job in the more prestigious institution, telling her that if she did not accept the job there, she would always wonder what would have happened if she had. Bad advice: She went there and never fit in well. Eventually she left, and now she is at an institution that values the kind of work she does. Now I always advise people to go for the best fit.

By building a constant appreciation of the importance of person-environment fit, teachers prepare their children for choosing environments that are conducive to their creative success. Encourage children to examine environments to help them select and match environments with their skills. And while encouraging the children to do it, do it yourself!

People who are uncreative, and perhaps especially people who are smart in a traditional sense but uncreative, are particularly susceptible to four fallacies.

The first, the *should-be fallacy*, is the belief that what is, should be. The second, the *must-be fallacy*, is the belief that what is, must be. In Leibnizian philosophy, it is the principle of sufficient reason – that whatever exists can exist only if there is a sufficient reason for it to exist. The third fallacy is the *always-will-be fallacy*, the belief that the way things are now is the way they always will be. And the fourth fallacy is the *safety fallacy*, which is the belief that regardless of what should be or must be, doing what others are doing is the safe way to live.

5

The Propulsion Theory of Creative Contributions

There are tens of thousands of artists, musicians, writers, scientists, and inventors today. What makes some of them stand out from the rest? Why will some of them become distinguished contributors in the annals of their field and others be forgotten? Although many variables may contribute to who stands out from the crowd, certainly creativity is one of them. The standouts are often those who are doing particularly creative work in their line of professional pursuit. Are these highly creative individuals simply doing more highly creative work than their less visible counterparts, or does the creativity of their work also differ in quality? One possibility is that creative contributors make different *decisions* regarding *how* to express their creativity. This section describes a propulsion theory of creative contributions (Sternberg, 1999c; Sternberg, Kaufman, & Pretz, 2002) that addresses this issue of how people decide to invest their creative resources. The basic idea is that creativity can be of different kinds, depending on how it propels existing ideas forward. When developing creativity in children, we can develop different kinds of creativity, ranging from minor replications to major redirections in their thinking.

Creative contributions differ not only in their amounts but also in the types of creativity they represent. For example, both Sigmund Freud and Anna Freud were highly creative psychologists, but the nature of their contributions seems in some way or ways to have been different. Sigmund Freud proposed a radically new theory of human thought and motivation and Anna Freud largely elaborated on and modified Sigmund Freud's theory. How do creative contributions differ in quality and not just in quantity?

The type of creativity exhibited in a creator's works can have at least as much of an effect on judgments about that person and his or her work as does the amount of creativity exhibited. In many instances, it may have more of an effect. For example, a contemporary artist might have thought

Portions of this chapter are based on collaborative work with James Kaufman and Jean Pretz.

processes, personality, motivation, and even background variables similar to those of Monet, but that artist, painting today in the style of Monet, probably would not be judged to be creative in the way Monet was. He or she was born too late. Artists, including Monet, have experimented with impressionism, and unless the contemporary artist introduced some new twist, he or she might be viewed as imitative rather than creative.

The importance of context is illustrated by the difference, in general, between creative discovery and rediscovery. For example, BACON and related programs of Langley, Simon, Bradshaw, and Zytgow (1987) rediscover important scientific theorems that were judged to be creative discoveries in their time. The processes by which these discoveries are made via computer simulation are presumably not identical to those by which the original discoverers worked. One difference derives from the fact that contemporary programmers can provide, in their programming of information into computer simulations, representations and particular organizations of data that may not have been available to the original creators. Moreover, the programs solve problems, but do not define them. But putting aside the question of whether the processes are the same, a rediscovery might be judged to be creative with respect to the rediscoverer, but would not be judged to be creative with respect to its field at the time the rediscovery is made.

Given the importance of purpose, creative contributions must always be defined in some context. If the creativity of an individual is always judged in a context, then it will help to understand how the context interacts with how people are judged. In particular, what are the types of creative contributions a person can make within a given context? Most theories of creativity concentrate on attributes of the individual (see Sternberg, 1999b). But to the extent that creativity is in the interaction of person with context, we would need to concentrate as well on the attributes of the individual and the individual's work relative to the environmental context.

A taxonomy of creative contributions needs to deal with the question not just of in what domain a contribution is creative, but of what the type of creative contribution is. What makes one work in biology more creative or creative in a different way from another work in biology, or what makes its creative contribution different from that of a work in art? Thus, a taxonomy of domains of work is insufficient to elucidate the nature of creative contributions. A field needs a basis for scaling how creative contributions differ quantitatively and, possibly, qualitatively.

Creativity as Propulsion. A creative contribution represents an attempt to propel a field from wherever it is to wherever the creator believes the field should go. Thus, creativity is by its nature *propulsion*. It moves a field from some point to another. It also always represents a decision to exercise leadership. The creator tries to bring others to a particular point in the multidimensional creative space. The attempt may or may not succeed. There are different kinds of creative leadership that the creator may attempt to exercise, depending on how he or she decides to be creative.

Eight Types of Creative Contributions.   The propulsion model suggests eight types of contributions that can be made to a field of endeavor at a given time. Although the eight types of contributions may differ in the extent of creative contribution they make, the scale of eight types presented here is intended as closer to a nominal one than to an ordinal one. There is no fixed a priori way of evaluating *amount* of creativity on the basis of the *type* of creativity. Certain types of creative contributions probably tend, on average, to be greater in amounts of novelty than are others. But creativity also involves quality of work, and the type of creativity does not make any predictions regarding quality of work.

The panels of Figure 5.1 summarize the eight types of contributions and are referred to in the following discussion. To foreshadow the following discussion, the eight types of creative contributions are divided into three major categories, contributions that accept current paradigms, contributions that reject current paradigms, and paradigms that attempt to integrate multiple current paradigms. There are also subcategories within each of these two categories: paradigm-preserving contributions that leave the field where it is (Types 1 and 2), paradigm-preserving contributions that move the field forward in the direction it already is going (Types 3 and 4), paradigm-rejecting contributions that move the field in a new direction from an existing or pre-existing starting point (Types 5 and 6), paradigm-rejecting contributions that move the field in a new direction from a new starting point (Type 7), and paradigm-integrating contributions that combine approaches (Type 8).

Thus, Type 1, the limiting case, is not crowd-defying at all (unless the results come out the wrong way!). Type 2 may or may not be crowd-defying, if the redefinition goes against the field. Type 3 typically leads the crowd. Type 4 goes beyond where the crowd is ready to go, so may well be crowd-defying. And Types 5 to 8 typically are crowd-defying in at least some degree. Obviously, there is often no "crowd" out there just waiting to attack. Rather, there is a field representing people with shared views regarding what is and is not acceptable, and if those views are shaken, the people may not react well.

Types of Creativity that Accept Current Paradigms and Attempt to Extend Them

1. REPLICATION.   The contribution is an attempt to show that the field is in the right place. The propulsion keeps the field where it is rather than moving it. This type of creativity is represented by stationary motion, as of a wheel that is moving but staying in place.

2. REDEFINITION. The contribution is an attempt to redefine where the field is. The current status of the field thus is seen from different points of view. The propulsion leads to circular motion, such that the creative work leads back to where the field is, but viewed in a different way.

3. FORWARD INCREMENTATION. The contribution is an attempt to move the field forward in the direction it already is going. The propulsion leads to forward motion.

4. ADVANCE FORWARD INCREMENTATION. The contribution is an attempt to move the field forward in the direction it is already going, but beyond where others are ready for it to go. The propulsion leads to forward motion that is accelerated beyond the expected rate of forward progression.

Types of Creativity that Reject Current Paradigms and Attempt to Replace Them

5. REDIRECTION. The contribution is an attempt to redirect the field from where it is toward a different direction. The propulsion thus leads to motion in a direction that diverges from the way the field is currently moving.

6. RECONSTRUCTION/REDIRECTION. The contribution is an attempt to move the field back to where it once was (a reconstruction of the past) so that it may move onward from that point, but in a direction different from the one it took before. The propulsion thus leads to motion that is backward and then redirective.

7. REINITIATION. The contribution is an attempt to move the field to a different as yet unreached starting point and then to move from that point. The propulsion is thus from a new starting point in a direction that is different from the one the field previously pursued.

A Type of Creativity That Merges Disparate Current Paradigms

8. INTEGRATION. The contribution is an attempt to integrate two formerly diverse ways of thinking about phenomena into a single way of thinking about a phenomenon. The propulsion thus is a combination of two different approaches that are linked together.

The eight types of creative contributions described above are largely qualitatively distinct. Within each type there can be quantitative differences. For example, a forward incrementation can represent a fairly small step forward or a substantial leap. A reinitiation can restart a subfield (for example, the work of Leon Festinger on cognitive dissonance) or an entire field (for example, the work of Einstein on relativity theory). Thus, the theory distinguishes contributions both qualitatively and quantitatively.

In the discussion below, I demonstrate each type of creative contribution with exemplars from a variety of fields, including especially one of my own fields of research, the field of intelligence. The examples below are from Sternberg (1999c) and from Sternberg, Kaufman, and Pretz (2002).

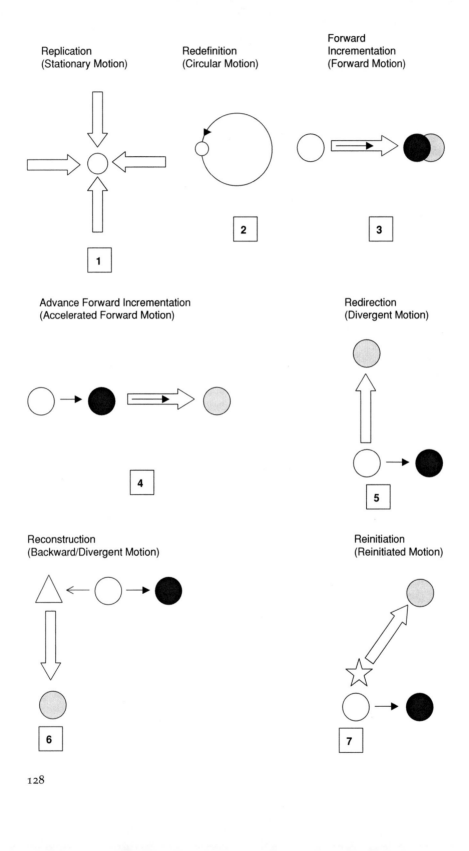

Replication
(Stationary Motion)

Redefinition
(Circular Motion)

Forward
Incrementation
(Forward Motion)

1

2

3

Advance Forward Incrementation
(Accelerated Forward Motion)

Redirection
(Divergent Motion)

4

5

Reconstruction
(Backward/Divergent Motion)

Reinitiation
(Reinitiated Motion)

6

7

Figure Key

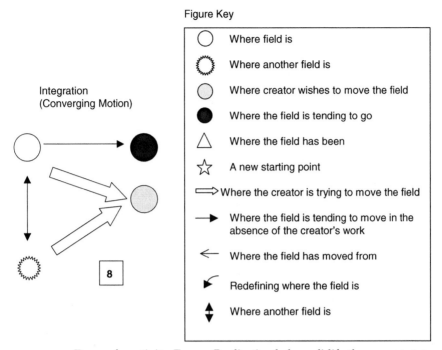

FIGURE 5.1. Types of creativity. Type 1: Replication helps solidify the current state of a field. Type 2: Redefinition involves a change in perception as to where the field is. Type 3: Incrementation occurs when a piece of work takes the field where it is and moves it forward from that point in the space of contributions in the direction it is already going. Type 4: Advance incrementation occurs when an idea is "ahead of its time." Type 5: Redirection involves taking the field where it is at a given time but attempting to move it in a new direction. Type 6: Reconstruction/redirection involves moving the field back to a point it previously was and then moving it in a different direction. Type 7: Reinitiation occurs when a contributor suggests that a field or subfield has reached an undesirable point or has exhausted itself moving in the direction it is moving. The contributor suggests moving in a different direction from a different point in the multidimensional space of contributions. Type 8: Integration occurs when a contributor suggests putting together ideas formerly seen as distinct and unrelated or even as opposed.

Paradigm-Preserving Contributions that Leave the Field Where It Is

TYPE 1: REPLICATION. Replication is illustrated in Panel 1 of Figure 5.1. Replications help solidify the current state of a field. The goal is not to move a field forward so much as to establish that it really is where it is supposed to be. Thus, in science, if a finding is surprising, then a replication can help establish that the finding is a serious one. If the replication fails then contributors in the field need to question whether they are where they have supposed themselves, or perhaps have hoped themselves, to be. In art or literature, replications essentially show that a style of work can be applied not just to a single artwork or literary work, but to other works as well.

Replications are limiting cases in that they in some sense seem, on their face, to offer the least that is new in terms of the types of creative contributions considered in this taxonomy of types of contributions. Yet replications are important because they can help either to establish the validity or invalidity of contributions, or the utility or lack of utility of approaches.

For example, consider the choice reaction-time paradigm and its implications. As background, Jensen (1982) and others argued that correlations between scores on choice reaction-time tests and scores on intelligence tests suggest that individual differences in human intelligence could be traced to individual differences in velocity of neural conduction. Because tests of choice reaction time in no way measure neural conduction velocity, such interpretations of results were wholly speculative.

Vernon and Mori (1992) tested and seemingly confirmed Jensen's hypothesis. They developed a paradigm whereby they could measure speed of neural conduction in the arm. They found that neural-conduction velocity did indeed predict scores on conventional tests of intelligence. This was a startling finding because it suggested that what previously had been a speculative claim that was at best very loosely tied to data was instead a serious empirically supported claim. However, Wickett and Vernon (1994) later reported a failure to replicate this result so its empirical status was cast into doubt. The Wickett and Vernon study was a replication study, and the failure to replicate arguably was as important to the field as would have been a replication. Failures to replicate can prevent a field from pursuing red herrings.

Although work designed to yield exact replications and conceptual replications (where the generality of a finding or kind of product is assessed by trying to replicate it under circumstances somewhat different from those that originally gave rise to it) is about as unglamorous as any kind of work can be, it is necessary for the development of a field. Without replications the field would be (and probably often is) very susceptible to Type 1 errors (false alarms). In science, replications help ensure the solidity of the base of empirical findings on which future researchers build.

In the arts and letters, replications help ensure that an approach is robust and can generate a number and variety of works. For example, many artists imitated Monet's impressionistic technique, and although they added nothing new, they showed the robustness of the technique. Perhaps the limiting case in the art world is the work of forgers, who attempt to reproduce exactly the work of a (usually well-known) creator. Replications are not limited to forgers, however. Many visitors to museums have encountered individuals studiously copying great works of art and proudly displaying their work for what it is.

Perhaps the crucial insight for the contributor is to know when there is a need for replication in the first place. In science, this need is associated with findings that are surprising or that seem on their face to be sufficiently dubious that either their existence or their generality needs to be demonstrated. In the arts and letters, this need is associated with techniques that may seem to be limited to a single artwork or artist, or literary work or writer, but that could be used more widely.

TYPE 2: REDEFINITION. Redefinition is illustrated in Panel 2 of Figure 5.1. Redefinition, like replication, involves little or even no change of where a field is. What redefinition involves is a change in perception as to where that is. A redefinition in a conceptual space leads people to realize that the field is not where they had thought. Work of this type is judged to be creative to the extent that the redefinition of the field is different from the earlier definition (novelty) and to the extent that the redefinition is judged to be plausible or correct (quality).

An example of a redefinition is provided by the work of Thomson (1939), who reinterpreted the work of Spearman (1904, 1927). Spearman was the English psychologist who invented factor analysis and who used this technique to argue that underlying performance on all tests of mental abilities is a general factor, which he labeled g. Spearman's analysis had a powerful effect on the field and continues to have such an effect today, with many theorists still believing in the existence and importance of the general factor (for example, Brand, 1996; Carroll, 1993; Horn, 1994; Jensen, 1998).

Spearman believed his work to show that a single mental entity was responsible for interesting and consequential individual differences in performance on mental tests. Spearman (1927) suggested that this entity was mental energy. Thomson (1939) proposed that although Spearman was correct in positing a general factor underlying performance on mental tests, he was incorrect in his interpretation of it. According to Thomson, the general factor actually represents the workings of multitudinous "bonds." These bonds are all alleged to be those mental processes common to performance on all mental tests. Thus, because all such tests require people to understand the instructions, read the terms of the problems, provide a response, and so forth, there might be many different sources of individual differences shared across these tests. They might appear via factor analysis to be a single entity, but in fact they are multifarious. Thus, Thomson proposed to change not the empirical status of work on intelligence, but how its empirical status was conceptualized. He argued that the field was not where Spearman and others thought it to be.

Similarly, Minkowski r-metrics represent a redefinition of the notion of spatial metaphors (see Kruskal, 1964a, 1964b). In computing distances in a multidimensional space, people traditionally had assumed that distance is Euclidean – to compute distances, one squares differences between coordinates and then takes the square root of the sum of the squared differences. Minkowski's generalization shows that there is nothing privileged about the r-value of 2. One can use any number at all as the basis for exponentiation. For example, an r-value of 1 yields a city-block metric, where distances are computed as they would be in a city where it is impossible to construct a hypotenuse through buildings. An r-value of infinity yields a max metric, where only the longest within-dimensional distance contributes to the total distance. Thus, the Minkowski r-metric shows that the way distances were computed was not unique but rather one of many possible cases: The r-metric redefines through a generalization the already existing distance construct.

An interesting example of redefinition in the arts is the work of the late Roy Lichtenstein. Lichtenstein took a form of art – the comic – that was viewed as debased and turned it into a serious art form. Lichtenstein's work originally met with tremendous opposition, which never really ended, at least in some quarters. Yet in his later career, his comic works of art brought large sums of money as well as the kind of serious study that showed what had been perceived as a base art form had come to be taken seriously, at least by many. Andy Warhol is a second example of an artist in this tradition, turning studies of soda bottles into pieces of art valued by many collectors.

Paradigm-Preserving Contributions that Move the Field Forward in the Direction It Already Is Going

TYPE 3: FORWARD INCREMENTATION.   This type of creative contribution is illustrated in Panel 3 of Figure 5.1. It probably represents the most common type of creative contribution. It occurs when a piece of work takes the field at the point where it is and moves it forward from that point in the space of contributions in the direction it is already going. There is no change in the trajectory of the field. Work of this type is judged to be creative to the extent that it seems to move the field forward from where it is and to the extent that the movement appears to be correct or desirable.

Hunt, Frost, and Lunneborg (1973) proposed that intelligence could be studied by investigators examining individual differences in cognitive performance on the kinds of tasks cognitive psychologists study in their laboratories. A few years later, Hunt, Lunneborg, and Lewis (1975) published an incrementation study that extended the range of tasks that could be studied using this paradigm, suggesting that certain of these tasks were particularly useful for studying individual differences in verbal ability. The second study was an incrementation study, building on a paradigm that Hunt and his colleagues had already established. The second study provided a fairly substantial increment in both increasing the range of tasks and in focusing in particular on verbal ability.

Most studies published in scientific journals can be characterized as forward incrementations. For example, after the initial groundbreaking study of Festinger and Carlsmith (1959) on cognitive dissonance, huge numbers of follow-up studies were done on phenomena of cognitive dissonance and cognitive consistency (Abelson et al., 1968). These studies helped elucidate the phenomenon and its limiting circumstances. As these forward incrementations made the limits of the cognitive-dissonance phenomenon clearer, other theories came to be proposed that provided alternative (Bem, 1967) or more refined explanations of when people exhibit cognitive dissonance and when they exhibit other kinds of reactions – such as self-perception reactions – in the face of cognitive inconsistencies (Fazio, Zanna, & Cooper, 1977).

Forward incrementations can also be found in genre fiction that pushes the envelope. The hard-boiled detective story pioneered by Dashiell Hammett and Raymond Chandler has been elaborated on by countless writers, some of them moving the genre forward in major ways, such as Ross MacDonald, who introduced identity confusions as a major theme in his work. But MacDonald's work and that of others have their roots in the paradigm introduced by Hammett and Chandler.

Jonathan Kellerman's psychological thrillers take the genre a step further by having the hero, Alex Delaware, actually be a clinical psychologist. Patricia Cornwell's suspense novels have Kay Scarpetta, a medical examiner, as the protagonist. Using these nonstandard professions instead of the usual cops and detectives adds an extra layer of authenticity to the stories, and allows for much more technical detail to be realistically added to the plots. Kellerman's plots, for example, often hinge on Delaware identifying various psychological syndromes (for example, Munchausen Syndrome by Proxy), whereas Cornwell has Scarpetta discover essential clues in her autopsies. The forward incrementations can also be found in the plots of genre fiction. Agatha Christie's classic *The Murder of Roger Ackroyd* (1926) is a fairly standard murder mystery . . . until the then-startling ending of the narrator turning out to be the killer. These advances certainly move the field forward, but in a nonstartling way. Kellerman and Cornwell still work within the pre-established conventions of the field, and Christie's famed novel still obeyed most of the "rules" of a murder mystery.

TYPE 4: ADVANCE FORWARD INCREMENTATION. This type of creative contribution is illustrated in Panel 4 of Figure 5.1. Advance incrementation occurs when an idea is "ahead of its time." The field is moving in a certain direction but is not yet ready to reach a given point ahead. Someone has an idea that leads to that point. The person pursues the idea and produces a work. The value of the work is often not recognized at the time because the field has not yet reached the point where the contribution can be adequately understood. The creator accelerates beyond where others in his or her field are ready to go – often "skipping" a step that others will need to take. The value of the work may be recognized later or some other creator who has the idea at a more opportune time may end up getting credit for it.

For example, Alfred Binet is best known for his work on intelligence, but as pointed out by Siegler (1992), Binet did work on the nature of expertise in outstanding chess play and on the validity of eyewitness testimony. That work, which did not even remotely fit into existing paradigms of the time, was largely ignored. By the second half of the twentieth century, these and other topics that Binet studied had gained prominence. Binet is virtually never cited in the current work on these topics, however.

Royer (1971) published an article that was an information-processing analysis of the digit–symbol task on the Wechsler Adult Intelligence Scale (WAIS). In the article, Royer showed how information-processing analysis could be used to decompose performance on the task and understand the elementary information processes underlying the performance. Royer's work foreshadowed the later work of Hunt (Hunt, Frost, & Lunneborg, 1973; Hunt, Lunneborg, & Lewis, 1975) and especially of Sternberg (1977, 1983), but his work went largely (although not completely) unnoticed. There could be any number of reasons for this, but it is likely the field was not quite ready for Royer's contribution. The field and possibly even Royer himself did not recognize fully the value of the approach he was taking.

Advance incrementations can occur in any field. For example, the ancient Greek philosopher Democritus was way ahead of his time in proposing ideas that later gave rise to the theory of atoms. In the nineteenth century, Ignaz Semmelweis, a Hungarian obstetrician, proposed the idea of microorganisms contaminating the hands of doctors and was so scoffed at that eventually he was driven crazy. It is often only later that the value of an idea is appreciated.

An advance forward incrementation is a work whose potential typically is not realized at its premiere, yet is later recognized as a step along the historical path of a genre, and then seen as a work ahead of its time. Perhaps the most memorable premiere in music history is that of Igor Stravinsky's ballet *The Rite of Spring* in 1913. This performance so shocked its Parisian audience that the instrumentalists could not hear themselves play over the riotous crowd. At the time, French ballet music was very backward-looking and accompanied a very stylized choreography. The usual ballet patrons were bound to be overwhelmed by the enactment of barbaric rituals accented by the pulsating rhythms and dissonant harmonies featured in Stravinsky's new work.

Although *The Rite* was vehemently rejected, Stravinsky's innovation was rooted in the past and proved to be an important step in the future course of music history. The pressing and irregular rhythms of ritual in this work continued the rhythmic experimentation begun by Stravinsky's teacher, Nikolai Rimsky-Korsakov. This de-emphasis of melody and harmony became characteristic of works later in the century. Just as Stravinsky borrowed elements from folk music for this piece, many twentieth century composers also made extensive use of diverse sources in their compositions. Although *The Rite* was so poorly received at its premiere, its contribution to the field of music can be considered simply ahead of its time (Machlis, 1979).

Paradigm-Rejecting Contributions that Move the Field in a New Direction from an Existing or a Pre-Existing Starting Point

TYPE 5: REDIRECTION. Redirection is illustrated in Panel 5 of Figure 5.1. Redirection involves accepting the field where it is at a given time but attempting to move it in a new direction. Work of this type is creative to the extent that it moves a field in a new direction (novelty) and to the extent that this direction is seen as desirable for research (quality).

The pioneering Hunt, Frost, and Lunneborg (1973) article mentioned earlier suggested that researchers of intelligence use cognitive-psychological paradigms to study intelligence. The basic idea was to correlate scores on cognitive tasks with scores on psychometric tests. Sternberg (1977) used cognitive techniques as a starting point, but suggested that research move in a direction different from that suggested by Hunt. In particular, he suggested that complex cognitive tasks (such as analogies and classifications) be used instead of simple cognitive tasks (such as lexical access) and that the goal should be to decompose information processing on these tasks into its elementary information-processing components. Sternberg argued that Hunt was right in suggesting the use of cognitive tasks, but wrong in suggesting the use of very simple ones, which he believed involved only fairly low levels of intelligent thought. Sternberg was thus suggesting a redirection in the kind of cognitive work Hunt had initiated.

Edward Tolman (1932) made an effort to redirect the field of learning, an effort that today has earned Tolman a place in virtually every serious textbook on learning or even on introductory psychology. Tolman accepted many of the conventions of the day – experiments with rats, use of mazes, and multi-trial laboratory learning experiments. But he proposed to take all these features of research in a new direction, one that would allow for purposiveness and latent learning on the part of the animals he was studying. Today, these concepts are widely accepted, although at the time Tolman proposed them, the reaction was mixed, at best.

Beethoven's work can also be viewed as a redirection from the classical style of music that had been employed so successfully by Haydn, Mozart, and others. Beethoven used many of the same classical forms as his predecessors, but he also showed that a greater level of emotionality could be introduced into the music without sacrificing those forms.

Vonnegut questioned the very fabric of what constitutes a war novel, and in doing so pointed a path for the field to take. Re-creations and straightforward stories of the horrors of war (such as Stephen Crane's *The Red Badge of Courage* or MacKinlay Kantor's *Andersonville*) are powerful, Vonnegut might argue, but to truly convey the nature of war an author must go beyond this. O'Brien picks up on Vonnegut's path and takes yet another direction: An author *cannot* convey the nature of war to someone who has not experienced it. All he or she can do is convey the feelings and thoughts one might have in these situations. O'Brien and Vonnegut are not re-initiators, as they accept the same starting point for war novels that other novelists have used. Their work is not merely a type of forward incrementation, however, because they have taken a radically different view of the way in which a war novel should be written.

TYPE 6: RECONSTRUCTION/REDIRECTION. This type of creative contribution is illustrated in Panel 6 of Figure 5.1. In using reconstruction, an individual suggests that the field should move *backward* to a previous point but from there move in a direction divergent from that it had taken. In other words, the individual suggests that at some time in the past, the field went off track. The individual suggests the point at which this occurred and how the field should have moved forward from that point. The work is judged as creative to the extent that the individual is judged as correctly recognizing that the field has gone off track and to the extent that the new direction is viewed as a useful one for the field to pursue.

In the early part of the century, intelligence tests seemed to have potential for helping society understand why certain groups rose to the top of the society and other groups fell to the bottom (see Carroll, 1982; Ceci, 1996; Gould, 1981). This often thinly disguised social Darwinism was based on the notion that those with more adaptive skills, on average, should and in fact did have more success in adapting to the demands of the social structure of the society. Those with fewer adaptive skills, on average, did and should fall to the bottom. This kind of thinking became unpopular in the latter half of the century. Environment came to be seen as much more important than it had before (Kamin, 1974; Lewontin, 1982). As a result, intelligence-test scores were no longer being looked at as a cause of group differences, but rather as an effect.

This balance was upset when Herrnstein and Murray (1994) argued that the older views were most likely correct in many respects: It is plausible, they argued, to believe that group differences in IQ are in fact due to genetic factors, and that these group differences result in social mobility. Herrnstein and Murray further suggested that what they considered a humane social policy could be constructed on the basis of these alleged facts. Many people who were more comfortable with the older views or who were ready to be persuaded of them found the Herrnstein-Murray arguments convincing. Others, especially those believing in multiple intelligences or the importance of environment, were not at all convinced.

My goal here is not to argue about the validity of the Herrnstein-Murray position, which I have discussed elsewhere (Sternberg, 1995). Rather, it is to suggest that the work of Herrnstein and Murray was serving a reconstructive function. Herrnstein and Murray were suggesting that the field had gone off course in the desire of its members to accept certain beliefs that, however charitable they might be, were incorrect. These authors suggested the field return to a point that many (although certainly not all) investigators had thought had been left behind, and advance from that point.

B. F. Skinner's (1972) analysis of creativity represents another example of reconstruction/redirection. Skinner apparently was perturbed that the analysis of creativity had moved further and further away from the kinds of behavioristic principles that he and his colleagues believed applied to *all* behavior. The 1972 paper was, in large part, an argument that the field of creativity had lost its foundations, and that it needed to return to the kinds of behavioristic analyses that Skinner believed he and others had shown could account for creative behavior.

Some literary scholars are now suggesting that literary criticism, too, has gone off track – that the kind of deconstructionism introduced by Derrida (1992) and others has produced a literary nihilism that has resulted in a degeneration of the field of literary criticism. These individuals, such as Bloom (1994), suggest that literary scholars return to their earlier tradition of finding specific meaning in literary works rather than asserting that virtually any meaning can be read into any literary work.

The musical "Take It Easy" (1996) is an exemplar of reconstruction/redirection. Author Raymond G. Fox's musical takes place in the 1940s, and the music is a reconstruction of the "swing" sound. The characters are intentionally stereotypes, such as The Bookworm and The All-American Hero. The ultimate goal of the show is to re-create the feel of a 1940s college musical, with young, good-looking, and patriotic characters. Several other recent Broadway shows, such as "Triumph of Love" (book by James Magruder, music by Jeffrey Stock, and lyrics by Susan Birkenhead) and "Big" (book by John Weidman, music by David Shire, and lyrics by Richard Maltby, Jr.) have been "throwback" musicals that reflect the more simplistic plot, characters, and musical tone of musicals of the 1950s. Unlike more modern shows, which tend to be entirely sung and have either an operatic or rock musical style, these shows take the structure and values of more classic musicals (such as "Oklahoma!" or "My Fair Lady") and update the topics and sensibilities to the 1990s (for example, in "Big," characters refer to rap music).

Paradigm-Rejecting Contributions that Restart the Field in a New Place and Move in a New Direction from There

TYPE 7: REINITIATION.   This type of creative contribution is illustrated in Panel 7 of Figure 5.1. In reinitiation, a contributor suggests that a field or subfield has reached an undesirable point or has exhausted itself moving in the direction in which it is moving. But rather than suggesting that the field or subfield move in a different direction from where it is (as in redirection), the contributor suggests moving in a different direction from a different point in the multidimensional space of contributions. In effect, the contributor is suggesting people question their assumptions and "start over" from a point that most likely makes different assumptions. This form of creative contribution represents a major paradigm shift.

Two notable examples of this type of creativity can be found in the contributions to the field of intelligence made by Spearman (1904) and by Binet and Simon (1916a). Spearman reinvented the field of intelligence theory and research by his invention of factor analysis and by proposing his two-factor theory (general ability and specific abilities), based on his factor-analytic results. Spearman's contribution was to put theorizing about intelligence on a firm quantitative footing, a contribution that lives on today, whether or not one agrees with either Spearman's theory or his methodology. Binet and Simon (1916a) reinvented the field of intelligence measurement. Whereas Galton (1883) had proposed that intelligence should be understood in terms of simple psychophysical processes, Binet and Simon proposed that intelligence should be understood in terms of higher-order processes of judgment. For the most part, the measurements of intelligence today are still based on this notion of Binet and Simon.

Spearman's (1904, 1927) reinitiating emphasis on general ability was not shared by all investigators. For example, Thurstone (1938), Guilford (1967), and many other theorists have suggested that intelligence comprises multiple abilities and that any general factor obtained in factor analyses was likely to be at best, unimportant, and at worst, epiphenomenal. In all cases, however, intelligence was accepted as a unitary construct. What differed were investigators' views on how, if at all, the unitary construct should be divided up.

Festinger and Carlsmith's (1959) initial paper on cognitive dissonance, mentioned earlier, represents a reinitiation, an attempt to make a new start in the field of social psychology. A more recent example of a reinitiation is Bem's (1996) theory of homosexuality, according to which what initially is exotic for an individual later in life becomes erotic. Bem's is a theory arguing for environmental causes of homosexuality at a time when biological theories have largely gained acceptance.

Revolutionary works tend to be major reinitiations. In the field of linguistics, Chomsky's (1957) transformational grammar changed the way many linguists looked at language. Linguists following Chomsky began analyzing deep syntactic structures, not just surface structures. And of course Einstein revolutionized physics, showing that Newtonian physics represented only a limiting case of physics, in general, and further showing the relativity of notions about space and time. Reinitiations can apply to entire fields, as in the case of Einstein, or to smaller subfields. In each case, however, the creators are arguing for a fresh approach to creative work.

Reinitiative contributions are often bold and daring gestures. One prime example can be found in sculpture, with Marcel Duchamp's 1917 *Fountain*. Duchamp's Dada piece is simply a urinal turned on its back. The very act of entering such a piece in an art show is a statement about art – Duchamp's sculpture made art-making focus on the definition of exactly what art is and what art can be. Duchamp's urinal became a piece of art, and he and his fellow Dada creators set the stage for other modern art that challenges our ideas of what "art" encompasses (Hartt, 1993).

Another radical reinitiator is one of Duchamp's friends, the composer John Cage. He often employed unconventional sound materials and for a period his compositional process (and often performance) was determined entirely by chance. The philosophy that led Cage to compose in this unorthodox manner can be considered essentially a rejection of some basic tenets of the Western musical tradition, including the definition of music itself. Cage declared music to be all sound, including the whispers and heartbeats we perceive while silent. His affinity for Eastern philosophy caused him to focus on the importance of awareness in the human experience, and he used his music to foster awareness in his listeners.

An illustration of this point is his piece 4' 33". The performance of this piece consists of four minutes and thirty-three seconds of "silence," or rather, in Cage's terminology, "unintentional sound." In performance, the instrumentalist approaches her instrument, prepares to play, and proceeds to sit, without sound, for four minutes and thirty-three seconds. The only pauses are those indicated by Cage which signal the change of movement. The music, therefore, is that sound that exists in the environment. Cage's statement is that there is music being played around us all the time; we must reject the notion of music as organized melody, harmony, and rhythm to include all sound, even the rush of traffic beyond the door and the buzzing of the fluorescent lights above our heads (Cage, 1961; Hamm, 1980).

TYPE 8: INTEGRATION. In this type of creative contribution, illustrated in Panel 8 of Figure 5.1, the creator puts together two types of ideas previously seen as unrelated or even as opposed. Formerly viewed as distinct ideas, they now are viewed as related and capable of being unified. Integration is a key means by which progress is attained in the sciences.

One example of an integration is *Fatherland* (Harris, 1992), Robert Harris's best-selling novel of historical speculation. In the genre of historical speculation the author imagines a world different from the one we live in because of a fundamental change in history, perhaps a world in which a famous event in the past did not occur (for example, if John F. Kennedy had not been assassinated). Or a world in which an event that did not occur had, in fact, happened (if Adolf Hitler had been assassinated). In *Fatherland*, Harris conceptualizes a world in which Germany defeated the Allies in World War II. But rather than devoting most of the book to setting up the world and describing the "new" history, Harris plunges right in and begins a suspense thriller. Harris took the two genres – historical speculation and suspense thriller – and fused them together into a well-received novel.

Another example of integration is the innovative artwork of Rob Silvers. Silvers (1997) takes Georges Seurat's pointillist technique of using many small dots to form a larger work and combines it with the field of photography. Silvers uses thousands of tiny photographs and puts them together to form a larger image. His type of work, called photo mosaics, has become well known; Silvers designed the movie poster for *The Truman Show* and has done portraits of such disparate individuals as Princess Diana, Abraham Lincoln, and Darth Vader.

General Issues. In considering the eight types of creative contributions, one must realize that certain types of creative contributions may be, in practice, more highly creative than others, but that there can be no claim, in principle, that contributions of one type are more creative than others (with the possible exception of replications). Contributions can vary in novelty and quality. Consider as an example a reinitiation versus a forward incrementation. A reinitiation is, on average, more defiant of existing paradigms than is a forward incrementation. But a reinitiation is not necessarily more creative than a forward incrementation. The reinitiation may differ only trivially from existing paradigms or it may differ in a way that moves the field in a fruitless direction. The forward incrementation, on the other hand, may be one that has eluded all or almost all other investigators and thus is highly novel; moreover, it may be a contribution that makes just the step that makes a great difference to a field, such as the step that yields a vaccine against a serious illness. Thus, types of creative contributions do not immediately translate into levels of creative contributions. The relative levels of creativity of two contributions have to be determined on other grounds.

Nevertheless, individual investigators or institutions may have preferences for one type of creative contribution over another. The management of one institution may feel threatened by redefinitions or reinitiations whereas the management of another institution welcomes them. One graduate advisor may encourage his or her students to strike out on their own in crowd-defying directions whereas another graduate advisor insists that students work only within existing paradigms or perhaps even only the advisor's own paradigm. Undoubtedly, graduate training plays an important role not only in socializing students with respect to doing worthwhile research but also with respect to the kinds of research considered to be worthwhile. As always, what is viewed as creative will depend on the match between what an individual has to offer and what the context is willing to value. We also need to keep in mind that contributions are judged on the basis of many attributes, not just their creativity. A contribution that is creative may be valued or devalued in a society for any number of reasons, for example, its "political correctness" or the gender, ethnic group, or status of its creator.

Understanding Creativity-Related Phenomena via the Propulsion Model.
The propulsion model may help explain several creativity-related phenomena, although it does not provide a unique explanation.

First, the propulsion model may help reconcile the fact that creativity tends to generate negative reactions with the fact that most people seem to believe that they support creativity (Sternberg & Lubart, 1995). The present model suggests that positive or negative reactions to a given contribution are likely to vary with the type of creativity evinced in a given creative contribution. For example, the kind of paradigm-rejecting, crowd-defying creativity dealt with by the investment theory of creativity (Sternberg & Lubart, 1995) is probably largely of the later three types: redirection (type 5), reconstruction/redirection (type 6), and especially reinitiation (type 7). Paradigm-accepting creativity is more likely to generate a favorable response, at least initially. Forward incrementations, for example, are creative but occur within existing paradigms and hence are more likely to engender favorable reactions, whether from journal editors, grant reviewers, or critics of music and art. In the short run, artists, scientists, and others who provide forward incrementations may have the easiest time getting their work accepted; in the long run, however, their contributions may not be the longest lasting or the most important.

Second, the propulsion model helps psychologists better understand the nature of the relation between creativity and leadership (see, for example, Gardner, 1993, 1995). Leadership, like creativity, is propulsion. Hence, creativity always represents at least a weak attempt to lead. In the case of replication, the attempt is rather trivial. In the case of redirection, reconstruction/redirection, or reinitiation, it may be quite dramatic. In each of these cases, the creative individual is trying to lead the field in a direction different from the one in which it is going. Even advance incrementation represents an impressive form of leadership, in that it attempts to lead a field rather far away from where it is in the multidimensional space, albeit in the same direction as the field already is going.

Examples of the application of the propulsion model to creative leadership can be inferred from an analysis of university presidents by Levine (1998). Levine provides examples of two failed presidents – Francis

Wayland of Brown (president from 1827 to 1855) and Henry Tappan of the University of Michigan (1852 to 1863) – both of whom failed because their ideas were ahead of their time. Their ideas would succeed in other institutions, but later. Both presidents exemplified forward advance incrementations in the attempts at creative leadership of their institutions. Robert Hutchins, president of the University of Chicago from 1929 to 1951, was removed from his presidency because his ideas were behind the times. Hutchins wished to set off in a new direction from a set of ideas that had become passé in the minds of his constituents. He illustrated reconstruction/redirection. Clark Kerr, president of the University of California, Berkeley, from 1959 to 1967, ultimately failed because he became the wrong person at the wrong time when Ronald Reagan became governor of California. In essence, Reagan moved the multidimensional space to a new point, one that left Kerr outside the realm viewed as acceptable. The mantle of creative leadership thus was taken on by a governor, leaving the university president out of a job.

Third, the propulsion model helps address the question of whether programs based on artificial intelligence are creative (see discussions in Boden, 1992, 1999; Csikszentmihalyi, 1988; Dreyfus, 1992). To the extent that computer programs *replicate* past discoveries, no matter how creative those discoveries were, they are nevertheless replications, which is creativity (type 1), although perhaps of a more modest type. To the extent that computers actually are able to move a field forward or in a new direction, they may be creative in other senses. My reading of the present literature is that these programs are certainly creative in the sense of replication and that they also probably have been creative in the sense of forward incrementations. It is not clear that they have shown the more crowd-defying forms of creativity (types 5–7: redirection, reconstruction/redirection, reinitiation).

Fourth, the propulsion model may be relevant to the long-standing issue (raised above) of the extent to which creativity is domain-specific or domain-general. I would speculate that the ability to do reasonably successful forward incrementations may be largely domain-general and may even be highly correlated with scores on tests of conventional (analytical) abilities. A forward incrementation seems to require, for the most part, a high level of understanding of an extant knowledge base and an analysis of the trajectory of that field. The ability to acquire, understand, and analyze a knowledge base is largely what is measured by conventional standardized tests (Sternberg, 1997b). But the ability to perform a reinitiation may be quite a bit more domain-specific, requiring a sense or even feeling for a field that goes well beyond the kinds of more generalized analytical abilities measured by conventional tests. People who engage in creativity of types 5 (redirection), 6 (reconstruction/redirection), and 7 (reinitiation) may be less susceptible than others to the entrenchment that can accompany expertise (Frensch & Sternberg, 1989; Sternberg & Lubart, 1995).

The propulsion model certainly has weaknesses and ambiguities. First, it is new and has yet to be quantitatively tested. Such tests are planned, based on classifications of creative contributions and analyses of various measures of their impact. Second, contributions cannot be unequivocally classified into the different types. Bach, for example, was viewed in his time as, at best, making small forward incremental contributions or even as being a replicator. Today he is perceived by many as having helped to redefine Baroque music. Moreover, because we are always making judgments from whatever perspective we may hold, it is impossible to ensure "objective" judgments of the type of creative contribution a particular work makes or has made. Third, the model proposed here is probably not exhaustive with respect to the types of creative contributions that can be made. There may well be others and the ones proposed here almost certainly could be subdivided. Fourth, a given contribution may have elements of more than one type of contribution. Finally, the spatial metaphor used as a basis for the theory obviously is an oversimplification. There is no one point in a multidimensional space that can adequately represent a field or a subfield, nor is all research in the field or subfield moving in a single direction.

Ultimately, it is unlikely that there is any one "right" model of types of creative contributions. Rather, models such as this one can help people expand their thinking about the types of creative contributions that can be made in a field. And to the extent this model accomplishes that goal, it is accomplishing what it should. Creative contributions differ not only in amounts but also in types, and the eight types represented here are ones that presumably occur in all fields at all times. We should be aware of them when they occur. We also may wish to steer our children and ourselves toward certain types of creative contributions, ideally the types that are most compatible with what these children or we wish to offer. Do we wish our children to be replicators, to be forward incrementers, to be redirectors, to know when to be which? These are the decisions we must make in socializing our children. Ultimately, the children will need to decide for themselves, as they grow older, how they wish to unlock and express their creative potential. But the thing that is certain is that they will decide, because creativity is a decision. How can one encourage people to decide for creativity? According to the view of creativity as a decision, fomenting creativity is largely a matter of fomenting a certain attitude toward problem solving and even toward life. Creativity researchers may have a great deal of academic knowledge about creativity, but they do not necessarily interact with students in a way that maximizes the chances that students will decide for creativity.

PART III

WISDOM

6

Background Work on Wisdom

Many societies today are preoccupied with the development of cognitive skills in schoolchildren. In U.S. society, cognitive skills have become practically equated with intellectual skills – the mental bases of intelligence.[1] This equation is a mistake.

Given that IQs have been rising (Flynn, 1998), what does our world have to show for it? Judging by the seriousness and sheer scale of global conflict, perhaps not much. There is no reason to believe that increasing IQs have improved people's or nations' relations with each other.

The memory and analytical skills so central to intelligence are certainly important for school and life success, but perhaps they are not sufficient. Arguably, wisdom-related skills are at least as important or even more important.

Wisdom can be defined as the "power of judging rightly and following the soundest course of action, based on knowledge, experience, understanding, etc." (*Webster's New World College Dictionary*, 1997, p. 1533). Such a power would seem to be of vast importance in a world that at times seems bent on destroying itself.

MAJOR APPROACHES TO UNDERSTANDING WISDOM

A number of psychologists have attempted to understand wisdom in different ways. The approaches underlying some of these attempts are summarized in Sternberg (1990b). A more detailed review of some of the major

---

[1] By *intellectual skills*, I refer to those skills that are relevant to a given theory of intelligence. For example, Spearman (1927) included among such skills apprehension of experience (encoding), eduction of relations (inference), and eduction of correlates (application). Binet and Simon (1916b) included judgment skills, Galton (1883), psychophysical skills. Such skills are a subset of cognitive skills, which include skills that both are and are not relevant to intelligence within a given theoretical framework. Which cognitive skills would count as intellectual skills will vary with the theory of intelligence.

approaches to wisdom can be found in Baltes and Staudinger (2000) or in Sternberg (1990b, 1998b, 2000c). The main approaches might be classified as philosophical approaches, implicit-theoretical approaches, and explicit-theoretical approaches.

Philosophical Approaches

Philosophical approaches have been reviewed by Robinson (1990; see also Robinson, 1989, with regard to the Aristotelian approach in particular, and Labouvie-Vief, 1990, for a further review). Robinson notes that the study of wisdom has a history that long antedates psychological study, with the Platonic dialogues offering the first intensive analysis of the concept of wisdom. Robinson points out that, in these dialogues, there are three different senses of wisdom: wisdom as (a) *sophia*, which is found in those who seek a contemplative life in search of truth; (b) *phronesis*, which is the kind of practical wisdom shown by statesmen and legislators; and (c) *episteme*, which is found in those who understand things from a scientific point of view.

Implicit-theoretical Approaches

Implicit-theoretical approaches to wisdom have in common the search for an understanding of people's folk conceptions of what wisdom is. Thus, the goal is not to provide a "psychologically true" account of wisdom, but rather an account that is true with respect to people's beliefs, whether these beliefs are right or wrong. Some of the earliest work of this kind was done by Clayton (1975, 1976; Clayton & Birren, 1980), who multidimensionally scaled ratings of pairs of words potentially related to wisdom for three samples of adults differing in age (younger, middle-aged, older). In her earliest study (Clayton, 1975), the terms scaled were such as *experienced, pragmatic, understanding*, and *knowledgeable*.

Holliday and Chandler (1986) also used an implicit-theories approach to understanding wisdom. Approximately five hundred participants were studied across a series of experiments. The investigators were interested in determining whether the concept of wisdom could be understood as a prototype (Rosch, 1975), or central concept. Principal-components analysis of one of their studies revealed five underlying factors: exceptional understanding, judgment and communication skills, general competence, interpersonal skills, and social unobtrusiveness.

Sternberg (1985b, 1990a) has reported a series of studies investigating implicit theories of wisdom. In one study, two hundred professors each of art, business, philosophy, and physics were asked to rate the characteristic-ness of each of the behaviors obtained in a prestudy from the corresponding population with respect to the professors' conception of an ideally wise, intelligent, or creative individual in their occupation. Laypersons were also asked to provide these ratings but for a hypothetical ideal individual without regard to occupation. Correlations were computed across the three ratings. In each group except philosophy, the highest correlation was between wisdom and intelligence; in philosophy, the highest correlation was between intelligence and creativity. The correlations between wisdom and intelligence ratings ranged from .42 to .78 with a median of .68. For all groups, the lowest correlation was between wisdom and creativity (which ranged from −.24 to .48 with a median of .27).

In a second study, forty college students were asked to sort three sets of forty behaviors each into as many or as few piles as they wished. The forty behaviors in each set were the top-rated wisdom, intelligence, and creativity behaviors from the previous study. The sortings were subjected to nonmetric multidimensional scaling. For wisdom, six components emerged: *reasoning ability, sagacity, learning from ideas and environment, judgment, expeditious use of information,* and *perspicacity.* These components can be compared with those that emerged from a similar scaling of people's implicit theories of intelligence, which were *practical problem-solving ability, verbal ability, intellectual balance and integration, goal orientation and attainment, contextual intelligence,* and *fluid thought.* In both cases, cognitive abilities and their use are important. In wisdom, however, some kind of balance appears to emerge as important that does not emerge as important in intelligence, in general.

In a third study, fifty adults were asked to rate descriptions of hypothetical individuals for wisdom, intelligence, and creativity. Correlations were computed between pairs of ratings of the hypothetical individuals' levels of the three traits. Correlations between the ratings were .94 for wisdom and intelligence, .62 for wisdom and creativity, and .69 for intelligence and creativity, again suggesting that wisdom and intelligence are highly correlated in people's implicit theories, at least in the United States.

Explicit-Theoretical Approaches

Explicit-theoretical approaches have in common a formal theory of wisdom that is proposed to account for wisdom. The most extensive program of research has been that conducted by Baltes and his colleagues. This program of research is related to Baltes's long-standing program of research on intellectual abilities and aging. For example, Baltes and Smith (1987, 1990) gave adult participants life-management problems, such as "A fourteen-year-old girl is pregnant. What should she, what should one, consider and do?" and "A fifteen-year-old girl wants to marry soon. What should she, what should one, consider and do?" This same problem might be used to measure the pragmatics of intelligence, about which Baltes has written at length. Baltes and Smith tested a five-component model of wisdom on participants' protocols in answering these and other questions, based on a notion of wisdom as expert knowledge about fundamental life matters (Smith & Baltes, 1990) or of wisdom as good judgment and advice in important but uncertain matters of life (Baltes & Staudinger, 1993).

Three kinds of factors – general person factors, expertise-specific factors, and facilitative experiential contexts – were proposed to facilitate wise judgments. These factors are used in life planning, life management, and life review. Wisdom is in turn reflected in five components: (a) rich factual knowledge (general and specific knowledge about the conditions of life and its variations), (b) rich procedural knowledge (general and specific knowledge about strategies of judgment and advice concerning matters of life), (c) life span contextualism (knowledge about the contexts of life and their temporal [developmental] relationships), (d) relativism (knowledge about differences in values, goals, and priorities), and (e) uncertainty (knowledge about the relative indeterminacy and unpredictability of life and ways to manage). An expert answer should reflect more of these components, whereas a novice answer should reflect fewer. The data collected to date generally have been supportive of the model. These factors seem to reflect the pragmatic aspect of intelligence but go beyond it, for example, in the inclusion of factors of relativism and uncertainty.

Over time, Baltes and his colleagues (for example, Baltes, Smith, & Staudinger, 1992; Baltes & Staudinger, 1993) have collected a wide range of data showing the empirical utility of the proposed theoretical and measurement approaches to wisdom. For example, Staudinger, Lopez and Baltes (1997) found that measures of intelligence (as well as personality) overlap with, but are nonidentical to, measures of wisdom in terms of constructs measured and Staudinger, Smith, and Baltes (1992) showed that human-services professionals outperformed a control group on wisdom-related tasks. They also showed that older adults performed as well on such tasks as did younger adults, and that older adults did better on such tasks if there was a match between their age and the age of the fictitious characters about whom they made judgments. Baltes, Staudinger, Maercker, and Smith (1995) found that older individuals nominated for their wisdom performed as well as did clinical psychologists on wisdom-related tasks. They also showed that up to the age of eighty, older adults performed as well on such tasks as did younger adults. In a further set of studies, Staudinger and Baltes (1996) found that performance settings that were ecologically relevant to the lives of their participants and that provided for actual or "virtual" interaction of minds increased wisdom-related performance substantially.

Some theorists have viewed wisdom in terms of postformal–operational thinking, thereby viewing wisdom as extending beyond the Piagetian stages of intelligence (Piaget, 1972). Wisdom thus might be a stage of thought beyond Piagetian formal operations. For example, some authors have argued that wise individuals are those who can think reflectively or dialectically, in the latter case with the individuals realizing that truth is not always absolute but rather evolves in an historical context of theses, antitheses, and syntheses (for example, Basseches, 1984; Kitchener, 1983, 1986; Kitchener & Brenner, 1990; Kitchener & Kitchener, 1981; Labouvie-Vief, 1980, 1982, 1990; Pascual-Leone, 1990; Riegel, 1973). Other theorists have viewed wisdom in terms of finding important problems to solve (Arlin, 1990).

Although most developmental approaches to wisdom are ontogenetic, Csikszentmihalyi and Rathunde (1990) have taken a philogenetic or evolutionary approach, arguing that constructs such as wisdom must have been selected for over time, at least in a cultural sense. They have defined wisdom as having three basic dimensions of meaning: (a) that of a cognitive process or a particular way of obtaining and processing information; (b) that of a virtue or socially valued pattern of behavior; and (c) that of a good or a personally desirable state or condition.

Several of the theories described above emphasize the importance of various kinds of integrations or balances in wisdom. At least three major kinds of balances have been proposed: among various kinds of thinking (for example, Labouvie-Vief, 1990), among various self-systems, such as the cognitive, conative, and affective (for example, Kramer, 1990), and among various points of view (for example, Kitchener & Brenner, 1990). Baltes has also argued for the importance of balance (Baltes, 1993, 1994; Baltes & Staudinger, 2000; Staudinger, Lopez, & Baltes, 1997). The view presented here expands on but also differs from these kinds of notions in also providing for particular kinds of balance in wisdom.

7

The Balance Theory of Wisdom

The current theory views successful intelligence and creativity as the bases for wisdom. Successful intelligence and creativity are necessary, but not sufficient, conditions for wisdom. Particularly important is tacit knowledge, which is critical to practical intelligence.

THE BALANCE THEORY

Wisdom as Successful Intelligence and Creativity Balancing Interests

Wisdom is defined as the application of successful intelligence and creativity as mediated by values toward the achievement of a common good through a balance among (a) intrapersonal, (b) interpersonal, and (c) extrapersonal interests, over (a) short and (b) long terms, in order to achieve a balance among (a) adaptation to existing environments, (b) shaping of existing environments, and (c) selection of new environments, as shown in Figure 7.1.

Thus, wisdom is not just about maximizing one's own or someone else's self-interest, but about balancing various self-interests (intrapersonal) with the interests of others (interpersonal) and of other aspects of the context in which one lives (extrapersonal), such as one's city or country or environment or even God. Wisdom also involves creativity, in that the wise solution to a problem may be far from obvious.

An implication of this view is that when one applies successful intelligence and creativity, one may deliberately seek outcomes that are good for oneself and bad for others. In wisdom, one certainly may seek good ends for oneself, but one also seeks common good outcomes for others. If one's motivations are to maximize certain people's interests and minimize other people's, wisdom is not involved. In wisdom, one seeks a common good, realizing that this common good may be better for some than for others. A

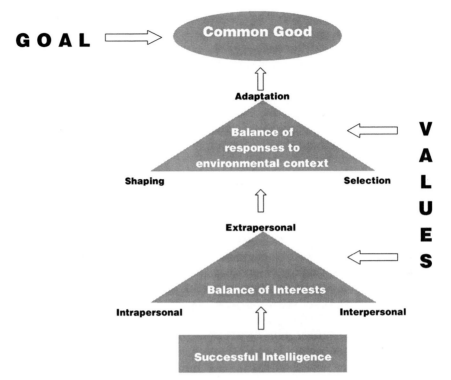

FIGURE 7.1. Wisdom as successful intelligence balancing goals, responses, and interests. The individual applies successful intelligence in order to seek a common good. Such application involves balancing of intrapersonal, interpersonal, and extrapersonal interests to adapt to, shape, and select environments. Judgments regarding how to achieve a common good inevitably involve the infusion of values.

terrorist may be academically intelligent; he may be practically intelligent; he cannot be wise.

Problems requiring wisdom always involve at least some element of each of intrapersonal, interpersonal, and extrapersonal interests. For example, one might decide that it is wise to take a particular teaching position, a decision that seemingly involves only one person. But many people are typically affected by an individual's decision to take a job – significant others, children, perhaps parents and friends. And the decision always has to be made in the context of what the whole range of available options is. Thus, people have to know what the options are and what they mean. To be wise, one must know what one knows, know what one does not know, know what can be known, and know what cannot be known at a given time or place.

What kinds of considerations might be included under each of the three kinds of interests? Intrapersonal interests might include the desire to enhance one's popularity or prestige, to make more money, to learn more, to increase one's spiritual well-being, to increase one's power, and so forth. Interpersonal interests might be quite similar, except as they apply to other people rather than oneself. Extrapersonal interests might include contributing to the welfare of one's school, helping one's community, contributing to the well-being of one's country, or serving God, and so forth. Different people balance these interests in different ways. At one extreme, a malevolent dictator might emphasize his or her own personal power and wealth; at the other extreme, a saint might emphasize only serving others and God.

Failures in balancing intrapersonal, interpersonal, and extrapersonal interests can have devastating effects. Consider some examples.

Although both Richard Nixon and Bill Clinton, as presidents, were rather self-absorbed, neither was wise. Wisdom involves a balancing not only of the three kinds of interests, but also of three possible courses of action in response to this balancing: adaptation of oneself or others to existing environments; shaping of environments in order to render them more compatible with oneself or others; and selection of new environments. In adaptation, the individual tries to find ways to conform to the existing environment that forms his or her context. Sometimes adaptation is the best course of action under a given set of circumstances. But typically one seeks a balance between adaptation and shaping, realizing that fit to an environment requires not only changing oneself, but changing the environment as well. When an individual finds it impossible or at least implausible to attain such a fit, he or she may decide to select a new environment altogether, leaving, for example, a job, a community, a marriage, or whatever.

Wisdom manifests itself as a series of processes, which are typically cyclical and can occur in a variety of orders. These processes are the meta-components of thought, including (a) recognizing the existence of a problem, (b) defining the nature of the problem, (c) representing information about the problem, (d) formulating a strategy for solving the problem, (e) allocating resources to the solution of a problem, (f) monitoring one's solution of the problem, and (g) evaluating feedback regarding that solution. In deciding about a teaching job, for example, one first has to see both taking the position and not taking it as viable options (problem recognition); then figure out exactly what taking or not taking the position would mean for oneself (defining the problem); then consider the costs and benefits to oneself and others (representing information about the problem); and so forth.

Wisdom is typically acquired by what I have referred to earlier as knowledge-acquisition components (Sternberg, 1985a). Its acquisition depends on (a) selectively encoding new information that is relevant for one's purposes in learning about that context; (b) selectively comparing this information to old information to see how the new fits with the old; and

(c) selectively combining pieces of information to make them fit together into an orderly whole (Sternberg, Wagner, & Okagaki, 1993).

This treatment of wisdom, which emphasizes the role of tacit knowledge, should not be interpreted to mean that formal knowledge is not or cannot be relevant to wise judgments and decision making. Quite the contrary: Obviously formal knowledge can be and often is extremely relevant to wise judgments and decision making. For example, consider the story of Solomon's judgment regarding the two women claiming to be the mother of the same infant. Stories of wise leadership are often learned in formal settings. But these aspects of knowledge, although relevant to wise judgments, need to be connected to such judgments via tacit knowledge. For example, consider the decision of Nelson Mandela in school to unify his country. But when to apply this knowledge, where to apply it, how to apply it, to whom to apply it, even why to apply it – these are the stuff of tacit knowledge. They are not and cannot be directly taught in school lessons. They are the lessons learned from experience. They can be learned in school, but they are not directly taught out of textbooks or lectures.

SOURCES OF DEVELOPMENTAL AND INDIVIDUAL
DIFFERENCES IN WISDOM

The balance theory suggests a number of sources of developmental and individual differences in wisdom. In particular, there are two kinds of sources, those directly affecting the balance processes and those that are antecedent.

Individual and Developmental Differences Directly Affecting the Balance Processes

There are seven sources of differences directly affecting the balance processes. Consider, as an example, a teacher who has been instructed by a principal to spend almost all of his time teaching in a way to maximize students' scores on a statewide assessment test, but who believes that the principal is essentially forcing him to abandon truly educating his students.

1. Goals. People may differ in terms of the extent to which they seek a common good, and thus in the extent to which they aim for the essential goal of wisdom. They also may differ in terms of what they view as the common good. The teacher may believe it is not in the children's best interest to engage in what he views as mindless drills for a test. The principal, however, may have a different view. The teacher is thus left with the responsibility of deciding what is in the best interests of all concerned.

2. *Balancing Responses to Environmental Contexts.* People may differ in their balance of responses to environmental contexts. Responses always reflect in the interaction of the individual making the judgment and the environment, and people can interact with contexts in myriad ways. The teacher may adapt to the environment and do exactly what the principal has told him to do, or shape the environment and do exactly what he believes he should do, or try to find some balance between adaptation and shaping that largely meets the principal's goals but also largely meets his own. Or the teacher may decide that the environment of the school is sufficiently aversive to his philosophy of teaching that he would prefer to teach elsewhere.

3. *Balancing of Interests.* People may balance interests in different ways. The teacher must decide how to balance his own interests in good teaching and also in staying on good terms with the principal; the children's interests in learning but also doing well on the statewide tests; the parents' interests in having well-educated children; and so on.

4. *Balancing of Short and Long Terms.* People may differ in their emphases. The teacher may believe that, in the long run, a proper education involves much more than preparing for statewide tests, but at the same time realize that, in the short run, the children's scores on the tests will affect their future as well as his future and possibly those of his principal and school.

5. *Acquisition of Tacit Knowledge.* People differ in the extent to which they acquire tacit knowledge. The teacher may bring relatively sophisticated tacit knowledge to solving this problem of how to teach the children, or may bring virtually no tacit knowledge and may have no clear option other than to do what the principal says.

6. *Utilization of Tacit Knowledge.* People differ in how well and how fully they utilize the tacit knowledge they have acquired. The teacher may decide to teach in a way that represents a compromise between his own views and those of the principal, but the way in which this decision is implemented will depend on his knowledge of how to balance the various interests involved in the decision.

7. *Values.* People have different values mediating their utilization of intelligence and creativity in the balancing of interests and responses. Values may vary somewhat across space and time, as well as among individuals within a given cultural context. The teacher's values may require him to diverge at least somewhat from the instructions of the principal. Another teacher's values might lead him to do what the principal says, regardless of how he personally feels. Nevertheless, there seem to be certain core values that are common to the world's great ethical systems and religions. They include values such as honesty, sincerity, reciprocity, compassion, and courage.

These sources of differences produce variations in how wise people are and in how well they can apply their wisdom in different kinds of situations. To the extent that wisdom is typically associated with greater intellectual and even physical maturity, it is presumably because the development of tacit knowledge and of values is something that unfolds over the course of the life span, not in childhood or in the early years of adulthood.

The above sources of individual differences pertain to the balancing processes. Other sources are antecedent to these processes.

Relations of Wisdom to Other Skills

Wisdom is related to other psychological constructs but not identical to any of them. In particular, it is related to knowledge, as well as to analytical, creative, and practical aspects of intelligence, and other aspects of intelligence.

First, wisdom requires knowledge, but the heart of wisdom is tacit, informal knowledge of the kind learned in the school of life, not the kind of explicit formal knowledge taught in schools. One could be a "walking encyclopedia" and show little or no wisdom because the knowledge one needs to be wise is not found in encyclopedias or even, generally, in the type of teaching found in most schools (with the possible exception of those that teach Socratically).

Second, wisdom requires analytical thinking, but it is not the kind of analytical thinking typically emphasized in schools or measured on tests of academic abilities and achievements (discussed in Sternberg, 1980b). Rather it is the analysis of real-world dilemmas where clean and neat abstractions often give way to messy and disorderly concrete interests. The kind of abstract analytical thinking that may lead to outstanding performance on a test such as the Raven Matrices, which present figural reasoning items, will be of some but not much use in complex real-world dilemmas such as how to defuse the conflict between India and Pakistan.

An important part of analytical thinking is metacognition. Wisdom seems related to metacognition because the metacomponents involved in wisdom are similar or identical to those that follow from other accounts of metacognition (for example, Campione, Brown, & Ferrara, 1982; Nelson, 1999). Thus, in wisdom, as in other types of thinking, one needs to define problems, formulate strategies to solve problems, allocate resources to the solution of these problems, and so forth. These processes are used in wisdom, as they are in other types of thinking, but in wisdom they are used to balance different types of interests in order to seek a common good.

Third, wise solutions are often creative ones, as King Solomon demonstrated in cleverly determining which of two women was truly the mother of a child. But the kind of crowd-defying, buy-low, sell-high attitude that leads to creative contributions does not in itself lead to wisdom. Creative people often tend toward extremes, although their later contributions may be more integrative (Gardner, 1993). Creative thinking is often brash whereas wise thinking is balanced. This is not to say that the same people cannot be both creative and wise. It is to say, however, that the kinds of thinking required to be creative and wise are different and thus will not necessarily be found in the same person. Moreover, teaching people to think creatively (see, for example, Sternberg & Williams, 1996) will not teach them to think wisely.

Wisdom is also related to creatively insightful thinking. According to Sternberg and Davidson (1982), the three knowledge-acquisition components correspond to three kinds of insights, and these three components of knowledge acquisition are also used in the acquisition of wisdom and other kinds of thinking. Selective comparison insights, for example, are used in analogical problem solving when one solves a current problem by applying information obtained in the past in solving a related kind of problem. For example, deciding whether a military campaign will prove to be another "Vietnam" involves selective comparison: Is the new campaign going to be enough like the Vietnam campaign to lead to a similar disaster?

It is important to note that although wise thinking must be, to some extent, creative, creative thinking (as discussed above) need not be wise. Wise thinking must be creative to some extent because it generates a novel and problem-relevant high-quality solution involving balancing of interests, and novelty and appropriate quality are the two hallmarks of creativity (see essays in Sternberg, 1999b). But a solution can be creative – as in solving a mathematical proof – but have no particular characteristics of wisdom. The proof involves no balancing of interests and no search for a common good. It is simply an intellectual problem involving creative thinking.

Fourth, practical thinking is closer to wisdom than are analytical and creative thinking, but again, it is not the same. Wisdom is a particular kind of practical thinking. It (a) balances competing intrapersonal, interpersonal, and extrapersonal interests, over short and (b) long terms, (c) balances adaptation to, shaping of, and selection of environments, in (d) the service of a common good. Thus, people can be good practical thinkers without being wise but they cannot be wise without being good practical thinkers. Good practical thinking is necessary but not sufficient for the manifestation of wisdom.

Fifth, wisdom also seems to bear at least some relation to constructs such as social intelligence (Cantor & Kihlstrom, 1987; Kihlstrom & Cantor, 2000; Sternberg & Smith, 1985), emotional intelligence (Goleman, 1995; Mayer &

Salovey, 1993; Salovey & Mayer, 1990), and interpersonal and intrapersonal intelligences (Gardner, 1983, 1999). There are also differences, however. Social intelligence can be applied to understanding and getting along with others, to any ends, for any purposes. Wisdom seeks out a good through a balancing of interests. Thus, a salesperson who figures out how to sell a worthless product to a customer might do so through using social intelligence to understand the customer's wants, but has not applied wisdom in the process. Emotional intelligence involves understanding, judging, and regulating emotions. These skills are an important part of wisdom. But making wise judgments requires going beyond the understanding, regulation, or judgment of emotions. It requires processing the information to achieve a balance of interests and formulating a judgment that makes effective use of the information to achieve a common good. Moreover, wisdom may require a balance of interpersonal and intrapersonal intelligences, but it also requires an understanding of extrapersonal factors, and a balance of these three factors to attain a common good. Thus wisdom seems to go somewhat beyond these theoretically distinct kinds of intelligences as well. Perhaps the most salient difference among constructs is that wisdom is applied toward the achievement of ends that are perceived as yielding a common good, whereas the various kinds of intelligences may be applied deliberately toward achieving either good ends or bad ones, at least for some of the parties involved. It is interesting that the conception of wisdom proposed here is substantially closer to Chinese than to American conceptions of intelligence (Yang & Sternberg, 1997a, 1997b). One of the words used in Chinese to characterize intelligence is the same as the word used to characterize wisdom.

MEASUREMENT OF TACIT KNOWLEDGE IN WISDOM

Can wisdom be measured? We believe so. Consider problems we have used in the past to measure the tacit knowledge underlying practical intelligence, for which we have collected extensive data, and then consider problems we are using in our current research to measure wisdom.

We have devised a series of twenty-four problems to measure wisdom. The validity of these problems is currently being assessed. Here is an example of one (see below for a further example being used at a lower level of schooling).

"Felicia and Alexander have been in an intimate relationship for their entire four years of college. Felicia has now been accepted for graduate school in French by a prestigious graduate program in northern California. Alexander was not admitted to the law school in this university, nor to any other law school in the northern California area. Alexander was admitted to a good although not outstanding law school in southern California, but he was also admitted to an outstanding law school in Massachusetts. Felicia has no viable opportunities for graduate study on the East Coast, at least at this time. Alexander is trying to decide whether to attend the less prestigious law school in southern California or the more prestigious one in Massachusetts. He would like to continue the relationship, as would Felicia, and both ultimately hope to marry. A complicating factor is that the law school in Massachusetts has offered Alexander a half-scholarship, whereas the law school in southern California has not offered financial aid for the first year, although it has indicated that there is a possibility of financial aid in subsequent years. Alexander's parents have indicated that while they would be willing to pay his half-tuition for the more prestigious law school, they do not believe it is fair to ask them to pay full tuition for the less prestigious one. They also believe his going to the less prestigious law school will only hurt Alexander's career advancement. Felicia is torn and is leaving it to Alexander to decide what to do. What should Alexander do and why?"

FOOLISHNESS

Foolishness is the absence of wisdom. Smart people can be foolish and, are at times especially susceptible to foolishness. Foolish people are susceptible to four fallacies in thinking.

The *fallacy of egocentrism* occurs when an individual starts to think that the world centers around him or her. In life, it's all about that individual. Other people come to be seen merely as tools in the attainment of one's goals. Why would smart people think egocentrically, when one would expect that they would have abandoned the stage of egocentrism many years ago? The reason is, I believe, that conventionally smart people have been so highly rewarded for being smart that they lose sight of their own limitations. Wisdom requires one to know what one does know and does not know. Smart people often lose sight of what they do not know, leading to the second fallacy.

The *fallacy of omniscience* results from having available at one's disposal essentially any knowledge one might want that, is, in fact, knowable. With a phone call, a powerful leader can have almost any kind of knowledge made available to him or her. At the same time, people look up to the powerful leader as extremely knowledgeable or even close to all-knowing. The powerful leader may then come to believe that he or she really is all-knowing. So may his or her staff, as illustrated by Janis (1972) in his analysis of victims of groupthink. In case after case, brilliant government officials made the most foolish of decisions, in part because they believed they knew much more than they did.

The *fallacy of omnipotence* results from the extreme power one wields. In certain domains, one essentially can do almost whatever one wants to do. The risk is that the individual will start to overgeneralize and believe that this high level of power applies in all domains.

The *fallacy of invulnerability* comes from the illusion of complete protection, such as from a huge staff. People and especially leaders seem to have many friends ready to protect them at a moment's notice. The leaders may shield themselves from individuals who are anything less than sycophantic. Harry Truman suggested that high-powered (Washington) leaders who want friends ought to buy themselves a dog. As soon as things turn bad, many individuals who once seemed friends prove to be anything but.

In terms of the balance theory of wisdom, foolishness always involves interests going out of balance. Usually, the individual places self-interest way above other interests. But not always. Chamberlain may truly have believed he was doing the best for Great Britain. But in ignoring the interests of all the other countries being crushed under Hitler's brutal reign, Chamberlain was ignoring the common good, and, as it turned out, the long-term good of his own country.

Occasionally people sacrifice everything for another individual, only to be crushed by their own foolishness. The "classic" case is that of the prolonged war between Greece and Troy. Was Helen of Troy worth the war? Many wars have started over slights or humiliations, and the interests of the slighted or humiliated have taken precedence over the interests of the thousands who have been sacrificed to avenge the slight. There are those who believe that the war in Chechnya resulted in part from the humiliation suffered by the Russian army in the earlier war there. Certainly events in post–World War I contributed to Germany's humiliation after that war.

Wisdom involves a balancing not only of the three kinds of interests, but also of three possible courses of action in response to this balancing: adaptation of oneself or others to existing environments; shaping of environments to render them more compatible with oneself or others; and selection of new environments. Foolishness is reflected in action that represents poor use and balance of these processes. Wars are examples of shaping of the environment that often have proved to be of little avail. What, for example, did the Hundred Year War have to show for itself in the end? Or, for that matter, the more-recent Cold War? National leaders shaped environments in ways that caused great harm, suffering, and distress. In much of the world, they are continuing to do so.

Foolishness does not only derive from inappropriate shaping of the environment. One can adapt to a tyrannical environment to save one's own skin, only to find oneself paying the ultimate price. An example of this principle is shown in this quotation from Pastor Martin Niemöller:

> In Germany first they came for the communists
> and I did not speak out –
> because I was not a communist.

Then they came for the Jews
and I did not speak out –
because I was not a Jew.

Then they came for the trade unionists
and I did not speak out –
because I was not a trade unionist.

Then they came for the Catholics
and I did not speak out –
because I was a Protestant.

Then they came for me –
and there was no one left
to speak out for me.
                    — Pastor Martin Niemöller

Selection also can be foolish, as when old individuals leave good or at least acceptable marriages for much younger partners whose main goal appears to be sharing the older person's financial success. Selection can be with respect to environments rather than people. An individual may love the idea of living in a place, move to the place, and then find that the reality bears little resemblance to the ideal. An American living abroad commented to me somewhat bitterly that the reasons one moved to the country in which he lived were inevitably different from the reasons for which one stayed. Those who hoped to find some satisfaction abroad inevitably returned to the United States, because they never found it.

How can we teach people to think wisely rather than foolishly?

DEVELOPING WISE THINKING

Why Should Wisdom be Included in the School Curriculum?

The development of wisdom is beneficial because the judgments it yields can improve our quality of life and conduct (Kekes, 1995). Knowledge can and indeed must accompany wisdom. People need knowledge to draw on in rendering judgments – knowledge of human nature, of life circumstances, or strategies that succeed and strategies that fail. Although knowledge is necessary for wisdom, it is not sufficient for it. Merely having knowledge does not entail its use in judging rightly, soundly, or justly. Many highly knowledgeable individuals lead lives that are unhappy. Some of them make decisions that are poor or even reprehensible. This century provides many examples of such decisions.

There are several reasons why schools should seriously consider including instruction in wisdom-related skills in the school curriculum.

First, as noted above, knowledge is insufficient for wisdom and certainly does not guarantee satisfaction or happiness. Wisdom seems a better vehicle for the attainment of these goals.

Second, wisdom provides a mindful and considered way to enter considered and deliberative values into important judgments. One cannot be wise and at the same time impulsive or mindless (Langer, 1997) in one's judgments.

Third, wisdom represents an avenue to creating a better, more harmonious world. Dictators such as Adolf Hitler and Joseph Stalin may have been knowledgeable and may even have been good critical thinkers, at least with regard to the maintenance of their own power. Given the definition of wisdom, however, it would be hard to argue they were wise.

Fourth and finally, students – who will later become parents and leaders – are always part of a greater community and hence will benefit from learning to judge rightly, soundly, or justly on behalf of their community (Ardelt, 1997; Sternberg, 1990b, 1998b, 1999d; Varela, 1999).

If the future is plagued with conflict and turmoil, this instability does not simply reside *out there somewhere*; it resides and has its origin *in ourselves*. For all these reasons, we endorse teaching students not only to recall facts and to think critically (and even creatively) about the content of the subjects they learn, but to think wisely about it, too.

Some Past Orientations and Programs Relevant to the Development of Wisdom

What would education that fostered wisdom look like? Three previous programs seem particularly related to the goals of the proposed orientation of teaching for wisdom. All have been proposed by educators with a primarily philosophical orientation. The first program, *Philosophy for Children* (Lipman, 1982; Lipman, Sharp, & Oscanyan, 1980), uses a set of novels to develop analytical-thinking skills in children. Children read the novels and learn to evaluate information in them and to make judgments about the characters in the novels and the kinds of choices they should make in their lives. The second program is Paul's (1987) program, which emphasizes dialogical thinking, or seeing problems from a variety of perspectives. The third program is that of Perkins (1986), which emphasizes understanding of "knowledge by design" – in other words, how knowledge is designed and used to solve problems in the world. Ennis (1987) has provided a taxonomy of critical-thinking skills, many of which are required for wise thinking, and Bransford and Stein (1993), Feuerstein (1980), and Halpern (1996) have all provided systematic courses that teach skills of critical thinking needed for wise thinking. Feuerstein's (1980) program has been the most widely used of this group. Other programs also touch on aspects of the proposed instruction described here (see Reigeluth's [1999] book on instructional-design theories and models for descriptions of a variety of programs).

It is impossible to speak of wisdom outside the context of a set of values, which in combination may lead one to a moral stance, or, in Kohlberg's (1969, 1983) view, stage. The same can be said of all practical intelligence: Behavior is viewed as practically intelligent as a function of what is valued in a societal/cultural context. Values mediate how one balances interests and responses, and collectively contribute even to how one defines a common good. The intersection of wisdom with the moral domain can be seen in the overlap between the notion of wisdom presented here and that of moral reasoning as it applies in the two highest stages (4 and 5) of Kohlberg's (1969) theory. Wisdom also involves caring for others as well as oneself (Gilligan, 1982). At the same time, wisdom is broader than moral reasoning. It applies to any human problem involving a balance of intrapersonal, interpersonal, and extrapersonal interests, whether or not moral issues are at stake.

Sixteen Principles of Teaching for Wisdom Derived from the Balance Theory of Wisdom

There are sixteen principles derived from the balance theory that form the core of how wisdom can be developed in the classroom:

1. Explore with students the notion that conventional abilities and achievements are not enough for a satisfying life. Many people become trapped in their lives and, despite feeling conventionally successful, feel that their lives lack fulfillment. Fulfillment is not an alternative to success, but is an aspect of it that, for most people, goes beyond money, promotions, large houses, and so forth.
2. Demonstrate how wisdom is critical for a satisfying life. In the long run, wise decisions benefit people in ways that foolish decisions never do.
3. Teach students the usefulness of interdependence – a rising tide raises all ships; a falling tide can sink them.
4. Teach role-model wisdom because what you do is more important than what you say. Wisdom is action-dependent and wise actions need to be demonstrated.
5. Have students read about wise judgments and decision making so they understand that there are such means of judging and decision making.
6. Help students to recognize their own interests, those of other people, and those of institutions.
7. Help students to balance their own interests, those of other people, and those of institutions.

8. Teach students that the "means" by which the end is obtained matters, not just the end.
9. Help students learn the roles of adaptation, shaping, and selection, and how to balance them. Wise judgments are dependent in part on selecting among these environmental responses.
10. Encourage students to form, critique, and integrate their own values in their thinking.
11. Encourage students to think dialectically, realizing that both questions and their answers evolve over time, and that the answer to an important life question can differ at different times in one's life (such as whether to go to college).
12. Show students the importance of dialogical thinking, whereby they understand interests and ideas from multiple points of view.
13. Teach students to search for and then try to reach the common good – a good where everyone wins, not only those with whom one identifies.
14. Encourage and reward wisdom.
15. Teach students to monitor events in their lives and their own thought processes about these events. One way to recognize others' interests is to begin to identify one's own.
16. Help students understand the importance of inoculating oneself against the pressures of unbalanced self-interest and small-group interest.

Procedures to Follow in Teaching for Wisdom

There are several procedures a teacher can follow in teaching for wisdom. First, students would read classic works of literature and philosophy (whether Western or otherwise) to learn and reflect on the wisdom of the sages. The rush to dump classic works in favor of modern ones makes sense only if the wisdom the modern works impart equals or exceeds that of the classic works.

Second, students would engage in class discussions, projects, and essays that encourage them to discuss the lessons they have learned from the classic works, and how they can be applied to their own lives and the lives of others. A particular emphasis would be placed on the development of dialogical and dialectical thinking. Dialogical thinking (see Principle 12) involves understanding significant problems from multiple points of view, how others can legitimately conceive of things in a way quite different from one's own. Dialectical thinking (see Principle 11) involves understanding that ideas and the paradigms under which they fall evolve and keep evolving, not only from the past to the present, but from the present to the future (Hegel, 1807/1931; see also Sternberg, 1998c).

Third, students would study not only "truth," as we know it, but values as well. They would not be force-fed a set of values, but would be encouraged to develop their own values.

Fourth, such instruction would place an increased emphasis on critical, creative, and practical thinking in the service of good ends – ends that benefit not only the individual doing the thinking but others as well. All these types of thinking would be valued, not just critical thinking.

Fifth, students would be encouraged to think about how almost everything they study might be used for better or worse ends, and to realize that the ends to which knowledge is put *do* matter.

Finally, teachers would realize that the only way they can develop wisdom in their students is to serve as role models of wisdom themselves. This would, I believe, take a much more Socratic approach to teaching than teachers customarily employ. Students often want large quantities of information spoon-fed or even force-fed to them. They attempt to memorize this material for exams, only to forget it soon thereafter. In a wisdom-based approach to teaching, students will need to take a more active role. But a wisdom-based approach is not tantamount to a constructivist approach to learning. Students have not achieved or even come close to achieving wisdom when they have merely constructed their own learning. They must be able to construct knowledge not only from their own point of view, but from the point of view of others. Constructionism from only a single point of view can lead to egocentric rather than balanced understanding.

Lessons taught to emphasize wisdom would have a rather different character from lessons as they are often taught today. Consider examples.

First, social studies and especially history lessons would look very different. High school American history books typically teach American history from only one point of view, that of the new Americans. Thus Columbus is referred to as having "discovered" America, a strange notion from the standpoint of the many occupants who already lived here when it was "discovered." The conquest of the Southwest and the fall of the Alamo are presented only from the point of view of the new settlers, not from the standpoint of, say, the Mexicans who lost roughly half their territory to the invaders. This kind of ethnocentric and frankly propagandistic teaching would have no place in a curriculum that sought to develop wisdom and an appreciation of the need to balance interests.

Second, science teaching would no longer be about facts presented as though they are the final word. Science is often presented as though it represents the end of a process of evolution of thought rather than one of many midpoints (Sternberg, 1998a). Students can scarcely realize from this kind of teaching that the paradigms of today, and thus the theories and findings that emanate from them, will eventually be superseded, as the paradigms, theories, and findings of yesterday were replaced by those of today. Students would learn that, contrary to the way many textbooks are written, the classical "scientific method" is largely a fantasy rather than a reality and that scientists are as susceptible to fads as are members of other groups.

Third, teaching literature would reflect a kind of balance often absent. Literature is often taught and characters judged in terms of the standards and context of the contemporary U.S. scene today, rather than those of the time and place in which the events took place. From the proposed standpoint, the study of literature must, to some extent, proceed in the context of the study of history. Banning books often reflects the application of certain contemporary standards of which an author from the past never could have been aware.

Fourth, foreign languages would be taught in the cultural context in which they are embedded. Perhaps American students have so much more difficulty learning foreign languages than do children in much of Europe not because they lack the ability but because they lack the motivation. They do not see the need to learn another language whereas, say, a Flemish-speaking child in Belgium does. Americans might be better off if they made more of an attempt wisely to understand other cultures rather than just expecting people from other cultures to understand them. Learning the language of a culture is a key to understanding. Americans might be less quick to impose their cultural values on others if they understood the cultural values of others. It is interesting to speculate on why Esperanto, a language designed to provide a common medium of communication across cultures, has been a notable failure. Perhaps it is because Esperanto is embedded in no culture at all. It is the language of no one.

Culture cannot be taught, in the context of foreign-language learning, in the way it now often is – as an aside divorced from the actual learning of the language. It should be taught as an integral part of the language, as a primary context in which the language is embedded. The vituperative fights we see about bilingual education and about the use of Spanish in the United States or French in Canada are not just, or even primarily, fights about language. They are fights about culture, and they are fights in need of wise resolutions.

Finally, as implied throughout these examples, the curriculum needs to be far more integrated. Literature needs to be integrated with history, science with history and social-policy studies, foreign language with culture. Even within disciplines, far more integration is needed. Different approaches to psychology, for example, are often taught as competing when in fact they are totally compatible. Thus, biological, cognitive, developmental, social, and clinical psychology provide complementary viewpoints on human beings. They do not each claim to be the "right approach." The study of the brain is important, for example, but most of the insights about learning and memory that can be applied to instruction have come from behavioral and cognitive approaches, not from the biological approach.

And some of the insights that have supposedly come from the biological approach – such as "left-brain" and "right-brain" learning – are based on ignorant or outdated caricatures of research in this area rather than on actual findings.

TESTING THE BALANCE THEORY IN THE CLASSROOM

Can these ideas be applied and tested in an educational setting? In collaboration with Elena L. Grigorenko and others at the PACE center at Yale, I am currently working on a project funded by the W. T. Grant Foundation to determine whether wisdom can be successfully taught to students at the middle-school level. It will take several years to complete this project and I show here how the theory is being tested, rather than providing concrete results. I hope the paradigm described will be of interest to others who would apply teaching for wisdom in the classroom.

We are working with roughly three dozen middle-school teachers and roughly six hundred middle-school students. This particular selection is based on several considerations.

First, students in middle school represent an age group ripe for the development of unbalanced thinking, with potentially devastating consequences. Students in middle school are close to the age when they will begin to make important life decisions involving sex, drugs, smoking tobacco, and violence. Wisdom-related skills need to be imparted and nurtured before the children start deciding their course of action on such vital life matters.

Second, students in middle school have acquired a level of cognitive development that renders them suitable to understand the different aspects of wisdom-related skills. Middle-school students can think abstractly about concepts, in which myriad possibilities are explored and weighed in the path to a solution (Piaget, 1952). Thinking abstractly is central to dialectical thinking. They have also developed metacognitive skills adequate for thinking wisely (Sternberg, 1985a, 1988c).

Third, unlike teachers of higher grades, teachers in middle schools often teach all subject-matter areas and so have direct control over the manner in which the subject matter is taught. This makes it possible to integrate a wisdom-related curriculum seamlessly into their regular teaching.

We are planning to develop an infused curriculum for teaching wisdom. We prefer an infused model of teaching rather than a separate "wisdom curriculum" for several reasons. First, most teachers seem to believe that they do not have the time in the school day to teach yet another subject. Second, infusion helps students transfer wisdom-related skills to skills they acquire in the course of their regular school learning. Third, we believe an infused program is more likely to result in knowledge that will interconnect with children's lives.

Finally, we believe that the curriculum in middle schools is in need of a richer, more penetrating program targeted not only at accumulating various academic skills, but also at adding richness, depth, and orientation to the formation of the higher-order thinking skills that the present curriculum sometimes appears to lack.

Wisdom-Related Curriculum

The following twelve major topics are covered in the wisdom-related curriculum we are developing, one per week, over a twelve-week curriculum (roughly one semester). The curriculum will be written for teachers to teach to their students:

1. What is wisdom – Part 1 (analyzing people's implicit theories)?
2. What is wisdom – Part 2 (analyzing famous definitions)?
3. Why is wisdom important to individuals, society, and the world?
4. Some big ideas about wisdom – Part 1 (the common good)
5. Some big ideas about wisdom – Part 2 (the role of values)
6. Some big ideas about wisdom – Part 3 (the role of interests)
7. Some big ideas about wisdom – Part 4 (the role of environmental responses)
8. Integration: Famous examples of wise individuals and why they were considered wise
9. Applying wisdom across the ages – Part 1 (earlier times)
10. Applying wisdom across the ages – Part 2 (present times)
11. Applying wisdom in students' daily life
12. Applying wisdom to create a better world

The design of the project involves three conditions: two experimental conditions and one control condition. Each condition includes twelve teachers and at least two hundred students. The first experimental condition incorporates the "Teaching for Wisdom" curriculum, the second experimental condition incorporates a critical-thinking skills curriculum, and the third control condition incorporates the regular curriculum. There are two reasons for including the critical-thinking condition.

First, we wish to avoid the possibility of a Hawthorne effect (Parsons, 1974). That is, if we find positive effects associated with the wisdom condition in relation to the regular-curriculum control, we want to know that the effects originated from the wisdom curriculum specifically and not from the implementation of a new curriculum generally.

Second, including a critical-thinking condition can inform us whether any new curriculum involving critical thinking, whether it focuses explicitly on wisdom or not, potentially can increase wisdom-related skills. We believe that critical thinking is not sufficient for wise thinking, but this remains to be shown.

Teachers in the wisdom condition are to implement the twelve-week course for teaching for wisdom. We are developing a curriculum handbook for teachers to use in their preparation and teaching. We are constructing this curriculum handbook along the same lines as the handbook for helping teachers develop students' Practical Intelligence For School ("PIFS"; Williams, Blythe, White, Li, Sternberg, & Gardner, 1996). In the wisdom handbook, as in the PIFS handbook, each chapter is dedicated to implementing a part of the curriculum. For example, one chapter introduces the notion of wisdom and why it is important. Other chapters instruct teachers how to incorporate wisdom-related skills in daily lesson plans in language arts, social science, and natural science following the sixteen principles mentioned above. Some topics might include wisdom and foolishness in literature, analysis of historical decisions using wisdom-related skills as criteria, and the costs of pollution to the world. The handbook can also help teachers coordinate the activities required for developing wisdom-related skills, such as generating dialectical thinking, group discussions, and ideas for modeling.

In addition, before they start teaching the curriculum, teachers are to attend twenty hours of professional development in-service meetings, where they will have an opportunity to orient themselves to, discuss, and use the information presented in the handbook. An additional ten hours of in-service are scheduled while the curriculum is running to give feedback to the teachers and the investigators.

We are implementing a twelve-week course for teaching critical-thinking skills. As in the wisdom condition, we are developing a curriculum handbook for teachers to use in their preparation and teaching along the same lines as the handbook for teaching for wisdom. The teaching of critical-thinking skills to middle-school students has been implemented before in past studies of Sternberg's triarchic theory of intelligence (see Sternberg, Torff, & Grigorenko, 1998b). Teaching these skills involves explaining to students the uses of analytical reasoning along with the strategies that foster and actualize critical thinking. For example, teachers might have students analyze flaws in an historical figure's political strategy, in a science experiment, or in a commentary devoted to a piece of literature.

The conventional instructional condition does not involve any specific course, per se. However, we provide the same level of in-service to teachers. The in-services are on effective assessment, including both conventional and performance assessments. We are preparing a handbook comparable to those in the other conditions.

The same evaluations are used in all conditions. The main dependent variables in this study are measures of students' levels of wisdom-related skills. These will be measured in three phases. We are also evaluating how closely teachers in the two experimental conditions followed their corresponding curricula, as well as the overall impressions of the curricula of teachers and students.

The first evaluation will be administered prior to the beginning of the twelve-week period (pre-test); a second evaluation will be administered during the curriculum delivery period (intervention stage); a third evaluation will be administered at the end of the twelve-week period (post-test); and a fourth evaluation will take place after an interval of two to three months following the twelve-week period (durability test). The first evaluation is designed to measure students' baseline levels of wisdom-related skills by condition. The second is designed to monitor the change during the curriculum delivery. The third is conceived to measure the effectiveness of each curriculum condition on students' wisdom-related skills immediately following the twelve-week curriculum. The fourth is designed to measure the durability of the effect of each curriculum condition on students' wisdom-related skills.

The materials with which we will assess students' level of wisdom-related skills include conflict-resolution scenarios (Sternberg & Dobson, 1987; Sternberg & Soriano, 1984) and unanticipated but highly plausible dilemmas, including dilemmas prepared by us and by others (for example, Staudinger, 1996; Staudinger & Baltes, 1996). This latter method of evaluating wisdom-related judgment has been successfully used in past research (for example, Staudinger & Baltes, 1996).

Conflict-resolution scenarios involve problematic situations with multiple interests that can be considered in finding a resolution to the problem. One such scenario for middle-school students is presented below:

Mary is fighting with her parents over a sleepover she wants to go to at her friend Lisa's house. Her parents have told her that they are worried about the lack of supervision at the sleepover and are worried about whether the children's behavior may get out of hand. Mary has had a number of problems with her classmates in the past year and sees this sleepover as an opportunity to strengthen friendships she has made or would like to make. What should Mary do?

The unanticipated but highly plausible dilemmas also require students to respond to open-ended scenarios. Students' responses will then be evaluated by trained raters according to a pre-specified set of criteria derived from the balance theory of wisdom. Ultimately, each response will be associated with a set of ratings corresponding to the set of criteria as well as an overall rating. There will be at least two raters per response to be rated.

The particular ratings (on a seven-point Likert scale) will consider

1. demonstration of attempt to reach a common good;
2. balancing of intrapersonal, interpersonal, and extrapersonal interests;

3. taking into account both short- and long-term factors;
4. justification for adaptation to, shaping of, and selection of environments;
5. mindful use of values;
6. overall quality (wisdom) of process of solution;
7. overall quality (wisdom) of the solution itself.

We will also collect other, more qualitative measures of students' wisdom-related skills. These other measures include evaluations of students' assignments completed during the twelve-week curriculum. For example, we will collect weekly journals, homework assignments, and reports that the students complete in each of the conditions. These measures will be rated according to the above criteria from the balance theory of wisdom.

Evaluating students' wisdom-related skills is only one part of a complete evaluation of the teaching for wisdom initiative. A second part is evaluating how closely and how well the wisdom and critical-thinking curricula were observed by teachers. Evaluating how closely the curricula were followed is essential to evaluation of the students' wisdom-related skills. For example, only if the wisdom curriculum is properly implemented can we expect students' wisdom-related skills to increase. Only if the critical-thinking curriculum is properly implemented can we expect to compare it against the effect of the wisdom curriculum. We plan to monitor the implementation of both curricula in four ways.

First, we are providing in-service professional training for teachers and helping them instantiate the curriculum as described in the curriculum handbook and we will assess their performance in the in-services. Second, we plan periodically to visit participating school classrooms and sit in on lectures and view lesson plans. Third, we intend to look at students' daily journals to check the content of the actual lesson plans they received. Fourth, we intend to survey the participating teachers for their thoughts on the curricula and on how well it was realized. Finally, we need to survey participating children for their evaluation of the curricula.

In addition to the above evaluations, we will ask students to complete two related measures: The Cornell Critical Thinking Test (CCTT; Ennis, 1987) and the Sternberg Triarchic Abilities Test, Level 1 (STAT; Sternberg, 1993). The Cornell Critical Thinking Test is a seventy-one-item, paper-and-pencil measure used to assess a student's ability to decide whether a set of premises supports a given conclusion, to judge the reliability of information, and whether specific statements follow from others. The STAT contains thirty-six multiple-choice and three essay items measuring analytical, creative, and practical thinking in the verbal, quantitative, and figural domains. Both these measures are designed to assess quality of thinking in middle-school students. They are included to assess whether effects from the wisdom and critical-thinking curricula are positively or negatively related to critical thinking and related skills.

We will also ask teachers to rate student achievements of various kinds in each condition before and after the twelve-week period to assess any possible transfer of the curricula to school performance.

CONCLUSIONS

The road to this new approach of teaching for wisdom is bound to be a rocky one. First, entrenched structures, whatever they may be, are difficult to change, and wisdom is neither taught in schools nor even discussed. Second, many people will not see the value of teaching something that shows no promise of raising conventional test scores. These scores, which formerly were predictors of more interesting criteria, have now become criteria, or ends in themselves. The society has lost track of why they ever mattered in the first place and they have engendered the same kind of mindless competition we see in people who relentlessly compare their economic achievements with those of others. Third, wisdom is much more difficult to develop than is the kind of achievement that can be developed and readily tested via multiple-choice tests. Finally, people who have gained influence and power in a society via one means are unlikely to want either to give up that power or to see a new criterion established on which they might not rank so favorably. Thus, there is no easy path to wisdom. There never was, and probably never will be.

Wisdom might bring us a world that would seek to better itself and the conditions of all the people in it. At some level, we as a society have a choice. What do we wish to maximize through our schooling? Is it just knowledge? Is it just intelligence? Or is it also wisdom? If it is wisdom, then we need to put our students on a much different course. We need to value not only how they use their outstanding individual abilities to maximize their attainments but also how they use their individual abilities to maximize the attainments of others. We need, in short, to value wisdom.

PART IV

SYNTHESIS

8

WICS: The Relations among Intelligence, Creativity, and Wisdom

The goal of this book is not only to discuss intelligence, creativity, and wisdom, but also to explore the interrelationships among them. These interrelationships can be assessed at two levels, at least based on the research we have done. The first level is that of implicit theories, the second, that of explicit theories.

IMPLICIT THEORIES

Sternberg (1985b), as mentioned earlier, assessed people's implicit theories of intelligence, creativity, and wisdom, as well as the implicit theories among these constructs. The study was done among experts and laypersons in the United States, and hence does not necessarily apply beyond this country.

Nonmetric multidimensional scaling was used to assess the dimensions for each construct. Table 8.1 shows the results of these scalings. Table 8.2 shows the intercorrelations of ratings of behaviors on a master list for different occupations of individuals. Note that there are differences in the correlations, and that, in business, creativity and wisdom show a negative correlation!

The data show that people's conceptions of intelligence overlap with, but go beyond, the skills measured by conventional intelligence tests. Thus, the problem-solving (fluid ability) and verbal-comprehension (crystallized ability) skills measured by intelligence tests appear most prominently in the dimensions of the derived implicit theory of intelligence. Thus, the intelligent individual is perceived as solving problems well, reasoning clearly, thinking logically, displaying a good vocabulary, and drawing on a large store of information – just the kinds of things conventional intelligence tests measure. But also embedded within people's conceptions of intelligence are ability to balance information, to be goal-oriented and aim for achievement of one's goals, and to show intelligence in worldly, as opposed to

TABLE 8.1. *Nonmetric multidimensional scaling solutions for behaviors*[a]

Intelligence	Creativity	Wisdom
I. Practical problem-solving ability	*I. Nonentrenchment*	*I. Reasoning ability*
Tends to see attainable goals and accomplish them	Makes up rules as he or she goes along	Has the unique ability to look at a problem or situation and solve it
Is good at distinguishing between correct and incorrect answers	Is impulsive	Has good problem-solving ability
Has good problem-solving ability	Takes chances	Has a logical mind
Has ability to change directions and use another procedure	Tends not to know own limitations and tries to do what others think is impossible	Is good at distinguishing between correct and incorrect answers
Has rationality: ability to reason clearly	Is emotional	Is able to apply knowledge to particular problems
Is able to apply knowledge to particular problems	Has a free spirit	Is able to put old information, theories, and so forth, together in a new way
Has the unique ability to look at a problem or situation and solve it	Builds castles in the sky	Has a huge store of information
Has a logical mind	Is a nonconformist	Has the ability to recognize similarities and differences
II. Verbal ability	Is unorthodox	Has rationality: ability to reason clearly
Can converse on almost any topic	*II. Integration and intellectuality*	Makes connections and distinctions between ideas and things
Attaches importance to ideas	Makes connections and distinctions between ideas and things	*II. Sagacity*
Is inquisitive	Has the ability to understand and interpret his or her environment	Displays concern for others
Studies and reads quite a lot	Has the ability to recognize similarities and differences	Considers advice
Has demonstrated a good vocabulary	Is able to grasp abstract ideas and focus his or her attention on those ideas	Understands people through dealing with a variety of people
Expresses broad concepts concisely	Is productive	Feels he or she can always learn from other people
Has a good command of language	Has a high IQ level	Knows self best
Has a huge store of information	Attaches importance to ideas	Is thoughtful
Attaches importance to well-presented ideas	Possesses ability for high achievement	Is fair
III. Intellectual balance and integration	Is always thinking	Is a good listener
Has the ability to recognize similarities and differences	Is able to put old information, theories, and so forth together in a new way	Is not afraid to admit making a mistake, will correct the mistake, learn, and go on
Makes connections and distinctions between ideas and things	*III. Aesthetic taste and imagination*	Listens to all sides of an issue
Listens to all sides of an issue	Has an appreciation of art, music, and so forth	*III. Learning from ideas and environment*
Is able to grasp abstract ideas and focus his or her attention on those ideas		Attaches importance to ideas

178

Is perceptive
Has the ability to integrate information
Has the ability to grasp complex situations

IV. *Goal orientation and attainment*
Tends to obtain and use information for specific purposes
Possesses ability for high achievement
Seeks out information, especially details
Is motivated by goals
Is inquisitive at an early age
Sees opportunities and knows when to take them

V. *Contextual intelligence*
Learns and remembers and gains information from past mistakes or successes
Has the ability to understand and interpret his or her environment
Knows what's going on in the world

VI. *Fluid throught*
Has a thorough grasp of mathematics, or good spatial ability, or both
Has a high IQ level
Thinks quickly

Likes to be alone when creating something new
Can write, draw, compose music
Has good taste
Uses the materials around him or her and makes something unique out of them
Is in harmony with the materials or processes of expression
Is imaginative

IV. *Decisional skill and flexibility*
Follows his or her gut feelings in making decisions after weighing the pros and cons
Has ability to change direction and use another procedure

V. *Perspicacity*
Questions societal norms, truisms, assumptions
Is perceptive
Is willing to take a stand

VI. *Drive for accomplishment and recognition*
Is motivated by goals
Likes to be complimented on his or her work
Is energetic
Has a sense of humor

VII. *Inquisitiveness*
Is inquisitive at an early age
Is inquisitive

VIII. *Intuition*
Has intuition

Is perceptive
Learns from other people's mistakes

IV. *Judgment*
Acts within own physical and intellectual limitations
Is sensible
Has good judgment at all times
Thinks before acting or making decisions
Is able to take the long view (as opposed to considering only short-term outcomes)
Thinks before speaking
Is a clear thinker

V. *Expeditious use of information*
Is experienced
Seeks out information, especially details
Has age, maturity, or longexperience
Learns and remembers and gains information from past mistakes or successes
Changes mind on basis of experience

VI. *Perspicacity*
Has intuition
Can offer solutions that are on the side of right and truth
Is able to see through things – read between the lines
Has the ability to understand and interpret his or her environment

---

[a] After Sternberg (1985b, pp. 614–616). Behaviors are listed in order of decreasing weights within dimension.
Note: Stress (formula 1) = .14, R^2 = .87.

179

strictly academic, contexts. People thus seem to be more concerned with the practical and worldly side of intelligence than are intelligence testers.

Conceptions of creativity overlap with those of intelligence, but there is much less emphasis in implicit theories of creativity on analytical abilities, whether they be directed toward abstract problems or toward verbal materials. For example, the very first dimension shows a greater emphasis on nonentrenchment, or the ability and willingness to go beyond ordinary limitations of self and environment and to think and act in unconventional and even dreamlike ways. The creative individual has a certain freedom of spirit and an unwillingness to be bound by the unwritten canons of society, characteristics not necessarily found in the highly intelligent individual. Implicit theories of creativity encompass a dimension of aesthetic taste and imagination absent in implicit theories of intelligence, and also encompass aspects of inquisitiveness and intuitiveness that do not seem to enter into the implicit theories of intelligence. Implicit theories of creativity go far beyond conventional psychometric creativity tests. A person's ability to think of unusual uses for a brick, or to form a picture based on a geometric outline, scarcely does justice to the kind of freedom of spirit and intellect captured in implicit theories of creativity.

Finally, the wise individual is perceived as having much the same analytical reasoning ability as the intelligent individual. But the wise person has a certain sagacity not necessarily found in the intelligent person: He or she listens to others, knows how to weigh advice, and knows how to deal with a variety of different kinds of people. In seeking as much information as possible for decision making, the wise individual reads between the lines as well as making use of the obviously available information. The wise individual is especially able to make clear, sensible, and fair judgments, and in doing so, takes a long-term as well as a short-term view of the consequences of the judgments made. The wise individual is perceived as profiting from the experience of others, and learning from others' mistakes, as well as from his or her own mistakes. This individual is not afraid to change his or her mind as experience dictates, and the solutions offered to complex problems tend to be the right ones. It is not surprising that the correlations between creativity and wisdom are the lowest of the three possible pairs (intelligence–creativity, intelligence–wisdom, creativity–wisdom) and in one case, the correlation is even negative: Whereas the wise person is perceived to be a conserver of worldly experience, the creative person is perceived to be a defier of such experience.

EXPLICIT THEORIES

The WICS (Wisdom, Intelligence, and Creativity Synthesized) theory views intelligence, creativity, and wisdom as different, but as involving fundamental similarities.

TABLE 8.2. *Intercorrelations of ratings of behaviors on master list for each occupation providing ratings*[a]

Measures	Intelligence	Creativity	Wisdom
Art			
Intelligence	1.00	.55	.78
Creativity		1.00	.48
Business			
Intelligence	1.00	.29	.51
Creativity		1.00	−.24
Philosophy			
Intelligence	1.00	.56	.42
Creativity		1.00	.37
Physics			
Intelligence	1.00	.64	.68
Creativity		1.00	.14
Laypersons			
Intelligence	1.00	.33	.75
Creativity		1.00	.27

[a] Based on Sternberg (1985b, Table 2, p. 612).

The Basic Relationships

The basic relationship between intelligence, creativity, and wisdom is shown in Figure 8.1. The basis for "intelligence" narrowly defined, as it is measured by successful intelligence, is the analytical aspect of successful intelligence. The basis for creativity is the creative aspect of successful intelligence. And the basis for wisdom is the practical aspect of successful intelligence, and in particular, tacit knowledge. Thus, successful intelligence lies at the basis of conventional intelligence, creativity, and wisdom. But there is more to each of these constructs than just successful intelligence. What is that something more?

The Role of Components

Metacomponents.   Metacomponents play a key role in intelligence, creativity, and wisdom. They form the central executive functions without which none of these three attributes could operate. To think intelligently, creatively, or wisely, one needs to be able to recognize the existence of problems, define the problems, formulate strategies to solve the problems, and so forth. The difference in their application lies in the kinds of problems to which they are applied.

In intelligence they are applied to several kinds of problems. First, when they are applied to relatively familiar kinds of problems that are somewhat

Conventional Intelligence	Creativity	Wisdom

Analytical Aspect	Creative Aspect	Practical Aspect

SUCCESSFUL INTELLIGENCE

FIGURE 8.1. The basic relation between successful intelligence, conventional intelligence, creativity, and wisdom.

abstracted from the world of everyday experience, they are applied to problems requiring analytical intelligence. Second, when they are applied to relatively novel kinds of problems that are relatively nonentrenched in nature, then they are applied to problems requiring creative intelligence. Third, when they are applied to relatively practical problems that are highly contextualized in nature, then they are applied to problems requiring practical intelligence.

All problems requiring creativity require creative intelligence, but not all problems requiring creative intelligence require creativity. Creativity – at least according to the investment theory – requires more than just creative intelligence. It also requires knowledge, certain thinking styles, certain personality attributes, and certain motivational attributes. Thus people can be creatively intelligent but not creative. They may think in novel ways, but perhaps lack the persistence, or the propensity toward risk-taking, or the willingness to grow that one needs to be fully creative. Problems requiring full creativity thus tend to be more complex than problems requiring just creative intelligence. For example, a conceptual-projection problem (about grue and bleen), as described earlier, requires creative intelligence. But it does not require creativity in the same sense that writing an important novel does. The novel involves far more components of creativity than does the conceptual-projection problem. Thus, coping with novelty is only one aspect of creativity.

Metacomponents are especially important to define and redefine creative problems. As Getzels and Csikszentmihalyi (1976) have pointed out, finding and then clearly defining good problems is an essential element of creativity. Metacomponents are also important for monitoring and evaluating one's products. No one, no matter how creative, hits the creative heights every time. A creative individual needs to devise a system to separate his or her own wheat from the chaff.

Metacomponents also apply in the solution of problems requiring wisdom. Much of the difficulty of a wisdom-related problem is in figuring out exactly what the problem is, whose interests are involved, and what their interests are. One then needs to formulate a strategy to deal with the problem and a way of monitoring whether the strategy is working.

Performance Components.   Performance components also are involved in solving each of the three kinds of problems. For example, one almost inevitably needs to make inferences in solving each kind of problem, whether it is in inferring relations in test-like analogy problems, inferring analogical relations in order to propose a new model of a phenomenon based on a model of a phenomenon (such as Freud's applying the hydraulic model to the psyche), or inferring what a participant in a negotiation really is looking for so that one can offer a wise solution that balances interests.

Knowledge-Acquisition Components.   Finally, knowledge-acquisition components are involved in all three kinds of problems as well.

In learning the meanings of new words embedded in context, the reader has to separate helpful and relevant information in context from extraneous material that is irrelevant to, or may actually get in the way of, learning the meaning of the words. Moreover, the reader must combine the selected information into a meaningful whole, using past information about the nature of words as a guide. Deciding what things would be useful for defining a new word and deciding what to do with these useful things once they are isolated are processes that are guided by the use of old information. The reader constantly seeks to connect the context of the unknown word to something with which he or she is familiar. Thus, we see that processing the available information requires three distinct operations: (a) locating relevant information in context, (b) combining this information into a meaningful whole, and (c) interrelating this information to what the reader already knows. These processes will be referred to from now on as selective encoding, selective combination, and selective comparison, respectively.

Selective encoding involves sifting out relevant from irrelevant information. When you encounter an unfamiliar word in context, cues relevant to deciphering its meaning are embedded within large amounts of unhelpful or possibly even misleading information. You must separate the wheat from the chaff by sifting out the relevant cues. Most readers selectively encode information without being aware that they are doing it. By becoming more aware of this process, you are in a better position to improve your use of it.

When you encounter an unfamiliar word, imagine the word to be the center of a network of information. Seek out cues concerning its meaning in the sentence where the unknown word occurs. Then expand your systematic search, checking the sentences surrounding it.

Consider the brief passage below. Even in this rather obvious example, there is much information to weed out. For instance, in order to figure out the meaning of the word *macropodida*, we need not know that the man in the passage was on a business trip, that he was tired, or that he squinted in the bright sunlight. Although such information may be quite relevant to the story as a whole, it is entirely irrelevant to our purpose of figuring out the meaning of the unknown word.

He first saw a *macropodida* during a trip to Australia. He had just arrived from a business trip to India, and he was exhausted. Looking out at the plain, he saw a *macropodida* hop across it. It was a typical marsupial. While he watched, the animal pranced to and fro, intermittently stopping to chew on the surrounding plants. Squinting because of the bright sunlight, he noticed a young *macropodida* securely fastened in an opening in front of the mother.

In the first sentence, there are two important cues: (1) the man saw a macropodida, so macropodidae must be visually perceptible, and (2) the man saw the macropodida in Australia, so macropodidae must be found in that continent. As we have seen, the second sentence does not contain any information relevant to the unknown word. The next sentence informs us that macropodidae hop and can be found on plains. In the fourth sentence, we learn that a macropodida is a marsupial, and in the fifth sentence, we find out something about what macropodidae eat. Finally, the last sentence informs us that mother macropodidae carry their young in openings on their front sides.

Normally, readers would not selectively encode all the available information before proceeding to combine and compare the relevant facts. Usually, readers will shift from one process to another as they proceed through the paragraph. Listing relevant data is merely an attempt to show you the kinds of information that can be selectively encoded.

Selective combination involves combining selectively encoded information in such a way as to form an integrated, plausible definition of the previously unknown word. Simply sifting out the relevant cues is not enough to arrive at a tentative definition of a word: We must know how to combine these cues into an integrated representation of the word. When we encounter an unfamiliar word, we must selectively encode information about the meaning of the word before we can do anything else, but we usually do not selectively encode all the relevant information before moving on to the selective combination of this information. The process of selective combination can begin just as soon as the second piece of information has been selectively encoded.

Typically, the available information can be combined in many ways, and inevitably, different persons will produce slightly different combinations. Usually, however, there is one optimal combination of information that exceeds in usefulness any other possibilities. You can imagine an analogy to the job detectives do. First, they have to decide what the relevant clues are in figuring out who committed the crime (selective encoding). Once they have figured out some relevant clues, they begin to combine them selectively in such a way as to build a plausible case against the suspect. Combining the clues in an improper way can result in a false lead, and ultimately, the apprehension of the wrong suspect. Just as the detective has to track down the individual who actually perpetrated the crime, you have to track down the meaning of the word that is appropriate in the given instance or instances.

Consider how the process of selective combination can be applied to the *macropodida* above. From the first sentence, we selectively encode the fact that macropodidae are something we can see, and that they are found in Australia. Thus, we know that they are something that we can see when we go to Australia. The third sentence provides us with the knowledge that macropodidae can be found on plains and that they hop. We thus now know that macropodidae are something that we can see hopping on the plains of Australia. We learn that they are marsupials, that they eat plants, and that they carry their young in front openings. In sum, we now know that macropodidae are plant-eating marsupials that can be seen hopping on the plains of Australia, and that may be carrying their young in openings in front of them.

We now have a fairly extensive network of information about the word macropodida. Putting all the information together in a systematic manner yields a definition: A macropodida is a kangaroo.

Selective comparison involves relating newly acquired information to information acquired in the past. As readers decide what information to encode and how to combine this information, what they already know about the topic can be quite useful as a guide. Any given bit of relevant information will probably be nearly useless if it cannot somehow be related to past knowledge. Without previous knowledge, the helpful hints that would normally lead readers to the definition of an unknown term will be meaningless, and the readers will probably not even recognize the hints as relevant information. New information can be related to old information, and vice versa, by the use of similes, metaphors, analogies, and models, but the goal is always the same: to give the new information meaning by connecting it to old information that is already known.

Look again at the passage above to analyze how selective comparison operates. In selective comparison, we try to establish how the new word is similar to and different from old words that we already have stored in memory. We may end up deciding either that the new word is a synonym for an old word that we already know, or that a new concept has to be constructed that expands on our old concepts. In the case of the macropodida, the more information we have, the more restricted is the range of things that it might be. Initially, it might be anything that we might see in Australia – a very long list. We are able to reduce our list as we learn that a macropodida is something seen on a plain and something that hops. We can restrict our list of possibilities further when we learn that it is a herbi-vorous marsupial. If our original list of things indigenous to or particularly characteristic of Australia included such items as Aborigines, kangaroos, sheep, and eucalyptus trees, our developing list can no longer include all these things. By the time we are done with the passage, the only item on the list that the passage could describe is the kangaroo. Thus, the process of selective comparison includes a whittling-down process whereby large numbers of possibilities are successively further reduced. Eventually, if only one possibility remains, that possibility is a likely synonym for the unknown word. If no possibilities remain, then we probably have to form a new concept that is related to, but different from, all old concepts we have stored in memory.

The knowledge-acquisition processes apply in creative thinking to in-sightful problem solving. The view of insight that we prefer (Davidson & Sternberg, 1984; Sternberg & Davidson, 1982) is that insight consists of not one, but three separate but related psychological processes.

Significant problems generally present us with large amounts of infor-mation, only some of which is relevant and worthy of selective encoding for problem solution. For example, the facts of a legal case are usually both numerous and confusing: An insightful lawyer must figure out which of the myriad facts are relevant to principles of law. Similarly, a doctor or a psychotherapist must sift out those facts that are relevant for diagnosis or treatment. Perhaps the occupation that most directly must employ se-lective encoding is that of the detective: In trying to figure out who has perpetrated a crime, the detective must figure out what the relevant facts are. Failure to do so may result in following up on false leads, or in having no leads to follow up on at all.

Selective combination involves combining what might originally seem to be isolated pieces of information into a unified whole that may or may not resemble its parts. For example, the lawyer must know how the relevant facts of a case fit together to make (or break) the case. A doctor or psy-chotherapist must be able to figure out how to combine information about various isolated symptoms to identify a given medical (or psychological) syndrome. A detective, having collected the facts that seem relevant to the case, must determine how they fit together to point at the guilty party rather than at anyone else.

Problem solving by analogy, for example, is an instance of selective comparison: The solver realizes that new information is similar to old in-formation in certain ways (and dissimilar from it in other ways) and uses this information better to understand the new information. For example, an insightful lawyer will relate a current case to past legal precedents; choos-ing the right precedent is absolutely essential. A doctor or psychotherapist relates the current set of symptoms to previous case histories. Again, choos-ing the right precedent is essential. A detective may have been involved in or know about a similar case where the same modus operandi was used to commit a crime. Drawing an analogy to the past case may be helpful to the detective both in understanding the nature of the crime and in figuring out who did it.

It should be evident that the processes of insight that are being proposed here are the same as the processes of knowledge acquisition proposed earlier. Is insight, then, really nothing at all special, but merely a mundane extension of knowledge-acquisition skills? We do not believe this to be the case. What seems to separate insightful use of selective encoding, selective combination, and selective comparison from ordinary use of these processes is the nonobviousness of how they are applied, or the nonobviousness of the appropriateness of their application. By contrast, the nature of the problem in learning vocabulary from context is very clear: The task is to define the unknown word. Moreover, the kinds of clues that are useful in defining an unknown word are circumscribed in scope. Thus, with practice, the finding and use of these clues can become fairly routine. In insightful selective encoding, selective combination, and selective comparison, it is not obvious how to apply these processes, and often it is not even obvious that they are appropriate in the first place.

The processes of insight are the same as ordinary cognitive processes, but the circumstances of their application are different. It is much more difficult to apply selective encoding, selective combination, and selective comparison in an insightful way than it is to apply them in a routine way.

Coping with Novelty Skills

Coping with novelty is relevant in conventional intelligence, creativity, and wisdom. In conventional intelligence, coping with novelty is involved in fluid abilities (see Carroll, 1993; Cattell, 1971). It is the essential ingredient of creative thinking. And most wisdom problems are at least somewhat novel; in other words, they present new aspects that old problems have not presented. When problems are more routine, they may be referred to as requiring common sense, but they are not likely to be referred to as requiring wisdom.

Practical Skills

Practical skills are involved in all three sets of skills as well. They are probably least involved in conventional intelligence. Here they are most likely to apply to knowing what kinds of strategies and solutions are expected in taking tests and in school (Williams et al., 1996, 2002). They are required in creativity to employ ideas so they can be implemented and one can convince others of their worth. And they are required in wisdom to solve the problems. Tacit knowledge is a basis for wise thinking.

IN SUM

In sum, the components of intelligence are at the base of successful intelligence, creativity, and wisdom. They are applied in intelligence, broadly defined, to experience in order to adapt to, shape, and select environments. When the components are involved in fairly abstract but familiar kinds of tasks, they are used analytically. When they are involved in relatively novel tasks and situations, they are used creatively. When they are involved in adaptation to, shaping of, and selection of environments, they are used practically.

Creative intelligence is a part of, but not the entirety of, human creativity. Creativity also involves aspects of knowledge, styles of thinking, personality, and motivation, as well as these psychological components in interaction with the environment. An individual with the intellectual skills for creativity but without the other personal attributes is unlikely to do creative work.

Wisdom results from the application of successful intelligence and creativity toward the common good through a balancing of intrapersonal, interpersonal, and extrapersonal interests over the short and long terms. Wisdom is not just a way of thinking about things; it is a way of doing things. If people wish to be wise, they have to act wisely, not just think wisely. We all can do this. Whether we do is our choice.

References

Abelson, R. P., Aronson, E., McGuire, W. J., Newcomb, T. M., Rosenberg, M. J., & Tannenbaum, P. H. (Eds.). (1968). *Theories of cognitive consistency: A sourcebook.* Chicago: Rand McNally.

Adams, J. L. (1974). *Conceptual blockbusting: A guide to better ideas.* San Francisco: Freeman.

Albert, R. S., & Runco, M. A. (1999). A history of research on creativity. In R. J. Sternberg (Ed.), *Handbook of creativity* (pp. 16–31). New York: Cambridge University Press.

Amabile, T. M. (1983). *The social psychology of creativity.* New York: Springer.

Amabile, T. M. (1996). *Creativity in context.* Boulder, CO: Westview.

Anastasi, A., & Urbina, S. (1997). *Psychological testing* (7th ed.). Upper Saddle River, NJ: Prentice-Hall.

Anderson, J. R. (1983). *The architecture of cognition.* Cambridge, MA: Harvard University Press.

Andrews, F. M. (1975). Social and psychological factors which influence the creative process. In I. A. Taylor & J. W. Getzels (Eds.), *Perspectives in creativity* (pp. 117–145). Chicago: Aldine.

Ardelt, M. (1997). Wisdom and life satisfaction in old age. *Journals of Gerontology Series B-Psychological Sciences & Social Sciences, 52B,* 15–27.

Arlin, P. K. (1990). Wisdom: the art of problem finding. In R. J. Sternberg (Ed.), *Wisdom: Its nature, origins, and development* (pp. 230–243). New York: Cambridge University Press.

Au, T. K., Sidle, A. L., Rollins, K. B. (1993). Developing an intuitive understanding of conservation and contamination: Invisible particles as a plausible mechanism. *Developmental Psychology, 29,* 286–299.

Azuma, H., & Kashiwagi, K. (1987). Descriptions for an intelligent person: A Japanese study. *Japanese Psychological Research, 29,* 17–26.

Baillargeon, R. L. (1987). Young infants' reasoning about the physical and spatial properties of a hidden object. *Cognitive Development 2*(3), 179–200.

Baltes, P. B. (1993). The aging mind: Potential and limits. *The Gerontologist, 33,* 580–594.

Baltes, P. B. (1994). *Wisdom*. Unpublished manuscript, Max-Planck-Institut für Bildungsforschung, Berlin.

Baltes, P. B., & Smith, J. (1987, August). *Toward a psychology of wisdom and its ontogenesis*. Paper presented at the Ninety-Fifth Annual Convention of the American Psychological Association, New York.

Baltes, P. B., & Smith, J. (1990). Toward a psychology of wisdom and its ontogenesis. In R. J. Sternberg (Ed.), *Wisdom: Its nature, origins, and development* (pp. 87–120). New York: Cambridge University Press.

Baltes, P. B., Smith, J., & Staudinger, U. (1992). Wisdom and successful aging. In T. B. Sonderegger (Ed.), *Psychology and aging* (pp. 123–167). Lincoln, NE: University of Nebraska Press.

Baltes, P. B., & Staudinger, U. (1993). The search for psychology of wisdom. *Current Directions in Psychological Science, 2,* 75–80.

Baltes, P. B., & Staudinger, U. M (2000). Wisdom: A metaheuristic (pragmatic) to orchestrate mind and virtue toward excellence. *American Psychologist, 55,* 122–135.

Baltes, P. B., Staudinger, U. M., Maercker, A., & Smith, J. (1995). People nominated as wise: A comparative study of wisdom-related knowledge. *Psychology and Aging, 10,* 155–166.

Bandura, A. (1977). Self-efficacy: Toward a unifying theory of behavioral change. *Psychological Review, 84,* 181–215.

Bandura, A. (1996). *Self-efficacy: The exercise of control*. New York: Freeman.

Barnes, M. L., & Sternberg, R. J. (1989). Social intelligence and decoding of nonverbal cues. *Intelligence, 13,* 263–287.

Barron, F. (1963). *Creativity and psychological health*. Princeton, NJ: Van Nostrand.

Barron, F. (1968). *Creativity and personal freedom*. New York: Van Nostrand.

Barron, F. (1969). *Creative person and creative process*. New York: Holt, Rinehart & Winston.

Barron, F., & Harrington, D. M. (1981). Creativity, intelligence, and personality. *Annual Review of Psychology, 32,* 439–476.

Basseches, J. (1984). *Dialectical thinking and adult development*. Norwood, NJ: Ablex.

Bateson, G. (1979). *Mind and nature*. London: Wildwood House.

Beilin, H. (1980). Piaget's theory: Refinement, revision, or rejection? In R. H. Kluwee & H. Spada (Eds.), *Developmental models of thinking* (pp. 245–261). New York: Academic Press.

Belmont, J. M., & Butterfield, E. C. (1971). What the development of short-term memory is. *Human Development, 14,* 236–248.

Belmont, J. M., Butterfield, E. C., & Ferretti, R. P. (1982). To secure transfer of training instruct self-management skills. In D. K. Detterman & R. J. Sternberg (Eds.), *How and how much can intelligence be increased*. Norwood, NJ: Ablex Publishing Company.

Bem, D. J. (1967). Self-perception: An alternative interpretation of cognitive dissonance phenomena. *Psychological Review, 74,* 183–200.

Bem, D. J. (1996). Exotic becomes erotic: A developmental theory of sexual orientation. *Psychological Review, 81,* 320–335.

Berry, J. W. (1974). Radical cultural relativism and the concept of intelligence. In J. W. Berry & P. R. Dasen (Eds.), *Culture and cognition: Readings in cross-cultural psychology* (pp. 225–229). London: Methuen.

Binet, A., & Simon, T. (1916a). *The development of intelligence in children*. Baltimore: Williams & Wilkins (originally published in 1905).

Binet, A., & Simon, T. (1916b). *The intelligence of the feeble-minded* (E. S. Kite, Trans.). Baltimore: Williams & Wilkins.

Bloom, B. S. (1976). *Human characteristics and school learning*. New York: McGraw-Hill.

Bloom, B. S., Engelhart, M. D., Frost, E. J., Hill, W. H., & Krathwohl, D. R. (1956). *Taxonomy of educational objectives. Handbook I: Cognitive domain*. New York: David McKay.

Bloom, H. (1994). *The Western canon: The books and school of the ages*. New York: Harcourt Brace.

Boden, M. A. (1992). *The creative mind: Myths and mechanisms*. New York: Basic Books.

Boden, M. A. (1999). Computer models of creativity. In R. J. Sternberg (Ed.), *Handbook of creativity* (pp. 351–372). New York: Cambridge University Press.

Boring, E. G. (1923, June 6). Intelligence as the tests test it. *New Republic*, 35–37.

Borkowski, J., & Wanschura, P. (1974). Mediational processes in the retarded. In N. Ellis (Ed.), *International review of research in mental retardation, Vol. 7*. New York: Academic Press.

Bouchard, T. J., Jr. (1997). IQ similarity in twins reared apart: Findings and responses to critics. In R. J. Sternberg & E. L. Grigorenko (Eds.), *Intelligence, heredity, and environment* (pp. 126–160). New York: Cambridge University Press.

Bouchard, T. J., Jr., Lykken, D. T., McGue, M., Segal, N. L., & Tellegen, A. (1990). Sources of human psychological differences: The Minnesota study of twins reared apart. *Science, 250*, 223–228.

Bowers, K. S., Regehr, G., Balthazard, C., & Parker, K. (1990). Intuition in the context of discovery. *Cognitive Psychology, 22*, 72–109.

Brainerd, C. J. (1978). The stage question in cognitive-developmental theory. *Behavioral and Brain Sciences, 1*, 173–182.

Brand, C. (1996). *The g factor: General intelligence and its implications*. Chichester, England: Wiley.

Bransford, J. D., & Stein, B. (1984). *The IDEAL problem solver*. New York: Freeman.

Bransford, J. D., & Stein, B. S. (1993). *The IDEAL problem solver: A guide for improving thinking, learning, and creativity* (2nd ed). New York: Freeman.

Bronfenbrenner, U., & Ceci, S. J. (1994). Nature-nurture reconceptualized in developmental perspective: A bioecological model. *Psychological Review, 101*, 568–586.

Brown, A. L., Bransford, J. D., Ferrara, R. A., & Campione, J. C. (1983). Learning, remembering, and understanding. In J. H. Flavell & E. M. Markman (Eds.), *Handbook of child psychology, Vol. III*. New York: Wiley.

Brown, A. L., & DeLoache, J. S. (1978). Skills, plans, and self-regulation. In R. Siegler (Ed.), *Children's thinking: What develops?* Hillsdale, NJ: Erlbaum.

Brown, A. L., & Ferrara, R. A. (1985). Diagnosing zones of proximal development. In J. V. Wertsch (Ed.), *Culture, communication, and cognition: Vygotskian perspectives* (pp. 273–305). New York: Cambridge University Press.

Brown, A. L., & French, A. L. (1979). The zone of potential development: Implications for intelligence testing in the year 2000. In R. J. Sternberg & D. K. Detterman (Eds.), *Human intelligence: Perspectives on its theory and measurement* (pp. 217–235). Norwood, NJ: Ablex.

Bryant, P. E., & Trabasso, T. (1971). Transitive inferences and memory in young children. *Nature, 232*(5311), 456–458.

Budoff, M. (1968). Learning potential as a supplementary assessment procedure. In J. Hellmuth (Ed.), *Learning disorders* (Vol. 3, pp. 295–343). Seattle, WA: Special Child.

Burt, C. (1949). Alternative methods of factor analysis and their relations to Pearson's method of "principal axis." *British Journal of Psychology, Statistical Section, 2,* 98–121.

Cage, J. (1961). *Silence.* Middletown, CT: Wesleyan University Press.

Campbell, D. T. (1960). Blind variation and selective retention in creative thought and other knowledge processes. *Psychological Review, 67,* 380–400.

Campione, J. C., Brown, A. L., & Ferrara, R. (1982). Mental retardation and intelligence. In R. J. Sternberg (Ed.), *Handbook of human intelligence* (pp. 392–490). New York: Cambridge University Press.

Cantor, N., & Kihlstrom, J. F. (1987). *Personality and social intelligence.* Englewood Cliffs, NJ: Prentice-Hall.

Carey, S. (1985). *Conceptual change in childhood.* Cambridge, MA: MIT Press.

Carroll, J. B. (1981). Ability and task difficulty in cognitive psychology. *Educational Researcher, 10,* 11–21.

Carroll, J. B. (1982). The measurement of intelligence. In R. J. Sternberg (Ed.), *Handbook of human intelligence* (pp. 29–120). New York: Cambridge University Press.

Carroll, J. B. (1993). *Human cognitive abilities: A survey of factor-analytic studies.* New York: Cambridge University Press.

Cattell, J. M. (1890). Mental tests and measurements. *Mind, 15,* 373–380.

Cattell, R. B. (1971). *Abilities: Their structure, growth and action.* Boston: Houghton Mifflin.

Cattell, R. B., & Cattell, H. E. P. (1973). *Measuring intelligence with the Culture Fair Tests.* Champaign, IL: Institute for Personality and Ability Testing.

Ceci, S. J. (1996). *On intelligence* (expanded ed.). Cambridge, MA: Harvard University Press.

Chadwick, W., & Courtivron, I. (Eds.). (1996). *Significant others: Creativity & intimate partnership.* New York: Thames & Hudson.

Chase, W. G., & Simon, H. A. (1973). The mind's eye in chess. In W. G. Chase (Ed.), *Visual information processing* (pp. 215–281). New York: Academic Press.

Chen, M. J. (1994). Chinese and Australian concepts of intelligence. *Psychology and Developing Societies, 6,* 101–117.

Chen, M. J., Braithwaite, V., & Huang, J. T. (1982). Attributes of intelligent behaviour: Perceived relevance and difficulty by Australian and Chinese students. *Journal of Cross-Cultural Psychology, 13,* 139–156.

Chen, M. J., & Chen, H. C. (1988). Concepts of intelligence: A comparison of Chinese graduates from Chinese and English schools in Hong Kong. *International Journal of Psychology, 223,* 471–487.

Chi, M. T. H., Feltovich, P. J., & Glaser, R. (1981). Categorization and representation of physics problems by experts and novices. *Cognitive Science, 5*, 121–152.

Chi, M. T. H., Glaser, R., & Farr, M. J. (Eds.). (1988). *The nature of expertise*. Hillsdale, NJ: Erlbaum.

Chi, M. T. H., Glaser, R., & Rees, E. (1982). Expertise in problem solving. In R. J. Sternberg (Ed.), *Advances in the psychology of human intelligence* (Vol. 1, pp. 7–75). Hillsdale, NJ: Erlbaum.

Chiesi, H. L., Spilich, G. J., & Voss, J. F. (1979). Acquisition of domain-related information in relation to high and low domain knowledge. *Journal of Verbal Learning and Verbal Behavior, 18*, 257–274.

Chomsky, N. (1957). *Syntactic structures*. The Hague, Netherlands: Mouton.

Clayton, V. (1975). Erickson's theory of human development as it applies to the aged: Wisdom as contradictory cognition. *Human Development, 18*, 119–128.

Clayton, V. (1976). *A multidimensional scaling analysis of the concept of wisdom*. Unpublished doctoral dissertation, University of Southern California.

Clayton, V., & Birren, J. E. (1980). The development of wisdom across the life-span: A reexamination of an ancient topic. In P. B. Baltes & O. G. Brim (Eds.), *Life-span development and behavior* (Vol. 3, pp. 103–135). New York: Academic Press.

Clement, J. (1989). Learning via model construction and criticism: Protocol evidence on sources of creativity in science. In G. Glover, R. Ronning, & C. Reynolds (Eds.), *Handbook of creativity* (pp. 341–381). New York: Plenum.

Collins, M. A., & Amabile, T. M. (1999). Motivation and creativity. In R. J. Sternberg (Ed.), *Handbook of creativity* (pp. 297–312). New York: Cambridge University Press.

Connolly, H., & Bruner, J. (1974). Competence: Its nature and nurture. In K. Connolly & J. Bruner (Eds.), *The growth of competence*. New York: Academic Press.

Cornell, E. H. (1978). Learning to find things: A reinterpretation of object permanence studies. In L. S. Siegel & C. J. Brainerd (Eds.), *Alternatives to Piaget: Critical essays on the theory* (pp. 11–27). New York: Academic Press.

Cox, C. M. (1926). *The early mental traits of three hundred geniuses*. Stanford, CA: Stanford University Press.

Craik, F. I. M., & Lockhart, R. S. (1972). Levels of processing: A framework for memory research. *Journal of Verbal Learning and Verbal Behavior, 11*, 671–684.

Cronbach, L. J. (1957). The two disciplines of scientific psychology. *American Psychologist, 12*, 671–684.

Crutchfield, R. (1962). Conformity and creative thinking. In H. Gruber, G. Terrell, & M. Wertheimer (Eds.), *Contemporary approaches to creative thinking* (pp. 120–140). New York: Atherton Press.

Csikszentmihalyi, M. (1988). Society, culture, and person: A systems view of creativity. In R. J. Sternberg (Ed.), *The nature of creativity* (pp. 325–339). New York: Cambridge University Press.

Csikszentmihalyi, M. (1996). *Creativity: Flow and the psychology of discovery and invention*. New York: HarperCollins.

Csikszentmihalyi, M., & Rathunde, K. (1990). The psychology of wisdom: An evolutionary interpretation. In R. J. Sternberg (Ed.), *Wisdom: Its nature, origins, and development* (pp. 25–51). New York: Cambridge University Press.

Cziko, Gary A. (1998). From blind to creative: In defense of Donald Campbell's selectionist theory of human creativity. *Journal of Creative Behavior, 32*, 192–208.

Darwin, C. (1859). *The origin of species.* London: Murray.

Das, J. P. (1994). Eastern views of intelligence. In R. J. Sternberg (Ed.), *Encyclopedia of human intelligence* (Vol. 1, pp. 387–391). New York: Macmillan.

Das, J. P., Kirby, J. R., & Jarman, R. F. (1979). *Simultaneous and successive cognitive processes.* New York: Academic Press.

Das, J. P., Naglieri, J. A., & Kirby, J. R. (1994). *Assessment of cognitive processes: The PASS theory of intelligence.* Needham Heights, MA: Allyn & Bacon.

Dasen, P. (1984). The cross-cultural study of intelligence: Piaget and the Baoule. *International Journal of Psychology, 19,* 407–434.

Davidson, J. E., & Sternberg, R. J. (1984). The role of insight in intellectual giftedness. *Gifted Child Quarterly, 28,* 58–64.

Davies, M., Stankov, L., & Roberts, R. D. (1998). Emotional intelligence: In search of an elusive construct. *Journal of Personality & Social Psychology, 75,* 989–1015.

Day, J. D., Engelhardt, J. L., Maxwell, S. E., & Bolig, E. E. (1997). Comparison of static and dynamic assessment procedures and their relation to independent performance. *Journal of Educational Psychology, 89*(2), 358–368.

De Bono, E. (1971). *Lateral thinking for management.* New York: McGraw-Hill.

De Bono, E. (1985). *Six thinking hats.* Boston: Little, Brown.

De Bono, E. (1992). *Serious creativity: Using the power of lateral thinking to create new ideas.* New York: HarperCollins.

DeGroot, A. D. (1965). *Thought and choice in chess.* The Hague: Mouton.

Derrida, J. (1992). *Acts of literature.* (D. Attridge, Ed.). New York: Routledge.

Dewey, J. (1933). *How we think.* Boston: Heath.

Donchin E., Ritter, W., & McCallum, W. C. (1978). Cognitive psychophysiology: The endogenous components of the ERP. In P. Tueting & S. H. Koslow (Eds.), *Event-related brain potentials in man* (pp. 349–441). New York: Academic Press.

Donders, F. C. (1868/1969). Over de snelheid van psychische processen. Onderzoekingen gedaan in het Physiologisch Laboratorium der Utrechtsche Hoogeschool. *Tweede reeks, II,* 92–120.

Dreyfus, H. L. (1992). *What computers still can't do.* Cambridge, MA: MIT Press.

Duncker, K. (1945). On problem solving. *Psychological Monographs, 68*(5), 270.

Durojaiye, M. O. A. (1993). Indigenous psychology in Africa. In U. Kim & J. W. Berry (Eds.), *Indigenous psychologies: Research and experience in cultural context* (pp. 211–220). Newbury Park, CA: Sage.

Dweck, C. S. (1999). *Self-theories: Their role in motivation, personality, and development.* Philadelphia: Psychology Press/Taylor & Francis.

Elkind, D. (1976). *Child development and education: a Piagetian perspective.* New York: Oxford University Press.

Ennis, R. H. (1987). A taxonomy of crticial thinking dispositions and abilities. In J. B. Baron & R. J. Sternberg (Eds.), *Teaching thinking skills: Theory and practice* (pp. 9–26). New York: Freeman.

Epstein, S. (1985). The implications of cognitive-experiential self-theory for research in social psychology and personality. *Journal for the Theory of Social Behaviour, 15,* 283–310.

Ericsson, K. A. (Ed.). (1996). *The road to excellence.* Mahwah, NJ: Lawrence Erlbaum Associates.

Ericsson, K. A., & Smith, J. (1991). Prospects and limits in the empirical study of expertise: An introduction. In K. A. Ericsson & J. Smith (Eds.), *Toward a general theory of expertise: Prospects and limits* (pp. 19–38). Cambridge, U.K.: Cambridge University Press.

Evans, J. (1989). Problem solving, reasoning and decision making. In A. D. Baddeley & N. O. Bernsen (Eds.), *Cognitive psychology: Research directions in cognitive science: European perspective* (Vol. 1, pp. 85–102). Hove, U.K.: Lawrence Erlbaum Associates.

Eysenck, H. J. (1993). Creativity and personality: A theoretical perspective. *Psychological Inquiry, 4,* 147–178.

Fazio, R. H., Zanna, M. P., & Cooper, J. (1977). Dissonance and self-perception: An integrative view of each theory's proper domain of application. *Journal of Experimental Social Psychology, 13,* 464–479.

Festinger, L., & Carlsmith, J. M. (1959). Cognitive consequences of forced compliance. *Journal of Abnormal and Social Psychology, 58,* 203–210.

Feuerstein, R. (1979). *The dynamic assessment of retarded performers: The learning potential assessment device theory, instruments, and techniques.* Baltimore, MD: University Park Press.

Feuerstein, R. (1980). *Instrumental enrichment: An intervention program for cognitive modifiability.* Baltimore, MD: University Park Press.

Field, D. (1987). A review of preschool conservation training: An analysis of analyses. *Developmental Review, 7*(3), 210–251.

Findlay, C. S., & Lumsden, C. J. (1988). The creative mind: Toward an evolutionary theory of discovery and invention. *Journal of Social and Biological Structures, 11,* 3–55.

Finke, R. (1990). *Creative imagery: Discoveries and inventions in visualization.* Hillsdale, NJ: Lawrence Erlbaum Associates.

Finke, R. A. (1995). Creative insight and preinventive forms. In R. J. Sternberg & J. E. Davidson (Eds.), *The nature of insight* (pp. 255–280). Cambridge, MA: MIT Press.

Finke, R. A., Ward, T. B., & Smith, S. M. (1992). *Creative cognition: Theory, research, and applications.* Cambridge, MA: MIT Press.

Flavell, J. H. (1971). Stage-related properties of cognitive development. *Cognitive Psychology, 2*(4), 421–453.

Flavell, J. H. (1981). Cognitive monitoring. In W. P. Dickson (Ed.), *Children's oral communication skills* (pp. 35–60). New York: Academic Press.

Flavell, J. H., & Wellman, H. M. (1977). Metamemory. In R. V. Kail, Jr. & J. W. Hagen (Eds.), *Perspectives on the development of memory and cognition.* Hillsdale, NJ: Lawrence Erlbaum Associates.

Flescher, I. (1963). Anxiety and achievement of intellectually gifted and creatively gifted children. *Journal of Psychology, 56,* 251–268.

Flynn, J. R. (1984). The mean IQ of Americans: Massive gains 1932 to 1978. *Psychological Bulletin, 95,* 29–51.

Flynn, J. R. (1987). Massive IQ gains in 14 nations. *Psychological Bulletin, 101,* 171–191.

Flynn, J. R. (1998). WAIS-III and WISC-III gains in the United States from 1972 to 1995: How to compensate for obsolete norms. *Perceptual & Motor Skills, 86,* 1231–1239.

Fraser, S. (Ed.). (1995). *The bell curve wars: Race, intelligence and the future of America.* New York: Basic Books.

Frensch, P. A., & Sternberg, R. J. (1989). Expertise and intelligent thinking: When is it worse to know better? In R. J. Sternberg (Ed.), *Advances in the psychology of human intelligence* (Vol. 5, pp. 157–158). Hillsdale, NJ: Lawrence Erlbaum Associates.

Freud, S. (1908/1959). The relation of the poet to day-dreaming. In *Collected papers* (Vol. 4, pp. 173–183). London: Hogarth Press.

Freud, S. (1910/1964). *Leonardo da Vinci and a memory of his childhood.* New York: Norton (original work published in 1910).

Galton, F. (1869). *Hereditary genius: An inquiry into its laws and consequences.* London: Macmillan.

Galton, F. (1883). *Inquiry into human faculty and its development.* London: Macmillan.

Garcia, J., & Koelling, R. A. (1966). The relation of cue to consequence in avoidance learning. *Psychonomic Science, 4,* 123–124.

Gardner, H. (1983). *Frames of mind: The theory of multiple intelligences.* New York: Basic Books.

Gardner, H. (1993). *Multiple intelligences: The theory in practice.* New York: Basic Books.

Gardner, H. (1994). The stories of the right hemisphere. In W. D. Spaulding, et al. (Eds.), *Integrative views of motivation, cognition, and emotion. Nebraska symposium on motivation* (Vol. 41, pp. 57–69). Lincoln, NE: University of Nebraska Press.

Gardner, H. (1995). *Leading minds.* New York: Basic Books.

Gardner, H. (1999). *Intelligence reframed: Multiple intelligences for the 21st century.* New York: Basic Books.

Gardner, H., Krechevsky, M., Sternberg, R. J., & Okagaki, L. (1994). Intelligence in context: Enhancing students' practical intelligence for school. In K. McGilly (Ed.), *Classroom lessons: Integrating cognitive theory and classroom practice* (pp. 105–127). Cambridge, MA: MIT Press.

Gazzaniga, M. S., Ivry, R. B., Mangun, G. (1998). *Cognitive neuroscience: The biology of the mind.* New York: W.W. Norton & Co.

Getzels, J., & Csikszentmihalyi, M. (1976). *The creative vision: A longitudinal study of problem finding in art.* New York: Wiley–Interscience.

Getzels, J. W., & Jackson, P. W. (1962). *Creativity and intelligence: Explorations with gifted students.* New York: John Wiley & Sons.

Ghiselin, B. (Ed.). (1985). *The creative process: A symposium.* Berkeley, CA: University of California Press.

Gigerenzer, G., Todd, P. M., & The ABC Research Group. (1999). *Simple heuristics that make us smart.* New York: Oxford University Press.

Gill, R., & Keats, D. M. (1980). Elements of intellectual competence: Judgments by Australian and Malay university students. *Journal of Cross-Cultural Psychology, 11,* 233–243.

Gilligan, C. (1982). *In a different voice: Psychological theory and women's development.* Cambridge, MA: Harvard University Press.

Gleitman, H. (1986). *Psychology* (2nd Ed.). New York: W. W. Norton & Co.

Golann, S. E. (1962). The creativity motive. *Journal of Personality, 30,* 588–600.

Goleman, D. (1995). *Emotional intelligence.* New York: Bantam Books.

Goodman, N. (1955). *Fact, fiction, and forecast*. Cambridge, MA: Harvard University Press.

Goodnow, J. J. (1976). The nature of intelligent behavior: Questions raised by cross-cultural studies. In L. Resnick (Ed.), *The nature of intelligence* (pp. 169–188). Hillsdale, NJ: Lawrence Erlbaum Associates.

Gordon, W. J. J. (1961). *Synectics: The development of creative capacity*. New York: Harper & Row.

Gough, H. G. (1979). A creativity scale for the Adjective Check List. *Journal of Personality and Social Psychology, 37,* 1398–1405.

Gould, S. J. (1981). *The mismeasure of man*. New York: W. W. Norton & Co.

Gould, S. J. (1995). Curveball. In S. Fraser (Ed.), *The bell curve wars* (pp. 11–22). New York: Basic Books.

Green, D. R., Ford, M. P., & Flamer, G. B. (1971). *Measurement and Piaget*. New York: McGraw-Hill.

Greenfield, P. M. (1997). You can't take it with you: Why abilities assessments don't cross cultures. *American Psychologist, 52*(10), 1115–1124.

Grigorenko, E. L., Geissler, P. W., Prince, R., Okatcha, F., Nokes, C., Kenny, D. A., Bundy, D. A., & Sternberg, R. J. (2001). The organisation of Luo conceptions of intelligence: A study of implicit theories in a Kenyan village. *International Journal of Behavioral Development, 25*(4), 367–378.

Grigorenko, E. L., Gil, G., Jarvin, L., & Sternberg, R. J. (2000). Toward a validation of aspects of the theory of successful intelligence. Unpublished manuscript.

Grigorenko, E. L., Jarvin, L., & Sternberg, R. J. (2002). School-based tests of the triarchic theory of intelligence: Three settings, three samples, three syllabi. *Contemporary Educational Psychology, 27,* 167–208.

Grigorenko, E. L., & Sternberg, R. J. (1998). Dynamic testing. *Psychological Bulletin, 124,* 75–111.

Grigorenko, E. L., & Sternberg, R. J. (2001). Analytical, creative, and practical intelligence as predictors of self-reported adaptive functioning: A case study in Russia. *Intelligence, 29,* 57–73.

Grotzer, T. A., & Perkins, D. A. (2000). Teaching of intelligence: A performance conception. In R. J. Sternberg (Ed.), *Handbook of intelligence* (pp. 492–515). New York: Cambridge University Press.

Gruber, H. E. (1981). *Darwin on man: A psychological study of scientific creativity* (2nd ed.). Chicago: University of Chicago Press. (Original work published 1974.)

Gruber, H. E. (1989). The evolving systems approach to creative work. In D. B. Wallace & H. E. Gruber (Eds.), *Creative people at work: Twelve cognitive case studies* (pp. 3–24). New York: Oxford University Press.

Gruber, H. E., & Davis, S. N. (1988). Inching our way up Mount Olympus: The evolving-systems approach to creative thinking. In R. J. Sternberg (Ed.), *The nature of creativity* (pp. 243–270). New York: Cambridge University Press.

Gruber, H. E., & Wallace, D. B. (1999). The case study method and evolving systems approach for understanding unique creative people at work. In R. J. Sternberg (Ed.), *Handbook of creativity* (pp. 93–115). New York: Cambridge University Press.

Guilford, J. P. (1950). Creativity. *American Psychologist, 5,* 444–454.

Guilford, J. P. (1967). *The nature of human intelligence*. New York: McGraw-Hill.

Guilford, J. P. (1968). Intelligence has three facets. *Science, 160*(3828), 615–620.

Guilford, J. P. (1982). Cognitive psychology's ambiguities: Some suggested remedies. *Psychological Review, 89*, 48–59.

Guilford, J. P., & Hoepfner, R. (1971). *The analysis of intelligence.* New York: McGraw-Hill.

Gustafsson, J. E. (1984). A unifying model for the structure of intellectual abilities. *Intelligence, 8*, 179–203.

Gustafsson, J. E. (1988). Hierarchical models of the structure of cognitive abilities. In R. J. Sternberg (Ed.), *Advances in the psychology of human intelligence* (Vol. 4, pp. 35–71). Hillsdale, NJ: Lawrence Erlbaum Associates.

Guthke, J. (1993). Current trends in theories and assessment of intelligence. In J. H. M. Hamers, K. Sijtsma, & A. J. J. M. Ruijssenaars (Eds.), *Learning potential assessment* (pp. 13–20). Amsterdam: Swets & Zeitlinger.

Guttman, L. (1954). A new approach to factor analysis: The radix. In P. F. Lazarsfeld (Ed.), *Mathematical thinking in the social sciences* (pp. 258–348). New York: Free Press.

Guyote, M. J., & Sternberg, R. J. (1981). A transitive-chain theory of syllogistic reasoning. *Cognitive Psychology, 13*, 461–525.

Haier, R. J., Nuechterlein, K. H., Hazlett, E., Wu, J. C., Pack, J., Browning, H. L., & Buchsbaum, M. S. (1988). Cortical glucose metabolic rate correlates of abstract reasoning and attention studied with positron emission tomography. *Intelligence, 12*, 199–217.

Haier, R. J., Siegel, B., Tang, C., Abel, L., & Buchsbaum, M. S. (1992). Intelligence and changes in regional cerebral glucose metabolic rate following learning. *Intelligence, 16*, 415–426.

Halpern, D. F. (1996). *Thought and knowledge: An introduction to critical thinking* (2nd ed.). Mahwah, NJ: Lawrence Erlbaum Associates.

Halstead, W. C. (1951). Biological intelligence. *Journal of Personality, 20*, 118–130.

Hamm, C. (1980). John Cage. In *The new Grove dictionary of music and musicians* (Vol. 3, pp. 597–603). London: Macmillan.

Harris, Robert. (1992). *Fatherland.* New York: Random House.

Hartt, F. (1993). *Art: A history of painting, sculpture, architecture* (4th Ed.). Englewood Cliffs, NJ: Prentice Hall.

Hayes, J. R. (1989). Cognitive processes in creativity. In J. A. Glover, R. R. Ronning, & C. R. Reynolds (Eds.), *Handbook of creativity* (pp. 135–145). New York: Plenum.

Haywood, H. C., & Tzuriel, D. (Eds.). (1992). *Interactive assessment.* New York: Springer-Verlag.

Hebb, D. O. (1949). *The organization of behavior: A neuropsychological theory.* New York: Wiley.

Hedlund, J., Horvath, J. A., Forsythe, G. B., Snook, S., Williams, W. M., Bullis, R. C., Dennis, M., & Sternberg, R. J. (1998). *Tacit Knowledge in Military Leadership: Evidence of Construct Validity* (Technical Report 1080). Alexandria, VA: U.S. Army Research Institute for the Behavioral and Social Sciences.

Hegel, G. W. F. (1931). *The phenomenology of the mind* (2nd ed.; J. D. Baillie, Trans). London: Allen & Unwin (original work published 1807).

Hendrickson A. E., & Hendrickson, D. E. (1980). The biological basis for individual differences in intelligence. *Personality and Individual Differences, 1*, 3–33.

Hennessey, B. A., & Amabile, T. M. (1988). The conditions of creativity. In R. J. Sternberg (Ed.), *The nature of creativity* (pp. 11–38). New York: Cambridge University Press.

Herr, E. L., Moore, G. D., & Hasen, J. S. (1965). Creativity, intelligence, and values: A study of relationships. *Exceptional Children, 32,* 114–115.

Herrnstein, R. J., & Murray, C. (1994). *The bell curve.* New York: Free Press.

Hoffman, R. R. (Ed.). (1992). *The psychology of expertise: Cognitive research and empirical AI.* New York: Springer-Verlag.

Holliday, S. G., & Chandler, M. J. (1986). *Wisdom: explorations in adult competence.* Basel, Switzerland: Karger.

Holzinger, K. J. (1938). Relationships between three multiple orthogonal factors and four bifactors. *Journal of Educational Psychology, 29,* 513–519.

Horn, J. L. (1967). On subjectivity in factor analysis. *Educational and Psychological Measurement, 27,* 811–820.

Horn, J. L. (1994). Theory of fluid and crystallized intelligence. In R. J. Sternberg (Ed.), *The encyclopedia of human intelligence* (Vol. 1, pp. 443–451). New York: Macmillan.

Horn, J. L., & Knapp, J. R. (1973). On the subjective character of the empirical base of Guilford's structure-of-intellect model. *Psychological Bulletin, 80,* 33–43.

Horn, J. L., & Knapp, J. R. (1974). Thirty wrongs do not make a right: Reply to Guilford. *Psychological Bulletin, 81*(8), 502–504.

Howe, M. J., Davidson, J. W., & Sloboda, J. A. (1998). Innate talents: Reality or myth? *Behavioral & Brain Sciences, 21,* 399–442.

Humphreys, L. (1962). The organization of human abilities. *American Psychologist, 17,* 475–483.

Hunt, E. B. (1980). Intelligence as an information-processing concept. *British Journal of Psychology, 71,* 449–474.

Hunt, E. B. (1995). *Will we be smart enough? A cognitive analysis of the coming workforce.* New York: Russell Sage Foundation.

Hunt, E., Frost, N., & Lunneborg, C. (1973). Individual differences in cognition: A new approach to intelligence. In G. Bower (Ed.), *The psychology of learning and motivation* (Vol. 7, pp. 87–122). New York: Academic Press.

Hunt, E. B., Lunneborg, C., & Lewis, J. (1975). What does it mean to be high verbal? *Cognitive Psychology, 7,* 194–227.

Intelligence and its measurement: A symposium (1921). *Journal of Educational Psychology, 12,* 123–147, 195–216, 271–275.

Irvine, J. T. (1978). "Wolof magical thinking": Culture and conservation revisited. *Journal of Cross-Cultural Psychology, 9,* 300–310.

Jacoby, R. & Glauberman, N. (Eds.). (1995). *The bell curve debate.* New York: Times Books.

Janis, I. L. (1972). *Victims of groupthink.* Boston: Houghton-Mifflin.

Jensen, A. R. (1969). Intelligence, learning ability and socioeconomic status. *Journal of Special Education, 3,* 23–35.

Jensen, A. R. (1979). g: Outmoded theory or unconquered frontier? *Creative Science and Technology, 2,* 16–29.

Jensen, A. R. (1982). Reaction time and psychometric g. In H. J. Eysenck (Ed.), *A model for intelligence.* Heidelberg: Springer-Verlag.

Jensen, A. R. (1997). The puzzle of nongenetic variance. In R. J. Sternberg & E. L. Grigorenko (Eds.), *Intelligence, heredity, and environment* (pp. 42–88). New York: Cambridge University Press.

Jensen, A. R. (1998). *The g factor: The science of mental ability.* Westport, CT: Praeger/Greenwoood.

Jensen, A. R. (2002). Psychometric g: Definition and substantiation. In R. J. Sternberg & E. L. Grigorenko (Eds.), *The general factor of intelligence: How general is it?* (pp. 39–53). Mahwah, NJ: Lawrence Erlbaum Associates.

Johnson, R., Jr. (1986). A triarchic model of P300 amplitude. *Psychophysiology, 23,* 367–384.

Johnson, R., Jr. (1988). The amplitude of the P300 component of the vent-related potential: Review and synthesis. In P. K. Ackles, J. R. Jennings, & M. G. H. Coles (Eds.), *Advances in psychophysiology: A research manual* (Vol. 3, pp. 69–138). Greenwich, CT: CAI Press.

Johnson-Laird, P. N. (1988). Freedom and constraint in creativity. In R. J. Sternberg (Ed.), *The nature of creativity* (pp. 202–219). New York: Cambridge University Press.

John-Steiner, V. (2000). *Creative collaboration.* New York: Oxford University Press.

Kamin, L. (1974). *The science and politics of IQ.* Hillsdale, NJ: Lawrence Erlbaum Associates.

Kaplan, C. A., & Simon, H. A. (1990). In search of insight. *Cognitive Psychology, 22,* 374–419.

Katz, H., & Beilin, H. (1976). A test of Bryant's claims concerning the young child's understanding of quantitative invariance. *Child Development, 47,* 877–880.

Kauffman, S. (1995). *At home in the universe: The search for laws of self-organization and complexity.* New York: Oxford University Press.

Kaufman, A. S., & Kaufman, N. L. (1983). *Kaufman assessment battery for children: Interpretive manual.* Circle Pines, MN: American Guidance Service.

Keating, D. P., & Bobbit, B. (1978). Individual and developmental differences in cognitive processing components of mental ability. *Child Development, 49,* 155–169.

Keil, F. C. (1989). *Concepts, kinds, and cognitive development.* Cambridge, MA: MIT Press.

Kekes, J. (1995). *Moral wisdom and good lives.* Ithaca, NY: Cornell University Press.

Kihlstrom, J. F., & Cantor, N. (2000). Social intelligence. In R. J. Sternberg (Ed.), *Handbook of intelligence* (2nd ed.) (pp. 359–379). Cambridge, U.K.: Cambridge University Press.

Kipling, R. (1985). Working-tools. In B. Ghiselin (Ed.), *The creative process: A symposium* (pp. 161–163). Berkeley, CA: University of California Press (original article published 1937).

Kitchener, K. S. (1983). Cognition, metacognition, and epistemic cognition: A three-level model of cognitive processing. *Human Development, 4,* 222–232.

Kitchener, K. S. (1986). Formal reasoning in adults: A review and critique. In R. A. Mines & K. S. Kitchener (Eds.), *Adult cognitive development.* New York: Praeger.

Kitchener, K. S., & Brenner, H. G. (1990). Wisdom and reflective judgment: Knowing in the face of uncertainty. In R. J. Sternberg (Ed.), *Wisdom: Its nature, origins, and development* (pp. 212–229). New York: Cambridge University Press.

Kitchener, K. S., & Kitchener, R. F. (1981). The development of natural rationality: Can formal operations account for it? In J. Meacham & N. R. Santilli (Eds.), *Social development in youth: Structure and content*. Basel, Switzerland: Karger.

Koestler, A. (1964). *The act of creation*. New York: Dell.

Kohlberg, L. (1969). Stage and sequence: The cognitive-developmental approach to socialization. In G. A. Goslin (Ed.), *Handbook of socialization theory and research* (pp.347–380). Chicago: Rand McNally.

Kohlberg, L. (1983). *The psychology of moral development*. New York: Harper & Row.

Kramer, D. A. (1990). Conceptualizing wisdom: The primacy of affect-cognition relations. In R. J. Sternberg (Ed.), *Wisdom: Its nature, origins, and development* (pp. 279–313). New York: Cambridge University Press.

Kris, E. (1952). *Psychoanalytic exploration in art*. New York: International Universities Press.

Kroeber, A. L., & Kluckhohn, C. (1952). Culture: A critical review of concepts and definitions. *Papers. Peabody Museum of Archaeology & Ethnology, Harvard University, 47*, viii, 223.

Kruskal, J. B. (1964a). Multidimensional scaling by optimizing goodness of fit to a nonmetric hypothesis. *Psychometrika, 20*, 1–27.

Kruskal, J. B. (1964b). Nonmetric multidimensional scaling: A numerical method. *Psychometrika, 20*, 115–129.

Kubie, L. S. (1958). *The neurotic distortion of the creative process*. Lawrence: University of Kansas Press.

Kuhn, T. S. (1970). *The structure of scientific revolutions* (2nd ed.). Chicago: University of Chicago Press.

Laboratory of Comparative Human Cognition (1982). Culture and intelligence. In R. J. Sternberg (Ed.), *Handbook of human intelligence* (pp. 642–719). New York: Cambridge University Press.

Labouvie-Vief, G. (1980). Beyond formal operations: Uses and limits of pure logic in life span development. *Human Development, 23*, 141–161.

Labouvie-Vief, G. (1982). Dynamic development and mature autonomy. *Human Development, 25*, 161–191.

Labouvie-Vief, G. (1990). Wisdom as integrated thought: Historical and developmental perspectives. In R. J. Sternberg (Ed.), *Wisdom: Its nature, origins, and development* (pp. 52–83). New York: Cambridge University Press.

Langer, E. J. (1997). *The power of mindful learning*. Reading, MA: Addison-Wesley Publishing Co, Inc.

Langley, P., Simon, H.A., Bradshaw, G.L., & Zytkow, J.M. (1987). *Scientific discovery: Computational explorations of the creative processes*. Cambridge, MA: MIT Press.

Larkin, J. H., McDermott, J., Simon, D. P., & Simon, H. A. (1980). Expert and novice performance in solving physics problems. *Science, 208*, 1335–1342.

Lemann, N. (1999). *The big test: The secret history of the American meritocracy*. New York: Farrar, Straus & Giroux.

Levine, A. (1998). Succeeding as a leader; failing as a president. *Change*, January/February, 43–45.

Lewontin, R. (1982). *Human diversity*. New York: Freeman.

Lidz, C. S. (Ed.). (1987). *Dynamic assessment*. New York: Guilford Press.

Lidz, C. S. (1991). *Practitioner's guide to dynamic assessment*. New York: Guilford Press.

Lipman, M. (1982). *Harry Stottlemeier's discovery.* Upper Montclair, NJ: First Mountain Foundation.

Lipman, M., Sharp, A. M., & Oscanyan, F. S. (1980). *Philosophy in the classroom.* Philadelphia, PA: Temple University Press.

Loehlin, J. C. (1989). Group differences in intelligence. In R. J. Sternberg (Ed.), *Handbook of intelligence* (pp. 176–193). New York: Cambridge University Press.

Loehlin, J. C., Horn, J. M., & Willerman, L. (1997). Heredity, environment, and IQ in the Texas adoption project. In R. J. Sternberg & E. L. Grigorenko (Eds.), *Intelligence, heredity, and environment* (pp. 105–125). New York: Cambridge University Press.

Lubart, T. I. (1990). Creativity and cross-cultural variation. *International Journal of Psychology, 25,* 39–59.

Lubart, T. I. (1994). Creativity. In R. J. Sternberg (Ed.), *Thinking and problem solving* (pp. 290–332). San Diego: Academic Press.

Lubart, T. I., & Sternberg, R. J. (1995). An investment approach to creativity: Theory and data. In S. M. Smith, T. B. Ward, & R. A. Finke (Eds.), *The creative cognition approach.* Cambridge, MA: MIT Press.

Luria, A. R. (1973). *The working brain.* New York: Basic Books.

Luria, A. R. (1980). *Higher cortical functions in man* (2nd ed., rev & expanded). New York: Basic Books.

Lutz, C. (1985). Ethnopsychology compared to what? Explaining behaviour and consciousness among the Ifaluk. In G. M. White & J. Kirkpatrick (Eds.), *Person, self, and experience: Exploring Pacific ethnopsychologies* (pp. 35–79). Berkeley: University of California Press.

Machlis, J. (1979). *Introduction to contemporary music* (2nd ed.). New York: W. W. Norton & Co.

MacKinnon, D. W. (1965). Personality and the realization of creative potential. *American Psychologist, 20,* 273–281.

Mackintosh, N. J. (1998). *IQ and human intelligence.* Oxford: Oxford University Press.

Maduro, R. (1976). *Artistic creativity in a Brahmin painter community.* Research monograph 14, Berkeley, CA: Center for South and Southeast Asia Studies, University of California.

Maslow, A. (1967). The creative attitude. In R. L. Mooney & T. A. Rasik (Eds.), *Explorations in creativity* (pp. 43–57). New York: Harper & Row.

Maslow, A. (1968). *Toward a psychology of being.* New York: Van Nostrand.

Mayer, J. D., & Gehr, G. (1996). Emotional intelligence and the identification of emotion. *Intelligence, 22,* 89–114.

Mayer, J. D., & Salovey, P. (1993). The intelligence of emotional intelligence. *Intelligence, 17,* 433–442.

Mayer, J. D., Salovey, P., Caruso, D. (2000a). Emotional intelligence. In R. J. Sternberg (Ed.), *Handbook of intelligence* (pp. 396–421). New York: Cambridge University Press.

Mayer, J. D., Salovey, P., Caruso, D. (2000b). Emotional intelligence meets traditional standards for an intelligence. *Intelligence, 27,* 267–298.

Mayer, M. (1976). *Professor Wormbog in search of the Zipperump-a-zoo.* New York: Golden Press.

McClelland, D. C. (1985). *Human motivation.* New York: Scott Foresman.

McClelland, D. C., Atkinson, J. W., Clark, R. A., & Lowell, E. L. (1953). *The achievement motive.* New York: Appleton-Century-Crofts, Inc.

McClelland, D. C., Atkinson, J. W., Clark, R. A., & Lowell, E. L. (1976). *The achievement motive*. New York: Irvington.

McNemar, Q. (1951). The factors in factoring behavior. *Psychometrika, 16*, 353–359.

McNemar, Q. (1964). Lost: Our intelligence? Why? *American Psychologist, 19*, 871–882.

Mednick, M. T., & Andrews, F. M. (1967). Creative thinking and level of intelligence. *Journal of Creative Behavior, 1*, 428–431.

Mednick, S. A. (1962). The associative basis of the creative process. *Psychological Review, 69*, 220–232.

Miles, T. R. (1957). On defining intelligence. *British Journal of Educational Psychology, 27*, 153–165.

Miller, G. A., Galanter, E. H., & Pribram, K. H. (1960). *Plans and the structure of behavior*. New York: Holt, Rinehart & Winston.

Miller, S. A. (1976). Nonverbal assessment of Piagetian concepts. *Psychological Bulletin, 83*, 405–430.

Mumford, M. D., & Gustafson, S. B. (1988). Creativity syndrome: Integration, application, and innovation. *Psychological Bulletin, 103*, 27–43.

Mundy-Castle, A. C. (1974). Social and technological intelligence in Western or Nonwestern cultures. *Universitas, 4*, 46–52.

Naglieri, J. A., & Das, J. P. (1990). Planning, attention, simultaneous, and successive cognitive processes as a model for intelligence. *Journal of Psychoeducational Assessment, 8*, 303–337.

Naglieri, J. A., & Das, J. P. (1997). *Cognitive assessment system*. Itasca, IL: Riverside Publishing Company.

Neisser, U. (1976). *Cognition and reality: Principles and implications of cognitive psychology*. San Francisco: Freeman.

Neisser, U. (Ed.). (1998). *The rising curve*. Washington, D.C.: American Psychological Association.

Nelson, T. O. (1999). Cognition versus metacognition. In R. J. Sternberg (Ed.), *The nature of cognition* (pp. 625–641). Cambridge, MA: The MIT Press.

Newell, A., & Simon, H. A. (1972). *Human problem solving*. Englewood Cliffs, NJ: Prentice-Hall.

Noy, P. (1969). A revision of the psychoanalytic theory of the primary process. *International Journal of Psychoanalysis, 50*, 155–178.

Ochse, R. (1990). *Before the gates of excellence*. New York: Cambridge University Press.

Okagaki, L., & Sternberg, R. J. (1993). Parental beliefs and children's school performance. *Child Development, 64*(1), 36–56.

Osborn, A. F. (1953). *Applied imagination*. New York: Scribner.

Parsons, H. M. (1974). What happened at Hawthorne? *Science, 183*, 922–932.

Pascual-Leone, J. (1990). An essay on wisdom: Toward organismic processes that make it possible. In R. J. Sternberg (Ed.), *Wisdom: Its nature, origins, and development* (pp. 244–278). New York: Cambridge University Press.

Paul, R. W. (1987). Dialogical thinking: Critical thought essential to the acquisition of rational knowledge and passions. In J. B. Baron & R. J Sternberg (Eds.), *Teaching thinking skills: Theory and practice* (pp. 127–148). New York: Freeman.

Pedersen, N. L., Plomin, R., Nesselroade, J. R., & McClearn, G. E. (1992). A quantitative genetic analysis of cognitive abilities during the second half of the life span. *Psychological Science. Vol. 3*, 346–353.

Pellegrino, J. W., & Glaser, R. (1979). Cognitive correlates and components in the analysis of individual differences. In R. J. Sternberg & D. K. Detterman (Eds.), *Human intelligence: Perspectives on its theory and measurement* (pp. 61–88). Norwood, NJ: Ablex.

Pellegrino, J. W., & Glaser, R. (1980). Components of inductive reasoning. In R. E. Snow, P.-A. Federico, & W. E. Montague (Eds.), *Aptitude, learning, and instruction: Cognitive process analyses of aptitude* (Vol. 1, pp. 177–217). Hillsdale, NJ: Lawrence Erlbaum Associates.

Pellegrino, J. W., & Glaser, R. (1982). Analyzing aptitudes for learning: Inductive reasoning. In R. Glaser (Ed.), *Advances in instructional psychology* (Vol.2). Hillsdale, NJ: Lawrence Erlbaum Associates.

Perkins, D. N. (1981). *The mind's best work.* Cambridge, MA: Harvard University Press.

Perkins, D. N. (1986). *Knowledge as design.* Hillsdale, NJ: Lawrence Erlbaum Associates.

Perkins, D. N. (1995). *Outsmarting IQ: The emerging science of learnable intelligence.* New York: Free Press.

Perkins, D. N. (1998). In the country of the blind: An appreciation of Donald Campbell's vision of creative thought. *Journal of Creative Behavior. Vol. 32(3)*, 177–191.

Piaget, J. (1926). *Ideas of the world in children. A sequel to preceding studies on the thought of the child.* Paris: Alcan.

Piaget, J. (1928). *Judgement and reasoning in the child.* London: Routledge & Kegan Paul.

Piaget, J. (1952). *The origins of intelligence in children.* New York: International Universities Press.

Piaget, J. (1972). *The psychology of intelligence.* Totowa, NJ: Littlefield Adams.

Pinker, S. (1997). *How the mind works.* New York: W. W. Norton & Co.

Plomin, R. (1997). Identifying genes for cognitive abilities and disabilities. In R. J. Sternberg & E. L. Grigorenko (Eds.), *Intelligence, heredity, and environment* (pp. 89–104). New York: Cambridge University Press.

Plomin, R., DeFries, J. C., McClearn, G. E., & Rutter, M. (1997). *Behavioral genetics* (3rd ed.). New York: Freeman.

Plomin, R., McClearn, D. L., & Smith, D. L. (1994). DNA markers associated with high versus low IQ: The IQ QTL Project. *Behavior Genetics, 24,* 107–118.

Plomin, R., McClearn, D. L., & Smith, D. L. (1995). Allelic associations between 100 DNA markers and high versus low IQ. *Intelligence, 21,* 31–48.

Plomin, R., & Neiderhiser, J. M. (1992). Quantitative genetics, molecular genetics, and intelligence. *Intelligence, 15,* 369–387.

Plomin, R., & Petrill, S. A. (1997). Genetics and intelligence: What is new? *Intelligence, 24,* 53–78.

Polanyi, M. (1976). Tacit knowledge. In M. Marx & F. Goodson (Eds.), *Theories in contemporary psychology* (pp. 330–344). New York: Macmillan.

Policastro, E., & Gardner, H. (1999). From case studies to robust generalizations: An approach to the study of creativity. In R. J. Sternberg (Ed.), *Handbook of creativity* (pp. 213–225). New York: Cambridge University Press.

Poole, F. J. P. (1985). Coming into social being: Cultural images of infants in Bimin-Kuskusmin folk psychology. In G. M. White & J. Kirkpatrick (Eds.), *Person, self, and experience: Exploring Pacific ethnopsychologies* (pp. 183–244). Berkeley: University of California Press.

Popper, K. R. (1959). *The logic of scientific discovery*. London: Hutchinson.

Posner, M. I., & Mitchell, R. F. (1967). Chronometric analysis of classification. *Psychological Review, 74*, 392–409.

Putnam, D. B., & Kilbride, P. L. (1980). *A relativistic understanding of social intelligence among the Songhay of Mali and Smaia of Kenya.* Paper presented at the meeting of the Society for Cross-Cultural Research, Philadelphia, PA.

Raven, J. (1986). *Manual for Raven Progressive Matrices and Vocabulary Scales.* London: Lewis.

Reed, T. E., & Jensen, A. R. (1992). Conduction velocity in a brain nerve pathway of normal adults correlates with intelligence level. *Intelligence, 16*, 259–272.

Reigeluth, C. M. (Ed.) et al. (1999). *Instructional-design theories and models: A new paradigm of instructional theory, Vol. II.* Mahwah, NJ: Lawrence Erlbaum Associates.

Reitman, J. (1976). Skilled perception in GO: Deducing memory structures from interresponse times. *Cognitive Psychology, 8*, 336–356.

Renzulli, J. S. (1986). The three-ring conception of giftedness: A developmental model for creative productivity. In R. J. Sternberg & J. E. Davidson (Eds.), *Conceptions of giftedness* (pp. 53–92). New York: Cambridge University Press.

Riegel, K. F. (1973). Dialectical operations: The final period of cognitive development. *Human Development, 16*, 346–370.

Robinson, D. N. (1989). *Aristotle's psychology.* New York: Columbia University Press.

Robinson, D. N. (1990). Wisdom through the ages. In R. J. Sternberg (Ed.), *Wisdom: Its nature, origins, and development* (pp. 13–24). New York: Cambridge University Press.

Roe, A. (1952). *The making of a scientist.* New York: Dodd, Mead.

Roe, A. (1972). Patterns of productivity of scientists. *Science, 176*, 940–941.

Rogers, C. R. (1954). Toward a theory of creativity. *ETC: A Review of General Semantics, 11*, 249–260.

Rogoff, B. (1990). *Apprenticeship in thinking. Cognitive development in social context.* New York: Oxford University Press.

Rosch, E. (1975). Cognitive representations of semantic categories. *Journal of Experimental Psychology: General, 104*, 192–233.

Rothenberg, A. (1979). *The emerging goddess.* Chicago: University of Chicago Press.

Rothenberg, A., & Hausman, C. R. (Eds.). (1976). *The creativity question.* Durham, NC: Duke University Press.

Royer, F. L. (1971). Information processing of visual figures in the digit symbol substitution task. *Journal of Experimental Psychology, 87*, 335–342.

Royer, J. M., Carlo, M. S., Dufresne, R., & Mestre, J. (1996). The assessment of levels of domain expertise while reading. *Cognition & Instruction, 14*(3), 373–408.

Rubenson, D. L., & Runco, M. A. (1992). The psychoeconomic approach to creativity. *New Ideas in Psychology, 10*, 131–147.

Rumelhart, D. E., McClelland, J. L., & the PDP Research Group. (1986). *Parallel distributed processing. Explorations in the microstructure of cognition: Vol. 1. Foundations.* Cambridge, MA: MIT Press.

Ruzgis, P. M., & Grigorenko, E. L. (1994). Cultural meaning systems, intelligence and personality. In R. J. Sternberg and P. Ruzgis (Eds.), *Personality and intelligence* (pp. 248–270). New York: Cambridge University Press.

Ryle, G. (1949). *The concept of mind.* London: Hutchinson.

Sacks, P. (1999). *Standardized minds: The high price of America's testing culture and what we can do to change it.* Cambridge, MA: Perseus Books.

Salovey, P., & Mayer, J. D. (1990). Emotional intelligence. *Imagination, Cognition, and Personality, 9*, 185–211.

Scarr, S. (1997). Behavior-genetic and socialization theories of intelligence: Truce and reconciliation. In R. J. Sternberg & E. L. Grigorenko (Eds.), *Intelligence, heredity and environment* (pp. 3–41). New York: Cambridge University Press.

Schmidt, F. L., & Hunter, J. E. (1981). Employment testing: Old theories and new research findings. *American Psychologist, 36*, 1128–1137.

Schmidt, F. L., & Hunter, J. E. (1998). The validity and utility of selection methods in personnel psychology: Practical and theoretical implications of 85 years of research findings. *Psychological Bulletin, 124*, 262–274.

Schon, D. A. (1983). *The reflective practitioner.* New York: Basic Books.

Serpell, R. (1974). Aspects of intelligence in a developing country. *African Social Research*, No. 17, 576–596.

Serpell, R. (1982). Measures of perception, skills, and intelligence. In W. W. Hartup (Ed.), *Review of child development research* (Vol. 6, pp. 392–440). Chicago: University of Chicago Press.

Serpell, R. (1996). Cultural models of childhood in indigenous socialization and formal schooling in Zambia. In C. P. Hwang & M. E. Lamb (Eds.), *Images of childhood.* (pp. 129–142). Mahwah, NJ: Lawrence Erlbaum Associates.

Sharp, S. E. (1899). Individual psychology: A study in psychological method. *American Journal of Psychology, 10*, 329–391.

Siegler, R. S. (1988). Individual differences in strategy choices: Good students, not-so-good students, and perfectionists. *Child Development, 59*(4), 833–851.

Siegler, R. S. (1992). The Other Alfred Binet. *Developmental Psychology, 28*(2), 179–190.

Siegler, R. S. (1998). *Children's thinking* (3rd ed.). Upper Saddle River, NJ: Prentice-Hall.

Silver, H. R. (1981). Calculating risks: The socioeconomic foundations of aesthetic innovation in an Ashanti carving community. *Ethnology, 20*(2), 101–114.

Silvers, R. (1997). *Photomosaics.* Henry Holt.

Simon, R. (2000). Who's the dimmest dim bulb? *U.S. News and World Report*, April 3, 20.

Simonton, D. K. (1976). Biographical determinants of achieved eminence: A multivariate approach to the Cox data. *Journal of Personality and Social Psychology, 33*, 218–226.

Simonton, D. K. (1984). *Genius, creativity, and leadership.* Cambridge, MA: Harvard University Press.

Simonton, D. K. (1988). Age and outstanding achievement: What do we know after a century of research? *Psychological Bulletin, 104*, 251–267.

Simonton, D. K. (1994). *Greatness: Who makes history and why?* New York: Guilford.

Simonton, D. K. (1995). Foresight in insight: A Darwinian answer. In R. J. Sternberg & J. E. Davidson (Eds.), *The nature of insight* (pp. 495–534). Cambridge, MA: MIT Press.

Simonton, D. K. (1996). Creative expertise: A life-span developmental perspective. In K. A. Ericsson (Ed.), *The road to excellence* (pp. 227–253). Lawrence Erlbaum Associates.

Simonton, D. K. (1997). Creative productivity: A predictive and explanatory model for career trajectories and landmarks. *Psychological Review, 104*, 66–89.

Simonton, D. K. (1998). Donald Campbell's model of the creative process: Creativity as blind variation and selective retention. *The Journal of Creative Behavior, 32*, 153–158.

Simonton, D. K. (1999). Talent and its development: An emergenic and epigenetic mode. *Psychological Review, 106*, 435–457.

Skinner, B. F. (1972). A behavioral model of creation. In B. F. Skinner (Ed.), *Cumulative record: A selection of papers* (pp. 345, 350–355). Englewood Cliffs, NJ: Prentice-Hall.

Sloman, S. A. (1996). The empirical case for two systems of reasoning. *Psychological Bulletin, 119*, 3–22.

Smith, J., & Baltes, P. B. (1990). Wisdom-related knowledge: Age/cohort differences in response to life-planning problems. *Developmental Psychology, 26*, 494–505.

Smith, S. M., Ward, T. B., & Finke, R. A. (Eds.). (1995). *The creative cognition approach.* Cambridge, MA: MIT Press.

Snow, R. E., Kyllonen, P. C., & Marshalek, B. (1984). The topography of ability and learning correlations. In R. J. Sternberg (Ed.), *Advances in the psychology of human intelligence* (Vol. 2, pp. 47–103). Hillsdale, NJ: Lawrence Erlbaum Associates.

Spearman, C. (1904). 'General intelligence,' objectively determined and measured. *American Journal of Psychology. Vol 15(2)*, 201–293.

Spearman, C. (1923). Further note on the "theory of two factors." *British Journal of Psychology, 13*, 266–270.

Spearman, C. (1927). *The abilities of man.* London: Macmillan.

Sperry, R. W. (1961). Cerebral organization and behavior. *Science, 133*, 1749–1757.

Srivastava, A. K., & Misra, G. (1996). Changing perspectives on understanding intelligence: An appraisal. *Indian Psychological Abstracts and Review, 3*, 1–34.

Staudinger, U. M. (1996). Wisdom and the social-interactive foundation of the mind. In P. B. Baltes & U. M. Staudinger (Eds.), *Interactive minds* (pp. 276–315). New York: Cambridge University Press.

Staudinger, U. M., & Baltes, P. B. (1996). Interactive minds: A facilitative setting for wisdom-related performance? *Journal of Personality and Social Psychology, 71*, 746–762.

Staudinger, U. M., Lopez, D. F., & Baltes, P. B. (1997). The psychometric location of wisdom-related performance: Intelligence, personality, and more? *Personality & Social Psychology Bulletin, 23*, 1200–1214.

Staudinger, U. M., Smith, J., & Baltes, P. B. (1992). Wisdom-related knowledge in life review task: Age differences and the role of professional specialization. *Psychology and Aging, 7*, 271–281.

Sternberg, R. J. (1977). Intelligence, information processing, and analogical reasoning: The componential analysis of human abilities. Hillsdale, NJ: Lawrence Erlbaum Associates.

Sternberg, R. J. (1980a). The development of linear syllogistic reasoning. *Journal of Experimental Child Psychology, 29*, 340–356.

Sternberg, R. J. (1980b). Sketch of a componential subtheory of human intelligence. *Behavioral and Brain Sciences, 3*, 573–584.

Sternberg, R. J. (1981). Intelligence and nonentrenchment. *Journal of Educational Psychology, 73*, 1–16.

Sternberg, R. J. (1982). Nonentrenchment in the assessment of intellectual giftedness. *Gifted Child Quarterly, 26*, 63–67.

Sternberg, R. J. (1983). Components of human intelligence. *Cognition, 15*, 1–48.

Sternberg, R. J. (1984). Toward a triarchic theory of human intelligence. *Behavioral and Brain Sciences, 7*, 269–287.

Sternberg, R. J. (1985a). *Beyond IQ: A triarchic theory of human intelligence.* New York: Cambridge University Press.

Sternberg, R. J. (1985b). Implicit theories of intelligence, creativity, and wisdom. *Journal of Personality and Social Psychology, 49*(3), 607–627.

Sternberg, R. J. (1986). *Intelligence applied: Understanding and increasing your intellectual skills.* San Diego: Harcourt Brace Jovanovich.

Sternberg, R. J. (1987a). Most vocabulary is learned from context. In M. G. McKeown & M. E. Curtis (Eds.), *The nature of vocabulary acquisition* (pp. 89–105). Hillsdale, NJ: Lawrence Erlbaum Associates.

Sternberg, R. J. (1987b). The psychology of verbal comprehension. In R. Glaser (Ed.), *Advances in instructional psychology* (Vol. 3, pp. 97–151). Hillsdale, NJ: Lawrence Erlbaum Associates.

Sternberg, R. J. (1988a). Counting the ways: The scientific measurement of love. In J. Brockman (Ed.), *The reality club I* (pp. 151–173). New York: LYNX.

Sternberg, R. J. (Ed.). (1988b). *The nature of creativity: Contemporary psychological perspectives.* New York: Cambridge University Press.

Sternberg, R. J. (1988c). *The triarchic mind: A new theory of human intelligence.* New York: Viking.

Sternberg, R. J. (1990a). *Metaphors of mind: Conceptions of the nature of intelligence.* New York: Cambridge University Press.

Sternberg, R. J. (Ed.). (1990b). *Wisdom: Its nature, origins, and development.* New York: Cambridge University Press.

Sternberg, R. J. (1990c). Wisdom and its relations to intelligence and creativity. In R. J. Sternberg (Ed.), *Wisdom: Its nature, origins, and development* (pp. 142–159). New York: Cambridge University Press.

Sternberg, R. J. (1993). *Sternberg Triarchic Abilities Test.* Unpublished test.

Sternberg, R. J. (Ed.). (1994a). *Encyclopedia of human intelligence.* New York: Macmillan.

Sternberg, R. J. (1994b). The triarchic theory of human intelligence. In R. J. Sternberg (Ed.), *Encyclopedia of human intelligence* (pp. 1087–1091). New York: Macmillan.

Sternberg, R. J. (1995). For whom the bell curve tolls: A review of *The bell curve*. *Psychological Science, 6*, 257–261.

Sternberg, R. J. (1996). IQ counts, but what really counts is successful intelligence. *NASSP Bulletin, 80*, 18–23.

Sternberg, R. J. (1997a). Styles of thinking and learning. *Canadian Journal of School Psychology, 13(2)*, 15–40.

Sternberg, R. J. (1997b). *Successful intelligence*. New York: Plume.

Sternberg, R. J. (1998a). Abilities are forms of developing expertise. *Educational Researcher, 27*, 11–20.

Sternberg, R. J. (1998b). A balance theory of wisdom. *Review of General Psychology, 2*, 347–365.

Sternberg, R. J. (1998c). The dialectic as a tool for teaching psychology. *Teaching of Psychology, 25*, 177–180.

Sternberg, R. J. (1999a). A dialectical basis for understanding the study of cognition. In R. J. Sternberg (Ed.), *The nature of cognition* (pp. 51–78). Cambridge, MA: MIT Press.

Sternberg, R. J. (Ed.). (1999b). *Handbook of creativity*. New York: Cambridge University Press.

Sternberg, R. J. (1999c). A propulsion model of types of creative contributions. *Review of General Psychology, 3*, 83–100.

Sternberg, R. J. (1999d). The theory of successful intelligence. *Review of General Psychology, 3*, 292–316.

Sternberg, R. J. (2000a). Creativity is a decision. In A. L. Costa (Ed.), *Teaching for intelligence II* (pp. 85–106). Arlington Heights, IL: Skylight Training and Publishing Inc.

Sternberg, R. J. (Ed.). (2000b). *Handbook of intelligence*. New York: Cambridge University Press.

Sternberg, R. J. (2000c). Intelligence and wisdom. In R. J. Sternberg (Ed.), *Handbook of intelligence* (pp. 629–647). New York: Cambridge University Press.

Sternberg, R. J. (2001a). How wise is it to teach for wisdom? A reply to five critiques. *Educational Psychologist, 36(4)*, 269–272.

Sternberg, R. J. (2001b). Intelligence tests as measures of developing expertise. In C. Chiu, F. Salili, & Y. Hong (Eds.), *Multiple competencies and self-regulated learning: Implications for multicultural education* (pp. 17–27). Greenwich, CT: Information Age Publishing.

Sternberg, R. J. (2001c). Teaching psychology students that creativity is a decision. *The General Psychologist, 36(1)*, 8–11.

Sternberg, R. J., & Berg, C. A. (1986). Quantitative integration: Definitions of intelligence: A comparison of the 1921 and 1986 symposia. In R. J. Sternberg & D. K. Detterman (Eds.), *What is intelligence: Contemporary viewpoints on its nature and definition* (pp. 155–162). Norwood, NJ: Ablex.

Sternberg, R. J., Castejón, J. L., Prieto, M. D., Hautamäki, J., & Grigorenko, E. L. (2001). Confirmatory factor analysis of the Sternberg triarchic abilities test in three international samples: An empirical test of the triarchic theory of intelligence. *European Journal of Psychological Assessment, 17(1)*, 1–16.

Sternberg, R. J., & Clinkenbeard, P. R. (1995). A triarchic model of identifying, teaching, and assessing gifted children. *Roeper Review, 17* (4), 255–260.

Sternberg, R. J., Conway, B. E., Ketron, J. L., & Bernstein M. (1981). People's conceptions of intelligence. *Journal of Personality and Social Psychology*, *41*, 37–55.

Sternberg, R. J., & Davidson, J. E. (1982, June). The mind of the puzzler. *Psychology Today*, *16*, 37–44.

Sternberg, R. J., & Davidson, J. E. (Eds.). (1994). *The nature of insight*. Cambridge, MA: MIT Press.

Sternberg, R. J., & Detterman, D. K. (1986). *What is intelligence?* Norwood, N.J.: Ablex.

Sternberg, R. J., & Dobson, D. M. (1987). Resolving interpersonal conflicts: An analysis of stylistic consistency. *Journal of Personality and Social Psychology*, *52*, 794–812.

Sternberg, R. J., Ferrari, M., Clinkenbeard, P. R., & Grigorenko, E. L. (1996). Identification, instruction, and assessment of gifted children: A construct validation of a triarchic model. *Gifted Child Quarterly*, *40*, 129–137.

Sternberg, R. J., Forsythe, G. B., Hedlund, J., Horvath, J., Snook, S., Williams, W. M., Wagner, R. K., & Grigorenko, E. L. (2000). *Practical intelligence in everyday life*. New York: Cambridge University Press.

Sternberg, R. J., & Gardner, M. K. (1982). A componential interpretation of the general factor in human intelligence. In H. J. Eysenck (Ed.), *A model for intelligence* (pp. 231–254). Berlin: Springer-Verlag.

Sternberg, R. J., & Gardner, M. K. (1983). Unities in inductive reasoning. *Journal of Experimental Psychology: General*, *112*, 80–116.

Sternberg, R. J., & Gastel, J. (1989a). Coping with novelty in human intelligence: An empirical investigation. *Intelligence*, *13*, 187–197.

Sternberg, R. J., & Gastel, J. (1989b). If dancers ate their shoes: Inductive reasoning with factual and counterfactual premises. *Memory and Cognition*, *17*, 1–10.

Sternberg, R. J., & Grigorenko, E. L. (1997). The cognitive costs of physical and mental ill health: Applying the psychology of the developed world to the problems of the developing world. *Eye on Psi Chi*, *2(1)*, 20–27.

Sternberg, R. J., & Grigorenko, E. L. (2000). *Teaching for successful intelligence*. Arlington Heights, IL: Skylight Training and Publishing Inc.

Sternberg, R. J., Grigorenko, E. L., Ferrari, M., & Clinkenbeard, P. (1999). A triarchic analysis of an aptitude-treatment interaction. *European Journal of Psychological Assessment*, *15*, 1–11.

Sternberg, R. J., Grigorenko, E. L., Ngrosho, D., Tantufuye, E., Mbise, A., Nokes, C., Jukes, M., & Bundy, D. A. (2002). Assessing intellectual potential in rural Tanzanian school children. *Intelligence*, *30*, 141–162.

Sternberg, R. J., & Kalmar D. A. (1997). When will the milk spoil? Everyday induction in human intelligence. *Intelligence*, *25(3)*, 185–203.

Sternberg, R. J., & Kaufman, J. C. (Eds.). (2001). *The evolution of intelligence*. Mahwah, NJ: Lawrence Erlbaum Associates.

Sternberg, R. J., Kaufman, J. C., & Pretz, J. E. (2002). *The creativity conundrum: A propulsion model of kinds of creative contributions*. New York: Psychology Press.

Sternberg, R. J., & Lubart, T. I. (1991). Creating creative minds. *Phi Delta Kappan*, *8*, 608–614.

Sternberg, R. J., & Lubart, T. I. (1995). *Defying the crowd: Cultivating creativity in a culture of conformity*. New York: Free Press.

Sternberg, R. J., & Lubart, T. I. (1996). Investing in creativity. *American Psychologist*, *51*(7), 677–688.

Sternberg, R. J., & Nigro, G. (1980). Developmental patterns in the solution of verbal analogies. *Child Development*, *51*, 27–38.

Sternberg, R. J., Nokes, K., Geissler, P. W., Prince, R., Okatcha, F., Bundy, D. A., & Grigorenko, E. L. (2001). The relationship between academic and practical intelligence: A case study in Kenya. *Intelligence*, *29*, 401–418.

Sternberg, R. J., Okagaki, L., & Jackson, A. (1990). Practical intelligence for success in school. *Educational Leadership*, *48*, 35–39.

Sternberg, R. J., Powell, C., McGrane, P. A., & McGregor, S. (1997). Effects of a parasitic infection on cognitive functioning. *Journal of Experimental Psychology: Applied*, *3*, 67–76.

Sternberg, R. J., & Powell, J. S. (1983). The development of intelligence. In P. H. Mussen (Series Ed.), J. Flavell, & E. Markman (Volume Eds.), *Handbook of child psychology* (Vol. 3, 3rd ed., pp. 341–419). New York: Wiley.

Sternberg, R. J., Powell, J. S., & Kaye, D. B. (1983). Teaching vocabulary-building skills: A contextual approach. In A. C. Wilkinson (Ed.), *Classroom computers and cognitive science* (pp. 121–143). New York: Academic Press.

Sternberg, R. J., & The Rainbow Project Collaborators (in press). The Rainbow Project: Enhancing the SAT through assessments of analytical, practical, and creative skills. College Board Technical Report. New York: The College Board.

Sternberg, R. J., & Rifkin, B. (1979). The development of analogical reasoning processes. *Journal of Experimental Child Psychology*, *27*, 195–232.

Sternberg, R. J., & Smith, C. (1985). Social intelligence and decoding skills in nonverbal communication. *Social Cognition*, *2*, 168–192.

Sternberg, R. J., & Soriano, L. J. (1984). Styles of conflict resolution. *Journal of Personality and Social Psychology*, *47*, 115–126.

Sternberg, R. J., & Spear-Swerling, L. (1996). *Teaching for thinking*. Washington, D.C.: American Psychological Association.

Sternberg, R. J., Torff, B., & Grigorenko, E. L. (1998a). Teaching for successful intelligence raises school achievement. *Phi Delta Kappan*, *79*(9), 667–669.

Sternberg, R. J., Torff, B., & Grigorenko, E. L. (1998b). Teaching triarchically improves school achievement. *Journal of Educational Psychology*, *90*(3), 1–11.

Sternberg, R. J., & Turner, M. E. (1981). Components of syllogistic reasoning. *Acta Psychologica*, *47*, 245–265.

Sternberg, R. J., & Wagner, R. K. (1993). The g-ocentric view of intelligence and job performance is wrong. *Current Directions in Psychological Science*, *2*, 1–4.

Sternberg, R. J., Wagner, R. K., & Okagaki, L. (1993). Practical intelligence: The nature and role of tacit knowledge in work and at school. In H. Reese & J. Puckett (Eds.), *Advances in lifespan development* (pp. 205–227). Hillsdale, NJ: Lawrence Erlbaum Associates.

Sternberg, R. J., Wagner, R. K., Williams, W. M., & Horvath, J. A. (1995). Testing common sense. *American Psychologist*, *50*, 912–927.

Sternberg, R. J., & Williams, W. M. (1996). *How to develop student creativity*. Alexandria, VA: Association for Supervision and Curriculum Development.

Sternberg, R. J., & Williams, W. M. (1997). Does the *Graduate Record Examination* predict meaningful success in the graduate training of psychologists? A case study. *American Psychologist*, *52*, 630–641.

Sternberg, S. (1969). Memory-scanning: Mental processes revealed by reaction-time experiments. *American Scientist, 4,* 421–457.

Suler, J. R. (1980). Primary process thinking and creativity. *Psychological Bulletin, 88,* 555–578.

Super, C. M. (1976). Environmental effects on motor development: The case of African infant precocity. *Developmental Medicine and Child Neurology, 18,* 561–567.

Super, C. M., & Harkness, S. (1982). The development of affect in infancy and early childhood. In D. Wagner & H. Stevenson (Eds.), *Cultural perspectives on child development* (pp. 1–19). San Francisco: W. H. Freeman.

Super, C. M., & Harkness, S. (1986). The developmental niche: A conceptualization at the interface of child and culture. *International Journal of Behavioral Development, 9,* 545–569.

Super, C. M., & Harkness, S. (1993). The developmental niche: A conceptualization at the interface of child and culture. In R. A. Pierce & M. A. Black (Eds.), *Life-span development: A diversity reader* (pp. 61–77). Dubuque, IA: Kendall/Hunt Publishing Co.

Terman, L. M., & Merrill, M. A. (1937). *Measuring intelligence.* Boston: Houghton Mifflin.

Terman, L. M., & Merrill, M. A. (1973). *Stanford–Binet Intelligence Scale: Manual for the third revision.* Boston: Houghton Mifflin.

Tetewsky, S. J., & Sternberg, R. J. (1986). Conceptual and lexical determinants of nonentrenched thinking. *Journal of Memory and Language, 25,* 202–225.

Therivel, W. A. (1999). Why Mozart and not Salieri? *Creativity Research Journal, 12,* 67–76.

Thomson, G. H. (1939). *The factorial analysis of human ability.* London: University of London Press.

Thorndike, E. L., Bregman, E. D., Cobb, M. V., & Woodyard, E. I. (1926). *The measurement of intelligence.* New York: Teachers College.

Thorndike, R. L., Hagen, E. P., & Sattler, J. M. (1986). *Technical manual for the Stanford-Binet Intelligence Scale. (4th edition).* Chicago: Riverside.

Thurstone, L. L. (1938). *Primary mental abilities.* Chicago: University of Chicago Press.

Thurstone, L. L. (1947). *Multiple factor analysis.* Chicago: University of Chicago Press.

Thurstone, L. L., & Thurstone, T. C. (1941). *Factorial studies of intelligence.* Chicago: University of Chicago Press.

Tolman, E. C. (1932). *Purposive behavior in animals and men.* New York: Appleton-Century-Crofts.

Torrance, E. P. (1962). *Guiding creative talent.* Englewood Cliffs, NJ: Prentice-Hall.

Torrance, E. P. (1974). *Torrance tests of creative thinking.* Lexington, MA: Personnel Press.

Tzuriel, D. (1995). *Dynamic-interactive assessment: The legacy of L. S. Vygotsky and current developments.* Unpublished manuscript.

Varela, F. J. (1999). *Ethical know-how: Action, wisdom, and cognition.* Stanford, CA: Stanford University Press.

Vernon, P. A., & Mori, M. (1992). Intelligence, reaction times, and peripheral nerve conduction velocity. *Intelligence, 8,* 273–288.

Vernon, P. A., Wickett, J. C., Bazana, P. G., & Stelmack, R. M. (2000). The neuropsychology and psycholophysiology of human intelligence. In R. J. Sternberg (Ed.), *Handbook of intelligence* (pp. 245–264). New York: Cambridge University Press.

Vernon, P. E. (Ed.). (1970). *Creativity: Selected readings* (pp. 126–136). Baltimore, MD: Penguin Books.

Vernon, P. E. (1971). *The structure of human abilities*. London: Methuen.

von Oech, R. (1983). *A whack on the side of the head*. New York: Warner.

von Oech, R. (1986). *A kick in the seat of the pants*. New York: Harper & Row.

Vygotsky, L. S. (1978). *Mind in society: The development of higher psychological processes*. Cambridge, MA: Harvard University Press.

Wagner, R. K. (1987). Tacit knowledge in everyday intelligent behavior. *Journal of Personality and Social Psychology, 52,* 1236–1247.

Wagner, R. K. (2000). Practical intelligence. In R. J. Sternberg (Ed.), *Handbook of human intelligence* (pp. 380–395). New York: Cambridge University Press.

Wagner, R. K., & Sternberg, R. J. (1985). Practical intelligence in real-world pursuits: The role of tacit knowledge. *Journal of Personality and Social Psychology, 49,* 436–458.

Wagner, R. K., & Sternberg, R. J. (1986). Tacit knowledge and intelligence in the everyday world. In R. J. Sternberg & R. K. Wagner (Eds.), *Practical intelligence: Nature and origins of competence in the everyday world* (pp. 51–83). New York: Cambridge University Press.

Wahlsten, D., & Gottlieb, G. (1997). The invalid separation of effects of nature and nurture: Lessons from animal experimentation. In R. J. Sternberg & E. L. Grigorenko (Eds.), *Intelligence, heredity, and environment* (pp. 163–192). New York: Cambridge University Press.

Wallach, M., & Kogan, N. (1965). *Modes of thinking in young children*. New York: Holt, Rinehart, & Winston.

Wallas, G. (1926). *The art of thought*. New York: Harcourt, Brace.

Wanschura, P. B., & Borkowski, J. G. (1974). Development and transfer of mediational strategies by retarded children in paired-associate learning. *American Journal of Mental Deficiency, 78*(5), 631–639.

Ward, T. B. (1994). Structured imagination: The role of conceptual structure in exemplar generation. *Cognitive Psychology, 27,* 1–40.

Ward, T. B., Smith, S. M., & Finke, R. A. (1999). Creative cognition. In R. J. Sternberg (Ed.), *Handbook of creativity* (pp. 189–212). New York: Cambridge University Press.

Wechsler, D. (1991). *Manual for the Wechsler Intelligence Scales for Children* (3rd ed.), (WISC_III). San Antonio, TX: Psychological Corporation.

Wehner, L., Csikszentmihalyi, M., & Magyari-Beck, I. (1991). Current approaches used in studying creativity: An exploratory investigation. *Creativity Research Journal, 4*(3), 261–271.

Weisberg, R. W. (1986). *Creativity, genius and other myths*. New York: Freeman.

Weisberg, R. W. (1988). Problem solving and creativity. In R. J. Sternberg (Ed.), *The nature of creativity* (pp. 148–176). New York: Cambridge University Press.

Weisberg, R. W. (1993). *Creativity: Beyond the myth of genius*. New York: Freeman.

Weisberg, R. W. (1999). Creativity and knowledge: A challenge to theories. In R. J. Sternberg (Ed.), *Handbook of creativity* (pp. 226–250). New York: Cambridge University Press.

Weisberg, R. W., & Alba, J. W. (1981). An examination of the alleged role of "fixation" in the solution of several "insight" problems. *Journal of Experimental Psychology: General, 110,* 169–192.

Werner, H., & Kaplan, B. (1963). *Symbol formation.* Hillsdale, NJ: Lawrence Erlbaum Associates.

White, G. M. (1985). Premises and purposes in a Solomon Islands ethnopsychology. In G. M. White & J. Kirkpatrick (Eds.), *Person, self, and experience: Exploring Pacific ethnopsychologies* (pp. 328–366). Berkeley: University of California Press.

Wickett, J. C., & Vernon, P. A. (1994). Peripheral nerve conduction velocity, reaction time, and intelligence: An attempt to replicate Vernon and Mori. *Intelligence, 18,* 127–132.

Wigdor, A. K., & Garner, W. R. (Eds.). (1982). *Ability testing: Uses, consequences, and controversies.* Washington, D.C.: National Academy Press.

Willerman, L., Schultz, R., Rutledge, J. N., & Bigler, E. D. (1991). In vivo brain size and intelligence. *Intelligence, 15,* 223–228.

Willerman, L., Schultz, R., Rutledge, J. N., & Bigler, E. D. (1992). Hemisphere size asymmetry predicts relative verbal and nonverbal intelligence differently in the sexes: An MRI study of structure function relations. *Intelligence, 16,* 315–328.

Williams, W. M., Blythe, T., White, N., Li, J., Gardner, H., & Sternberg, R. J. (2002). Practical intelligence for school: Developing metacognitive sources of achievement in adolescence. *Developmental Review 22*(2), 162–210.

Williams, W. M., Blythe, T., White, N., Li, J., Sternberg, R. J., & Gardner, H. I. (1996). *Practical intelligence for school: A handbook for teachers of grades 5–8.* New York: HarperCollins.

Williams, W. M., & Sternberg, R. J. (2002). How parents can maximize children's cognitive abilities. In M. Borstein (Ed.), *Handbook of parenting (Vol. 5: Practical Issues in Parenting).* Mahwah, NJ: Lawrence Erlbaum Associates.

Wissler, C. (1901). The correlation of mental and physical tests. *Psychological Review, Monograph Supplement 3*(6).

Woodman, R. W., & Schoenfeldt, L. F. (1989). Individual differences in creativity: An interactionist perspective. In J. A. Glover, R. R. Ronning & C. R. Reynolds (Eds.), *Handbook of creativity.* New York: Plenum.

Yamamoto, K. (1964). Creativity and sociometric choice among adolescents. *Journal of Social Psychology, 64,* 249–261.

Yang, S., & Sternberg, R. J. (1997a). Conceptions of intelligence in ancient Chinese philosophy. *Journal of Theoretical and Philosophical Psychology, 17*(2), 101–119.

Yang, S., & Sternberg, R. J. (1997b). Taiwanese Chinese people's conceptions of intelligence. *Intelligence, 25*(1), 21–36.

Zenderland, L. (1998). *Measuring minds: Henry Goddard and the origins of American intelligence testing.* New York: Cambridge University Press.

Zuckerman, H. (1977). *Scientific elite: Nobel laureates in the United States.* New York: Free Press.

Zuckerman, H. (1983). The scientific elite: Nobel laureates' mutual influences. In R. S. Albert (Ed.), *Genius and eminence* (pp. 241–252). Oxford, U.K.: Pergamon.

Index

CPSIA information can be obtained at www.ICGtesting.com
Printed in the USA
267191BV00001B/5/P